THE
VOYNICH
MANUSCRIPT

THE
VOYNICH
MANUSCRIPT

The unsolved riddle of an extraordinary book which has defied interpretation for centuries

Gerry Kennedy
and Rob Churchill

ORION

First published in 2004 Orion Books Ltd
Orion House, 5 Upper St Martin's Lane, London WC2H 9EA

A CIP catalogue record for this book is available
from the British Library

ISBN 0 75285 996X

Typeset by Selwood Systems, Midsomer Norton

Printed in Great Britain by
Butler & Tanner Ltd, Frome and London

www.orionbooks.co.uk

For Zoey, Jemma and Morgan,
still the original and best line-up.

For my mother, Elizabeth Joan.
And for my father, Sidney Trevor, who
sadly never saw this book's completion.

⤳ CONTENTS ⤇

❖ ACKNOWLEDGEMENTS ❖

Particular thanks to Laurie Green whose chance remark set the ball rolling. This book would also never have been written without the encouragement and belief of Richard Gollner, Anthony Cheetham, who gave the project the go-ahead, and Alan Samson, who has guided it to completion. A big thank you to Georgina Laycock and all the dedicated staff at Orion, and our wonderful editors, Stacey McNutt and Lucinda McNeile, who provided innumerable creative suggestions and invaluable support to the authors.

Many thanks must go to Lucy Sandys-Winsch for the mountain of research she very kindly shared with us, and likewise all the team who worked on the Mentorn documentary, especially Paul Copeland. Similarly Nigel Acheson, who collaborated on the original documentary for BBC Radio 4.

A very large debt of gratitude is owed to that enthusiastic group of manuscript aficionados that we have come to know affectionately as the 'Voynicheros'. From this numerous band special mention must be made of René Zandbergen and Gabriel Landini, along with Jacques Guy, Nick Pelling, Dana Scott, Adam McLean et al. Thanks also to Jim Finn for contributing a precis of his theory, and Tim Mervyn for allowing us access to his research and (as yet) unpublished manuscript.

We also received much help in our researches from a variety of sources: Stephen Parkin and John Hopson at the British Library, Richard Aspin at the Wellcome Institute, Carol Spero and Margaret Till for access to Voynich archive material, Kevin Boole, Barbara Garlick, David Saunders, Andrew Cook, Brian Clegg, Karen Howell, and Dave Davies at Kew Gardens. Thanks also to Lol Henderson and Bob McCabe for various introductions and much advice, and Graham Meek for his technical support to two computer illiterates.

On a personal level we would like to thank all those friends and family who have provided encouragement and many sympathetic ears to our moans and worries during the sometimes painful writing period of this book. Honourable mentions in dispatches go to Ian Watson, Jenni Whiteside, K. Krombie, Ivan Davies, Monja Boonzaier, and special thanks to the unflagging spirit of the House of Peers.

✣ ILLUSTRATIONS ✣

xi

✦ INTRODUCTION ✦

This is a book about a book. More bizarrely, this is a book about a book no one can read or understand. A book that has puzzled, frustrated and ultimately confounded scholars, intellectuals and cryptologists for the last ninety years, and probably for many years before that. A book whose illustrations and cryptographic originality set it far apart from other medieval manuscripts, and whose impregnability makes it unique. The story of the book stretches back through time and across continents, and is interwoven with the lives of many astonishing characters, and generations of would-be solvers, over the last eight hundred years. This book attempts to tell that story; not just of the inscrutable manuscript, but of some of those people through whose hands it has passed. Inevitably, this story throws up more questions than the answers it provides.

One of the few incontrovertible facts about the manuscript is that it was first brought to the world's attention by the man whose name it still bears, Wilfrid Michael Voynich. Like a pebble dropped into a still pond, Voynich's discovery in 1912 sent ripples of interest in all directions. Since then, the manuscript has attracted the attention of academics, military and secret service cryptanalysts, and a vast swathe of keen amateur cipher breakers and puzzle solvers. Yet this most enduring of enigmas remains largely unknown to the average lay person, and the manuscript itself lies hidden from general view in the Beinecke Rare Book and Manuscript Library at Yale University. Gerry Kennedy, one of the authors of this book, was no different from so many others in his ignorance of the manuscript's existence, or of his very personal connection with its discovery, until a chance comment at a family gathering set in motion the three years of research that culminated in the writing of this book.

Sometimes, the benevolent aspect of a sad occasion like a funeral is the tribal coming together of an immediate family with its more distant kin, often far-flung both in terms of geography and familiarity. This was certainly true of the gathering to mark the passing of my aunt Doreen in November 2000. Her funeral in Staffordshire was an almost pleasant affair in the strange way that loss and a reminder of collective mortality can be soothed by the polite warmth of the following reception. Back at the house where she had lived I saw my two cousins and met their grown-up sons. I was chatting, teacup in hand, to Laurie, one of the latter, when he asked me whether I knew about a much further-flung relative of ours, Wilfrid Voynich. Did I know about the famous manuscript that Voynich had discovered?

The exotic name rang no bells at all. Our family was unequivocally English as far as I knew, and from working-class stock not given to literary discoveries. I vaguely remembered, however, some probably fusty Victorian antecedents named Boole (my maternal grandmother's maiden name), who were apparently a cut above the ordinary. My brother knew little of this ancestral line, but he did turn up a well-thumbed family tree, once owned by another aunt. On this yard-wide banner the descendants of John and Mary Boole, who both died around the time of the 1851 Great Exhibition, were hung like an elaborate mobile, a paper registry of names previously unknown to me but connected by a genealogical thread.

There were three main strands pendant from their sons, Charles, William and George. I dangled eventually from William; Charles, though prolific, did not seem to have spawned anyone exotic. It was George who provided the connection. I remembered then the talk of the famous mathematician, George Boole, who had invented the modern algebra of logic – not so fusty after all! He died in 1864, the same year that his wife Mary gave birth to the youngest of his five daughters, Ethel. It was she who had married Wilfrid Voynich. At the time this previously unknown family history seemed giddy stuff. A passing comment had offered a Lion, Witch and Wardrobe glimpse into unsuspected territory peopled with rare creatures.

Later I logged on the internet. 'Voynich' revealed over two thousand sites. I scrolled enthusiastically through the information that came tumbling on to the screen, and glimpsed the manuscript that my distant relative Wilfred had discovered. The tantalising, undeciphered script nuzzled up to the most extraordinary illustrations of herb-like plants, zodiac wheels and a whole bevy of plump little naked women holding stars aloft like toy balloons, or parading arm in arm whilst dipping their toes in baths of green liquid. It was at one and the same time fantastic yet down-to-earth, promising great secrets that could be unlocked with the right key to hand. Here was a sexy mystery-puzzle with which anyone could play detective.

In July 2001, while visiting my daughter in New York, I borrowed a car to drive the 120 miles north to New Haven, Connecticut, the home of Yale University. With similar buildings and pseudo-gothic towers, the place is a little like Oxford or Cambridge in so far as the university is its main industry, and 'gown' merges physically with 'town'. The occasional gilded dome reminded me presciently of the cathedrals within the Kremlin, but the Beinecke Library itself was ultra-modern, looking rather like a pile of black waffles stacked into a cube, the whole resting on four obelisk legs.

I boldly lunged through the revolving doors, feeling somewhat nervous, as if on a blind date. I had read and heard so much about the manuscript and its allure that I was not sure what to expect from a meeting in the flesh; an immediate falling-in-love or a limp disappointment? I was reminded of a description of the manuscript by Mary D'Imperio that I had recently read in preparation for my visit.

> The impression made upon the modern viewer...is one of extreme oddity, quaintness, and foreignness – one might almost say unearthliness. To the reader who has seen pictures of more typical illuminated medieval manuscripts, these pages look very different indeed from what one expects to find in such a book...the manuscript seems to stand totally apart from all other even remotely comparable documents. No one, to my knowledge, has so far discovered anything else at all like it.[1]

Having shown my passport at reception, Head of Public Services Ellen Cordes chaperoned me to a large classroom pushing a trolley-load of Voynichobilia. After showing me exactly where to sit, she extracted the Voynich manuscript from its protective packaging and laid it on a slab of extruded foam, ready for inspection. With rubber-gloved hands she opened the volume and began to turn the yellowish vellum pages. Their ancient creak and crackle lent an added satisfaction to the delights that unfolded. I was in love.

Gerry Kennedy
London
2003

THE UGLY DUCKLING

Just as with the provenance of his manuscript, a certain murkiness surrounds Wilfrid Voynich's origins. Anne Fremantle, who wrote about Voynich's wife Ethel, gives 31 October 1865 as his date of birth, and Kovno as his birthplace, an important polyglot town in Lithuania. Voynich himself, more precisely, on several documents gave Telschi, a town within the province of Kovno. According to Voynich scholar Rafal Prinke, his name was originally Michal Wojnics – later, understandably, anglicised – to which he added 'Wilfrid', used, perhaps, as a codename during his early political activities, and later adopted permanently. Fremantle states that his father was a 'petty official', but Wilfrid denotes 'barrister' on his marriage certificate. This sits better with one of his middle names, 'Habdank', indicating a connection to one of the old Polish clans, and helps explain the occasional reference to him as 'Count'. Certainly a former employee of Voynich, Millicent Sowerby, in her book *Rare Books and Rare People*,[1] elevates him to the nobility. Voynich often used the prefixes 'de' and 'von' before his surname when travelling on the continent in his later years, an affectation presumably designed to impress prospective clients of his rare-book business.

We know almost nothing about his early life, but he evidently secured a good enough education to allow him to attend Moscow University from where he graduated in chemistry and became a licensed pharmacist. According to E. Taratuta, biographer of Ethel, Voynich became engaged with the Polish Nationalist movement in Warsaw, which aimed to free Poland from oppressive Russian rule. Involved in a failed plot to free two of their number who had been condemned to death, Voynich was captured and imprisoned in 1885, suffering two years in isolation without trial in a tiny cell in the Warsaw

Citadel. This physical ordeal was to have two lasting effects on his life: a slight, though permanent deformity – one shoulder raised higher than the other – and generally weakened health.

Ethel Boole, born in 1864, the youngest of the five brilliant daughters of mathematical genius George Boole, had been brought up in relative poverty in Cork and Lancashire, before capitalising on a small legacy to study music in Berlin from 1882 to 1885. Here she fell under the influence of the writings of Sergei 'Stepniak' Kravchinsky, which vividly depicted the horrors of Tsarist rule. Stepniak had fled to London following the assassination of General Mezentsev in St Petersburg in 1879, and so on her return to England, Ethel sought him out. Having learnt Russian, and fired with revolutionary zeal, Ethel set out for St Petersburg to visit one of Stepniak's relatives. En route she stopped off in Warsaw, and some time during Easter week in 1887 came to stand below the Citadel fortress, where Voynich glimpsed her from his cell window.

Just before his later transportation to Siberia, Voynich met Stepniak's banished relatives. On learning of his determination to escape to London, he was given Ethel's name and Stepniak's address. Somehow Voynich managed to escape and so began the arduous journey that Ethel once described as 'five months of adventures and hairbreadth escapes'. It was perhaps on this odyssey that he received the scars that he later indicated to Sowerby in his pidgin English, 'Here I have sword, here I have bullet.'[2] Winifred Gaye, Ethel's adopted daughter, reported Voynich offering up the maxim of a true swashbuckler: 'However frightened you are you must never show it.' Putting it to the test during his escape to England, he would apparently court danger on trains by deliberately sitting next to railway officials.

When Voynich reached Hamburg docks he was penniless, having sold his waistcoat and glasses. He hid in a pile of lumber until managing to hitch a ride on a fruit-boat to England, even surviving shipwreck off the Scandinavian coast. Exhausted and dishevelled, he eventually disembarked in London and made his way to Stepniak's house in fashionable Chiswick. There, at last, on 5 October 1890, just as Ethel and company were sitting down to tea, he arrived and met her face to face, recognising her unmistakably as the woman he had seen outside the Warsaw fortress dressed completely in black

Wilfrid Voynich   *Ethel Voynich*

(a characteristically earnest homage to her Italian revolutionary hero Mazzini, and a reminder of the sad state of the
world).

Ethel was now a key figure in Stepniak's influential
'Society of Friends of Russian Freedom', patronised by leading
left-thinkers of the day such as Eleanor Marx and William
Morris, and had become co-editor of the society's publication,
Free Russia. Voynich wasted no time in establishing himself
with his new circle of friends. He took a bundle of copies the
very next day to sell on the streets, and seems to have become
as equally immersed as Ethel in the fight against the Tsar. But
more importantly, around this time, Voynich began his enduring involvement in the world of books when he became the
business manager of a bookshop selling revolutionary works
to the British public.

Voynich had now adopted the name Ivan Klecevski as a
cover in case of reprisals to his family in Europe. (Meanwhile
Ethel seems to have taken the surname 'Voynich', although
they were not in fact married until September 1902, allowing
his British naturalisation in April 1904.) Together, as part of
the League of Book Carriers, they smuggled proscribed literature into Russia, including copies of Marx, Engels and
Plekhanov. The more conventional account of Voynich's
book-dealing history is made by Millicent Sowerby. It begins,
she avers, Dick Whittington style, with his borrowing half a
crown from Stepniak – not a lot even in the 1890s – in order to

7

set up his own business; however, she perhaps wisely adds, 'at least that is the story we are told'.[3]

In 1895 Ethel set off on her own for Lvov to help organise the book-smuggling network, but a dramatic event back home was to bring an abrupt end to their revolutionary activities. Stepniak, their mentor and colleague, was knocked down and killed by a train at a level-crossing near his home. Perhaps in response to the change in leadership, they both appeared to withdraw from the movement. Letters show that 1895 was a year of bad health for Voynich and hardship for both of them. It marked a definite end to the chapter of their lives that had thrown them together.

We do not know the exact date on which Wilfrid started his antiquarian book business, but what is certain is that 'in a remarkably short time he had managed to acquire a large number of "unknown and lost" books, of which there were no copies in the British Museum'. H. P. Kraus, the book dealer who would eventually acquire the Voynich manuscript, similarly endorses Voynich's success. 'He rose like a meteor in the antiquarian sky and his catalogues testify to his ability.'[4] Voynich's first list was published in 1898, and by 1902 he had published a further eight. His success also allowed him rapidly to expand his business from the original premises in Soho Square to 68–70 Shaftesbury Avenue, and later to Piccadilly, as well as setting up offices abroad in Paris, Florence and Warsaw.

It is rather difficult to account for his achievement, especially since there is little evidence of his dealings. Sowerby, who worked at Shaftesbury Avenue between 1912 and 1914, puts it down to his instinct to 'hunt' for books in out-of-the-way places. Perhaps the enterprise and resourcefulness necessary while 'on the run' meant that he was well suited to the more congenial role reversal of sniffing out literary quarry. The gentle world of the auction house was clearly not for him; Voynich seems to have been a big-game hunter, described by Sowerby as 'forceful and inspiring', useful qualities on a bibliographic safari. Her strong attachment to Voynich (who inspired other women too) appears to go somewhat over the top, estimating him as '...immortal as any human being can be'. We can settle perhaps for her love of his 'sense of excitement and fun'.[5]

Some of this jollity was perhaps clouded by the legacy of his connection with Polish nationalism. Sowerby gives a number of anecdotes about 'spies' appearing in his bookshop and his hosting and helping Polish refugees. Voynich seemed to exhibit a gallant generosity in his dealings with both his compatriots and his staff. This did not preclude, however, his continued business shrewdness, put to work in his forays abroad looking for rare books and incunabula (books printed before 1500). Details of this period of their lives are few and sketchy. We have more solid evidence, provided by Voynich, relating to the episode that perhaps justifies Sowerby's intimations of his immortality.

In 1912, during one of my periodic visits to the Continent of Europe, I came across a most remarkable collection of precious illuminated manuscripts. For many decades these volumes had laid buried in the chest in which I had found them in an ancient castle in Southern Europe. While examining the manuscripts, with a view to the acquisition of at least part of the collection, my attention was especially drawn by one volume. It was such an ugly duckling compared with the others that my interest was aroused at once. I found that it was entirely written in cipher. Even a necessarily brief examination of the vellum upon which it was written, the calligraphy, the drawings and the pigments suggested to me as the date of its origin the latter part of the thirteenth century.[6]

So what was Wilfrid Voynich's strange find? What set it apart from all the other rare books in his collection? And what is it about the Voynich manuscript that still has the power to ensnare and entrance so many?

The Voynich manuscript is a small quarto, the leaves of which vary in size but average about nine inches by six. They are numbered in a sixteenth-century hand; the last bears the number 116, but eight leaves are missing. Several leaves are folded, thus being made equivalent to two or more, and one is a large folding sheet equivalent to six leaves. The manuscript contains at present the equivalent of 246 quarto pages; if the eight missing leaves be reckoned at two pages each it must originally have contained not less than 262 pages. The last

page contains the Key only, and f.57v bears a diagram, not yet
deciphered, which is probably a Key; of the remaining 244
pages, 33 contain text only, while 211 contain drawings,
usually touched up with watercolour, and nearly always
accompanied with some text... It is, on the whole, in an excellent state of preservation, although a few pages have suffered
somewhat from abrasion.[7]

More detail, and a greater sense of the mystery that pervades
the manuscript, comes from the following catalogue entry
from the Beinecke Library:

Almost every page contains botanical and scientific
drawings, many full-page, of a provincial but lively
character, in ink with washes in various shades of green,
brown, yellow, blue and red. Based on the subject matter of
the drawings, the contents of the manuscript falls into six
sections:

Part I
Folios 1r–66v Botanical sections containing drawings of 113
unidentified plant species. Special care is taken in the
representation of the flowers, leaves and the root systems
of the individual plants. Drawings accompanied by text.

Part II
Folios 67r–73v Astronomical or astrological section
containing 25 astral diagrams in the form of circles,
concentric or with radiating segments, some with the sun
or the moon in the center; the segments filled with stars
and inscriptions, some with the signs of the zodiac and
concentric circles of nude females, some free-standing,
other(s) emerging from objects similar to cans or tubes.
Little continuous text.

Part III
Folios 75r–84v 'Biological' section containing drawings of
small-scale female nudes, most with bulging abdomens and
exaggerated hips, immersed or emerging from fluids, or
interconnecting tubes and capsules. These drawings are the
most enigmatic in the manuscript and it has been

suggested that they symbolically represent the process of human reproduction and the procedure by which the soul becomes united with the body ...

Part IV
Folios 85r–86v This sextuple-folio folding leaf contains an elaborate array of nine medallions, filled with stars and cell-like shapes, with fibrous structures linking the circles. Some medallions with petal-like arrangements of rays filled with stars, some with structures resembling bundles of pipes.

Part V
Folios 87r–102v Pharmaceutical section containing drawings of over 100 different species of medicinal herbs and roots, all with identifying inscriptions. On almost every page drawings of pharmaceutical jars, resembling vases, in red, green and yellow, or blue and green. Accompanied by some continuous text.

Part VI
Folios 103r–117v Continuous text, with stars in inner margin on recto and outer margins verso. Folio 117v [sic] includes a 3-line presumed 'key' opening with a reference to Roger Bacon in anagram and cipher.

These descriptions do not begin to convey the sheer *weirdness* of the Voynich manuscript. On page after page one is confronted by images of exquisite uniqueness: here a plant drawn with such simplicity, almost naivety, that it produces a bold, striking image; there an interlocking set of 'medallions' or 'rosettes', mandala-like in its almost surreal complexity. Where the drawings lack representational felicity or artistic merit, it is the scale (over two hundred images) and dynamism of the creativity that impresses and fascinates. Certainly the illustrations are crude, at times childish, but the manuscript conveys a unity of style and visionary conviction.

Taking the 'Botanical' (or *Herbal*) section as an example, in well over a hundred drawings, which range from straightforward to highly intricate, there is not one *positively* identifiable plant. In a number of illustrations there is a passing, and sometimes quite close, resemblance to real plants from the natural world; but these are in the minority, and the identification is never without a degree of uncertainty. Furthermore, in many cases elements of the plants, in some examples the flowers or leaves, in others the roots, seem exaggerated, distorted or even expressionistic, but for what purpose remains unclear. Occasionally a plant seems to have mutated halfway through its growth, or undergone some form of grafting, with a root or stem ending abruptly, only to sprout again, sometimes in multiple branches, suggestive of an entirely different plant.

But if the plants leave one baffled, this is as nothing compared to the sense of vertiginous wonder when confronted by the 'Biological' (or *Balneological*) section. Myriad plump 'nymphs', often with headdresses, but otherwise completely naked, dance or recline in pools of limpid green liquid; the pools or baths themselves connected by streams, channels or 'plumbing' that appears more organic than architectural. Other individual figures stand alone in urns or tubs, arms upraised, either dispatching or receiving something from the interconnecting tubing. On one page (f82r), a figure with dark hair or headdress stands in a vessel, her left arm placed into a cruciform junction of pipes, from the other end of which issue flames, which themselves produce a star. Another star appears, leaving a trail from the original as it passes across the page to rest above another female figure, this one wrapped in a shroud, lying, either dead or asleep, on a tapering plinth. Above these figures two other women, one crowned, the other with long flowing blond hair, gesture towards two arching pipes that join and flow into a decorated vase; below, eleven nymphs, six of whom sport elaborate hats or crowns, stand around, and in, yet another green bath with ornate, curlicued edges. And this image is far from the exception: page after page is filled with equally strange scenes. There is something clearly sexual about these illustrations; not in the sense that they are designed to arouse (though of course they might), but that there is an underlying impression of fecundity, reproduction, birth and death. Streams of seeds or pollen issue from tubes, grape-like clusters of eggs produce flowing rivers which feed the pools in which the nymphs bathe and from which animals drink. Some images even bring to mind modern diagrams of human ovaries and fallopian tubes.

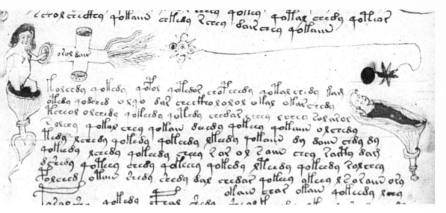

Detail from folio 82r

The overriding sense is that the creator of the manuscript had a purpose *other* than to create something of 'beauty', and was driven rather by a desire to convey meaning. The illustrations are therefore precisely that – illustrations or elucidations of the author's intent for the manuscript as a whole, and never designed to stand alone on their perceived artistic qualities. That is not to say, however, that the manuscript is without its own aesthetic appeal, which is bound up with a vivid and surprising use of colour. One American scholar of the 1940s takes considerable care in detailing the individual pigments he finds in the manuscript:

> Some of the colors appear to be colored ink or watercolor, some a kind of crayon, and some an opaque kind of paint like poster paint. There are many colors; the ink is good strong brown; there is an amber-like ink, like British-tan leather goods; a bright, not quite brilliant blue ink or watercolor; an opaque aquamarine; a good strong red, carmine rather than scarlet or vermillion; a dirty yellow…a red that looks like a bloodstain about a week old; a dirty green; an opaque green; a kind of green crayon; and several other greens of various hues, intensity, value, and texture; a red that looks like face rouge in color and texture; a thick red that makes dots of color that you could scrape with your fingernail; a red ink just like ordinary red ink today; [and] a blue that sparkles with tiny fragments.[8]

But the most mysterious and tantalising quality of the

manuscript that continues to draw experts back time and again is the unreadable text. Mary D'Imperio believes, 'However complex and interesting the drawings are, the script in which the bulk of the manuscript is written is undoubtedly the most intriguing part of the elegant enigma...a tour de force of artistry and ingenuity.'⁹ For all the compelling nature of the illustrations, it is the seductive quality of the text, and the intellectual challenge of 'breaking the code' that has led would-be solvers to concentrate their considerable and diverse talents on the manuscript.

For most of us, whose acquaintance with medieval manuscripts is limited to the odd page reproduced in books or the occasional glimpse on a television documentary, the 'Voynichese' hand looks little different from the other examples we may have seen. At first glance, the Voynich manuscript could be just another archaic text. It is therefore strange, yet oddly pleasing, to discover that this is exactly the same response that the Voynich manuscript generates in those people who are more familiar with texts from the Middle Ages. As cryptography expert David Kahn puts it: 'It looks like ordinary late medieval handwriting. The symbols preserve the general form of letters of their time, which they are not.'¹⁰

The first and most obvious statement to make is that the Voynich manuscript is not written in the Latin alphabet, or any other known script such as Cyrillic. The most common observation is that it appears to relate to what is known as the 'humanist hand'. This style of writing appeared just before 1400 in Florence as a conscious change of design, venerating antique styles rather than the angular Gothic of the Middle Ages, producing a more flowing style with a greater clarity and legibility. As this new style spread across Europe, the more slanted book and manuscript version became known as *italic* in recognition of its Florentine origins. From the similar characteristics seen in the Voynich script, which also displays a uniformity and balance in proportion, it has been suggested that the manuscript must date from the fifteenth century or later.

D'Imperio also draws comparisons with certain Latin abbreviations that were in use during the Middle Ages and the Renaissance, a version of which is still used in doctors' prescriptions today. The Voynichese symbol ᴄᴛ is the same as the Latin abbreviation used to represent 'ra', 'ci' or 'cri'; ⟨symbol⟩ is close to the shorthand ⟨symbol⟩, representing '-termi', and ⟨symbol⟩ a compound of ⟨symbol⟩ ('qu') and ⟨symbol⟩ ('is' or 's'), amongst more than a dozen or so likenesses. D'Imperio goes on to suggest that the 'inspiration' for the Voynich script comes at least in part from these shorthand signs, plus 'early forms of Arabic numerals and some common alchemical or astrological symbols'.[11] There are Voynichese characters that appear very similar to the numerals 0, 4, 8 and 9, but it is assumed they do not represent numbers as they do in current usage.

It is not even clear exactly how many different characters make up the Voynichese alphabet. Estimates range between twenty-three and forty, but many of the basic shapes can be joined together to create compound symbols, whilst others reoccur with the addition of 'hooks', 'tails' or 'commas', and still more are 'ligatured', joined together by a stroke bridging the top of two upright characters. The basic symbol ⟨symbol⟩ exists in thirteen added forms such as ⟨symbol⟩ and ⟨symbol⟩ and the ⟨symbol⟩ character combines with ᴄᴛ to produce ⟨symbol⟩.

The symbols seem to form words, and the script apparently runs from left to right, but beyond these facts, little that is certain can be ascertained. No one is even sure whether the text which accompanies each illustration is actually related to it. It does appear as if the drawings were produced first, as the lines of script end irregularly, running up to the edges of the illustrations; but whether the images refer to the text or are a decoy to lead the would-be reader on a false trail is unknown. The script flows smoothly, without any apparent corrections in the whole manuscript, and does seem to suggest an underlying meaning or sense, not just a stream of gibberish. Does the Voynichese alphabet represent an attempt to convey an unknown language? Or is it perhaps a code or cipher?

From the moment he acquired the codex, Wilfrid Voynich had been trying to trace its previous owners, its movements, and ultimately discover the identity of the author. Voynich believed the manuscript to be the work of the thirteenth-century English Franciscan friar Roger Bacon, and some of Voynich's surviving correspondence shows that he carried out his own research in an attempt to construct a viable history for the manuscript, a trail that crisscrossed Europe from England to Bohemia, and a list of previous owners that included emperors, scholars and charlatans. But however plausible his theory might be, gleaned as it was from the scant evidence he had uncovered, it was still essentially conjecture; only decipherment of the unrecognisable script could establish the author's identity. His only hope of achieving this was to enlist the help of experts in the fields of medieval texts and ciphers.

Returning to London in 1912, Voynich apparently lost no time in letting others know of his strange find. Millicent Sowerby recalled, 'Another treasure that he had found in some ancient castle in Southern Europe was...the cause of great excitement and a large number of scholarly visitors – botanists and astronomers as well as medieval experts. This was the famous Roger Bacon cypher...'[12] Voynich also seems to have taken the manuscript with him to Paris, where it was displayed to French scholars that same year. Yet despite obvious curiosity, no one came forward to venture an explanation of the document, or, more importantly for Voynich, to make a firm offer to purchase it.

By 1914 it must have been clear to him, as it was to many, that the military muscle-flexing of the great powers would sooner or later lead to war in Europe. Millicent Sowerby implies that Voynich's departure from England was caused by the likely curtailment of his book-foraging trips to the continent, and certainly the staff at Shaftesbury Avenue were cut, including Sowerby. In November 1914, Voynich sailed for America aboard the SS *Lusitania*, carrying many of his most valuable books and manuscripts with him.

Voynich's main concern upon arrival in New York seems to have been to set up his new shop at 33 West 42nd Street, and build a network of wealthy clients just like the one he had left behind in London. To this end he set about attracting favourable publicity for his collection. The catalogue of the Chicago Institute of Art records between 7 October and 3 November 1915 an 'Exhibition of Manuscripts and Books from the collection of W. M. Voynich, London', and the exhibition generated enough interest for it to be reported in the *Chicago Daily Tribune* of 9 October 1915, under the headline 'Art Works Worth $1,500,000 Arrive to Escape War'. Included among the exhibits was Voynich's 1912 discovery.

In early 1919 Voynich made photostatic copies of what he considered to be some of the more interesting pages and sent them to many 'distinguished American and European scholars'. From surviving correspondence we know a few of the people he contacted: Professor A. G. Little, an authority on Bacon; palaeographer H. Omort from the Bibliothèque Nationale in Paris; and even Cardinal Gasquet, Prefect of the Vatican Archives. Only one of these experts, however, claimed to have made some headway in understanding the process of encryption, Professor William Romaine Newbold, whose partial decipherment of the manuscript seemed to confirm Voynich's belief that Bacon was the author. By 1921, Voynich and Newbold were confident enough to present their Bacon hypothesis at a meeting of the College of Physicians of Philadelphia.

Voynich espoused his belief that it was the work of Bacon soon after he had obtained the manuscript. But his statement, quoted earlier in this chapter, that simply a 'brief examination of the vellum upon which it was written, the calligraphy, the drawings and the pigments suggested to me as the date of its origin the latter part of the thirteenth century', may have been somewhat disingenuous, because Voynich had been in possession of another piece of evidence all along. Luckily for him, and for all those who have subsequently taken up the investigative challenge, the few clues provided by the manuscript itself are augmented by an intriguing letter that was attached to its cover when it was found in 1912.

THE CIPHER OF ROGER BACON

REVEREND AND DISTINGUISHED SIR;
FATHER IN CHRIST:
This book bequeathed to me by an intimate friend, I
destined for you, my very dear Athanasius, as soon as it
came into my possession, for I was convinced it could be
read by no one except yourself. The former owner of this
book once asked your opinion by letter, copying and
sending you a portion of the book from which he believed
you would be able to read the remainder, but he at that
time refused to send the book itself. To its deciphering he
devoted unflagging toil, as is apparent from attempts of his
which I send you herewith, and he relinquished hope only
with his life. But his toil was in vain, for such Sphinxes as
these obey no one but their master, Kircher. Accept now
this token, such as it is and long overdue though it may be,
of my affection for you, and burst through its bars, if there
are any, with your wonted success. Dr Raphael, tutor in the
Bohemian language to Ferdinand III, then King of Bohemia,
told me the said book had belonged to the Emperor Rudolf
and that he presented the bearer who brought him the book
600 ducats. He believed the author was Roger Bacon, the
Englishman. On this point I suspend judgement; it is your
place to define for us what view we should take thereon, to
whose favour and kindness I unreservedly commit myself
and remain
At the command of your Reverence

Joannes Marcus Marci
of Cronland
Prague, 19 August, 1665? 6?

The above translation is of the letter that Wilfrid Voynich claimed to have found attached to the front of his new purchase. This single sheet, written in a scrawling, Latin hand, not only introduced a cast of fascinating characters into the story, but also seemed to suggest a verifiable history and provenance for the manuscript. In his address to the College of Physicians of Philadelphia, on 21 April 1921, Voynich rather surprisingly admitted that, at first, he paid little attention to the letter. He stated that it was not until 'some time after' that he read it, having regarded it as of 'no consequence'. This was rather strange for an experienced bibliophile skilled in looking for clues to provenance. He certainly changed his mind about its significance, however, and unlike the letter's author, Marcus Marci, who in his letter 'suspends judgement' as to the manuscript's author, Voynich later unequivocally attributed it to 'Roger Bacon the Englishman'. Even without the Marci letter, Voynich states that the moment he saw the manuscript he made up his mind to include it in his other purchases from the Villa Mondragone, the Jesuit college in Frascati, Italy, which Voynich rather cryptically referred to as 'an ancient castle in Southern Europe'. The fact that it was written in cipher, he thought, pointed to Bacon, whom he knew enough about to speculate that the philosopher had reasons to keep secrets from the Church. Much more in keeping with Voynich's bibliographic skills, that day in Frascati in 1912, was his further assumption of 'the fact' that it was thirteenth century.

As early as October 1915, at the Chicago Institute of Art, the manuscript had been exhibited in a collection, and described as 'a work by Roger Bacon in cipher to which the key has never been discovered'. In the 1921 lecture Voynich went on to sketch in the history to support his theory that the volume was penned by Bacon. Who was the key mysterious 'bearer' to whom Emperor Rudolf had given 600 ducats and who believed Bacon to be the author? Voynich had set to work diligently to find out, 'compelled to peruse the biographies of several hundred people', passing their lives 'through a veritable sieve until eventually retaining the nugget', the Elizabethan magus – John Dee.

How had Voynich arrived at this conclusion? Dee, a philosopher too, had certainly owned a large collection of works by

Bacon and had actually annotated one of his manuscripts. Dee had even claimed that he was descended from the great friar. There was clearly a strong affinity. Furthermore, Dee had been a friend of John Dudley, Duke of Northumberland, who, during the Dissolution of the Monasteries beginning in 1538, had 'amassed a large fortune by the unscrupulous pillaging of religious houses, chantries and churches'. It seemed entirely plausible that as part of the loot from their libraries, the famous manuscript, one amongst many, had been passed on to an eager Dee. As far as Voynich was concerned, he believed he had established a clear timeline to the equally fascinating Bacon.

Much of Bacon's life was spent questioning the Church's authority and asserting the importance of knowledge gained by experience rather than faith. For this reason he is generally considered to be the first Western scientist.

In January 1277 Pope Gregory X ordered the Bishop of Paris to enquire into and report on the 'errors' in academic thought circulating around the University of Paris, at that time the foremost seat of learning in the world. Less than six weeks later, on 7 March, a catalogue of dissent had been enumerated comprising 219 such errors, some trifling, some of great import. Number 150 states, 'That a man ought not to be content with authority in order to have certainty on any question.' Number 151, 'In order that a man may have certainty of any conclusion, he ought to be based on principles known by himself.'

Jerome d'Ascoli, the Franciscan General in charge of the Paris list, had condemned Bacon for 'certain suspected novelties'. Bacon had expressed these 'novelties' in his trenchant work of 1272 called *Compendium Studii Philosopiae*, where he directly challenged the moral authority of the Church from the Pope downwards: 'The whole clergy is given up to pride, luxury and avarice.' Nor were his contemporary theologian/ philosophers left unscathed for blindly adopting the 'scholastic' method of teaching, consisting mainly of the wordy debate of tired, hand-me-down nostrums.

The condemnation of General d'Ascoli had dire consequences for the English Franciscan Roger Bacon. He was imprisoned, as far as we know, for fourteen long years in a solitary cell in the friary at Ancona in Italy, forbidden to write or teach, his voraciously inquiring mind shut down, until his

Roger Bacon

release and return to Oxford in 1292. He died and was buried there two years later in the city that had nurtured this extraordinarily creative genius for the earlier part of his life.

Bacon's birth date is unknown. He was born in Ilchester, Somerset, of wealthy stock, around the year 1214. What is certain, though, is that at about thirteen years of age Bacon began his studies at Oxford University. This would have consisted of Latin, the lingua franca of the learned, plus basic maths, grammar, logic and rhetoric – a curriculum sufficient for a liberal Arts degree. Although Oxford at this time was no more than a collection of schools and houses of religious orders compared to the grandeur of Paris, it did have the advantage of a looser orthodoxy. Translations by Arabic scholars of Aristotle's works had found their way over the Pyrenees, only to be banned as pantheistic heresies in Paris, but acclaimed at Oxford for their materialism and down-to-earth examination of the world. Bacon's expertise with the Greek's work enabled him to take up a teaching post in Paris as this censorship lapsed in the early 1240s.

Here he came under the influence of Peter of Maricourt, of whom little is known except for Bacon's own praise of his practical experimentation with magnets and optics and his unashamed learning from the everyday experience of 'laymen, old women, soldiers, ploughmen', encouraging a wide interest in agriculture, magic, weapons and medicine. In Maricourt, Bacon found a prototype of the inquiring mind, as J. H. Bridges puts it, 'thirsting for reality in a barren land infested with metaphysical mirage'.[1]

According to most of his biographers, Bacon, whose thirst for knowledge could not be slaked by what must have been arduous travelling conditions, returned to his alma mater around the year 1250. Here he was again influenced by another Arabic, though purportedly Aristotelian work, the *Secretum Secretorum*, or *Secret of Secrets*. This compounded the belief in experimentation espoused by Maricourt by stressing the importance of an understanding of the real world of nature and man's creativity, as part of his overriding search for God. This spurred Bacon to spend the enormous sum of £2000, presumably of his family's money, on books, instruments and experiments, prompting a da Vinci-like spate of speculative invention. In *De Mirabile Potetate Artis et Natura – On the Marvellous Power of Art and Nature* – he sketches an absurdly prescient list of envisageable machines.

> First by the figurations of art, there may be made instruments of navigation without men to rowe in them, as great ships to brooke the sea, only with one man to steere them, and they shall sayle far more swiftly than if they were full of men: also chariots that shall move with an unspeakable force, without any living creature to stirre them. Likewise, an instrument may be made to fly withal, if one sit in the midst of the instrument, and doe turne an engine, by which the wings...may beat the ayre after the manner of a flying bird.

He adds to this breathtaking futurology the diving bell, the lift, and a system of pulleys 'by which a single man may violently pull 100 men greater than himself despite the opposition'. Less beneficially for the future of mankind he elucidates the composition of gunpowder to make a fire cracker (its propellant force was not utilised until a century later).

Given this fecund worldly outpouring of ideas, it seems rather strange that at some time in the 1250s Bacon opted to embrace the restrictive poverty of the Franciscan Order. We have no real idea why he made such a decision: it may have been that his own finances were exhausted, or that he had succumbed to illness, or even that the cloistered shelter of a friary offered an amenable climate in which to work. Any such felicity was short-lived, however. In 1257, John of Fidanza, later to be canonised as St Bonaventura, became Minister General of the Order, a promotion that, unlike his elevated name, offered Bacon no 'good fortune'. His orthodox and illiberal background ushered in repressive times. Bacon felt the impact by his despatch back across the Channel to Paris to endure a harsh monastic regime made many times worse by the prospective saint's less-than-saintly decree proscribing the publication or even harbouring of books.

Nevertheless, Bacon, forever mentally active, busied himself teaching and experimenting with lenses and making calculations on how to reform the Calendar. He also managed to contact the esteemed Cardinal Guy de Foulques, laying out a proposal for his sponsorship of an encyclopaedic work covering all the known sciences. After Foulques' ascendancy to become Pope Clement IV in 1265, he demanded to see the work assuming that it had already been written. Despite lack of funds for copyists, materials and the need to work in secrecy, Bacon knuckled down to write the three epics for which he is best remembered: the Opus Majus, Opus Minus and Opus Tertium, the last two being appendices to the main work. Despite Bacon's intention that the Opus Majus was no more than a preamble to an even larger exposition, he wrote the weighty tome of a million words in about a year. It was an amazing outpouring of knowledge and speculation embracing much that he had studied before, but also heading off in all kinds of new directions like a philosopher on amphetamines. Yet it must be borne in mind that the ultimate object of his writing was for the Pope as Head of the Church, the guardian of the highest interests of man. Despite his apparent secular free-thinking, ultimately, 'Human things have no value unless they be applied to divine things.'[2] Many of the subjects derive their validity from biblical reference: hence the computation of Christ's life, the length of the voyage of the Ark and the structure of musical instruments. However, his theological passions may have been something of a cover, an excuse for the study of science.

Bacon certainly seems capable of discussing anything under the sun to 'reverence the Creator', including a calculation of the sun's surface area. The importance of mathematics is central to Bacon's work; his mind is discursive but precise, as demonstrated by the profusion of diagrams exploring optics, for example. Perhaps less reverential, sailing close to a heretical wind, is his relationship with astrology and alchemy, which we shall explore briefly as an example of knowledge fraught with the doctrinal ambiguity of the time.

For Bacon and others, astrology, transmitted via Ptolemy and the Arabs, but stripped of Greek pagan associations and ordered by mathematical divinatory tables, provided a coherent theoretical system to explain daily life, one for which the Church had no alternative. It also seemed to proceed from common sense. If the sun so visibly affects the natural world and the moon the tides, God's other celestial bodies must also have functions to perform. Their high order and importance surely affected everything below them including human behaviour and health.

Man could comprehend how planetary influences operated by analysing the four elements, air, fire, water and earth, and their related qualities divided into hot/cold, dry/moist, in varying proportions. These components, too, operated from the highest order to the lowest – thus if the planet Mars was prominent at birth, being hot and dry it might influence a man's appearance, its heat disposing in later life towards a tall, slim build, to put to use as a smith or baker, occupations associated with hot processes. Any dispositions at birth, however, would be modified by celestial influences operating throughout one's lifespan, dependent too on other mediating factors such as gender and the seasons. Aiding an understanding of the body, in particular, lay the important notion of the four humours, each of which corresponded to a part of the body that in its turn was disposed to the influence of the heavens through their allotted qualities and elements.

Penetrating the mysteries of God's wonderful world was clearly incredibly complicated. A whole dizzying edifice of interrelationships of assigned properties was built up out of mathematical computations, observed congruences and intuited lore; a combination of the empiric and the poetic that 'worked' as long as enough vagueness within it accounted for the many inevitable failures to diagnose and predict. This inability to be truly deterministic was essential for astrology's survival; any notion that denied the freedom of the will (and the priest's powerful role to forgive) would be anathema to the Church. Error number 206 on the list of 1277 states a warning to those who believe 'That health, sickness, life and death are attributed to the position of the stars and the aspects of fortune.'

The medieval world is so different from our own that it is very hard to imagine. Not only is it difficult to empathise with the strength of an all-pervading faith in God and fear of transgression, but also the continual attempts to understand intellectually the workings of God's purpose. It seemed a necessary and appropriate task: if God's moral laws surely existed for our benefit, it must follow that there is an order in the natural world also capable of being understood. Everything placed by Him in the universe must serve some benevolent knowable purpose. To this end, all matter and the social organisation of man was seen as descending hierarchically from Him as part of His 'Great Plan' to bring a potential harmony to that which had been lost for us by Adam's original grand transgression. Man could seek to restore order by prayer and allegiance to Church teaching, but having the gift of a soul, and hence free will and reason, any understanding of the natural world beyond that revealed by God through scripture might lead to dangerous knowledge undermining its authority. Astrology, for example, teetered on the edge of the heretical.

Alchemy, too, accepted the relevance of astrology, which in its speculative state can be seen as a precursor to chemistry, using the same ideas about the building blocks of matter. In the twelfth chapter of the Opus Tertium, Bacon observes that alchemy 'treats of the generation of things from their elements, and of all inanimate things', without which 'we can know nothing of what follows of the generation of animate things – as vegetables, animals and man...Ignorance of this science will deny man for example the practice of medicine.'[3]

Alchemy also had an 'operative' side that employed astrological knowledge towards the twin goals of transmuting metals and prolonging life. In his short work, *The Mirror of Alchemy*, Bacon describes how to compose an elixir capable of realising both. Despite the fact that he always appeared to be a theoretician rather than a practitioner, it may be that the more esoteric nature of alchemy in general, compared to the relatively mundane vocabulary of astrology, contributed to his falling foul of the Church. This was not helped by his stated intention to disguise his work in case the hoi polloi 'seizes upon it and abuses it to the manifold disadvantage of persons and of the community'.[4] Despite espousing some rather odd magical notions himself, Bacon was very aware of how magic and sorcery were used by scoundrels to fool the public with 'collusions, darkness, fraudulent instruments or sleight of hand...in which matters the influence of the heavens is not operative'.[5] Either way, the problem for Bacon resided in the too forceful efforts he made to understand the world, appearing to ape the omniscient Creator rather than revere him.

The Opus Majus and possibly the Opus Minus were completed in 1267 and delivered to Clement IV by Bacon's trusty student John of London. Bacon seems to have returned yet again to Oxford having fulfilled his commission and preparing for an even larger and more comprehensive work. Life must have seemed to have changed for the better, his potential papal sponsorship auguring some real 'good fortune'. Sadly this was not to be. On 29 November 1268, Pope Clement IV died; and with his death, Bacon's hopes of an endorsement to continue his life's work evaporated. It remains unclear whether Clement ever saw the Opus Majus. To all intents and purposes Bacon had hit rock bottom. Despite his declared intention of subsuming his scientific work to the service of theology, his views were too wide-ranging and unorthodox to secure a permanently untroubled space in Christendom.

After his death, asserts Brian Clegg, 'Bacon's work became obscured by a smokescreen of legend and myth, transmuting the "First Scientist" into a pantomime figure.'[6] A sixteenth-century collection of tales, The Famous Historie of Fryer Bacon, portrayed the scientist as a vainglorious and diabolic conjuror, daring, for example, to construct a brass head that could talk and foretell the future. His life's work seems to have been largely ignored, except, as we have noted, for that champion of Doctor Mirabilis (as he became known), John Dee. Not until 1733 was the Opus Majus published. In 1861 Emile Charles made a comprehensive survey of Bacon's unpublished works in which he declared, 'The monk of Oxford has paid with his repose and with his liberty for the privilege of being in advance of his time.' Unsurprisingly, the Victorians, those masters of the appliance of science to the practical, less encumbered by ecclesiastical dogma, became enamoured with Bacon and more of his works became available to the public. However, some volumes have even yet to be translated from the Latin, and still others have been ascribed to him though his authorship is doubtful. Consequently, the newfound recognition of the neglected thinker led to several celebratory publications recognising the supposed seven hundredth anniversary of his birth in 1914. Voynich's announcement that he had discovered a manuscript possibly written by Bacon, which might not only throw light on his life but hold within it amazing discoveries in keeping with his genius, naturally aroused considerable interest.

William Romaine Newbold, Professor of Philosophy at the University of Pennsylvania, was the first person to announce decipherment of the manuscript, and the snippets of decrypted text he produced seemed to provide Voynich with corroborative evidence of Bacon's authorship.

Of all the inventions, few if any have contributed more to the increase of knowledge than those of the microscope and the telescope. The telescope has extended the range of vision far out into the depths of space; the microscope has revealed the existence of the unimagined realm of the infinitely little, and often exposes to view the secret mechanism by which the processes of nature are accomplished. That both of these indispensable instruments were known to and probably discovered by Roger Bacon, and that by their means he made discoveries of the utmost importance, the Voynich manuscript puts beyond the range of reasonable doubt.[7]

When Professor Newbold addressed the words above to the College of Physicians in Philadelphia, both he and Voynich believed they had solved the riddle, and were on the brink of wealth and recognition for their efforts. Newbold was sure he had uncovered Bacon's method of encryption, and so provided the key evidence to prove the identity of the manuscript's

William Newbold

creator. But it was not simply that Newbold seemed to confirm Voynich's historical research into the provenance of the codex, it was the nature of the information now revealed, with enormous implications for science and history, that led to their mounting optimism. So great were the hopes of Voynich in light of the discoveries that he predicted fame for Newbold and a fortune for himself.

Newbold first became aware of the manuscript in 1915, but did not begin studying it until early 1919, when Voynich sent him copies of three pages from which to work. At first, the choice of Newbold may seem strange, as he had at that time no experience of cryptography and code-breaking; but his wide-ranging academic interests must have attracted the attention of Voynich. Newbold, like Voynich, was born in 1865, and graduated first in his year from the philosophy department of the University of Pennsylvania in 1887, gaining his PhD in 1891 for his dissertation 'A Prolegomena to a Theory of Belief', and was subsequently appointed to the faculty. Originally a classicist, specialising in the history of ancient philosophy, he broadened his studies into the history of Christian thought and the theory of belief. He apparently read voraciously on many subjects, and his friend R. G. Kent gives the following example of Newbold's polymathy: 'One day, travelling to New York, he engaged his neighbour in conversation and found him to be a stock-broker; and so learnedly did he talk of stocks and bonds,

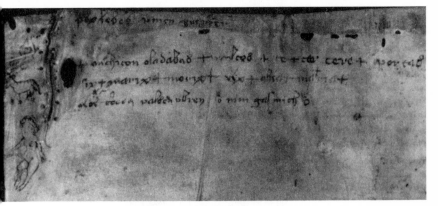

Folio 16v. Newbold's 'key'

and the conditions of finance, that the stock-broker presently asked him with what brokerage house he was connected; he was appalled to find that Newbold was a professor of philosophy, and of Greek philosophy, at that.'[8]

Between 1915, when Voynich first mentioned the manuscript to Newbold, and January 1919, the two men met several times but apparently did not discuss the document again. It was the casual mention of the photostats that Voynich had recently produced that prompted Newbold, out of simple curiosity, to request copies. Of the three photostats he received, one was of the last page of the manuscript. It contains only a small, doodle-like drawing of one of the naked nymphs, accompanied by an unidentifiable animal, and a few scribbled lines of text. Newbold was immediately struck by the feeling that this page was of great importance, and in his posthumously published work notes he recalled, 'within a very short time, an hour or two, of receiving the photostats, the idea occurred to me that the mysterious two and a half lines on the last page, written partly in cipher and partly in plain Latin, was nothing less than the Key to the cipher, and with the idea arose a desire to know what it meant'.[9] From this moment on Newbold was hooked, and he was to commit much of his spare time to the study of the manuscript over the following years. His process of discovery required a number of intuitive leaps and much inspired guesswork, but he felt the astonishing quality of his results more than justified his sometimes erratic methodology.

Newbold took the first line of this supposed key and, although it is not easily legible, made out the following phrase:

```
michiton oladabas multos te tccr cerc portas.
```

By discarding a number of letters, and changing one 'o' for an 'a', Newbold was able to produce a readable Latin phrase:

```
michi dabas multas portas
```

which he translated as 'To me thou gavest (or wast giving) many gates'.

At this point Newbold made an assumption that was to have a major effect on his subsequent studies; he decided to accept Voynich's assertion that Bacon was the author of the manuscript, and knowing that Bacon was familiar with the mystical Jewish tradition of the Cabala, he concluded that this held the key to understanding the 'many gates'.

The Cabala (from the Hebrew 'to receive') is a system of Jewish gnostic religious philosophy, developed in Spain during the Middle Ages. The most important work of Cabalistic lore is *The Zohar*, probably compiled in the thirteenth century and written in Aramaic. It consists largely of a commentary on the Pentateuch, the first five books of the Old Testament. It also contains an explanation of the essential doctrine of the Sephiroth, the ten emanations or attributes of God, and a theurgical or magical element through which the initiate can gain control over the supernatural world of spirits. It was believed that such esoteric knowledge lay hidden in the Hebrew scriptures, and could be accessed through the application of precise hermeneutical or interpretive skills. As R. G. Kent explains in the published notes of Newbold: 'the universe consists of God's thought; thought is expressed in speech; speech is composed of letters; hence the letters are the ultimate constituent of Things'.[10] To discover the mystical substrata which lay beneath the surface text, the adept could employ three methods of analysis.

The first method, known as Gematria, was the substitution of one word for another depending on a numerical value. The letters of the Hebrew alphabet were each designated a number, and so a Cabalist could calculate a value for any given word. This word could then be interchanged with another whose constituent letters produced the same total. The second process, the Temurah, involved the anagrammatising of words, whilst the Notarikon, the third process, allowed words to be constructed from the initial letters of other words, or sentences to be produced if the component letters of one word were used as the initial letters of others. As Mary D'Imperio notes: 'The names of God and of the Angels and the Hebrew letters were employed in ways strongly suggesting to us, today, cryptological techniques (and, in fact, the manipulations of the Cabala may have inspired at least some early cryptographic devices).'[11] As we shall see, Newbold seems to have reached just the same conclusion. Taking into account the almost sacred importance of individual letters and numerical value in the Cabalistic tradition, he made another of his intuitive leaps, interpreting the 'many gates' as an instruction to combine the letters of the Hebrew alphabet into pairs.

If each one of the 22 letters of Hebrew is combined with every other, and with itself, one can create 484 letter pairs. (The equivalent example using the Latin alphabet would be to combine A with A, giving AA; then A with B, AB; A with C, AC; and so on with all the other letters until one could start again with the letter B: BA, BB, BC, BD ... Newbold called these 484 letter combinations the 'biliteral alphabet', and suggested that Bacon could have applied this principle to a simplified, 22-letter Latin alphabet. To create a cipher, Bacon could have allocated each letter of the plain alphabet (that is, the alphabet in which the original text is written), with 22 letter pairs from the biliteral alphabet. Hence the letter 'a' could be represented by AD, AL, BT, FL, FR, GO and so on, followed by 22 different pairs for each of the other letters of the alphabet. Such a system would require a table showing the biliteral pairs for each plain alphabet letter, but with such a key in the possession of both the person enciphering the message and the person wishing to read it, the processes of encryption and decryption would be a simple matter of looking up the equivalents in the key table. According to Newbold, this was exactly what Bacon had done, and he was able to deduce the plaintext values of the biliteral pairs by examining the remaining scribbled lines on the photostat copy of the key page (though how exactly he achieved this was never made totally clear). Newbold believed that this encrypted set of instructions 'must have been intended for the use of some trusted friend who had been taught orally how to read it, and every device has been used to make it unintelligible to any unauthorised person'.[12]

But Newbold soon came to believe that Bacon had not stopped there. He began to suspect that the biliteral pairs would have allowed Bacon to produce a cipher text of readable Latin, rather than a meaningless string of random letters, and thus leave an untrained reader completely unaware that the text contained a hidden message. However, for this to be possible, a number of problems had to be overcome; the first and most obvious drawback being that the cipher text produced by this system would be twice as long as the original text, because it takes *two* letters from the biliteral alphabet to represent *one* in the plain text. Once again, Newbold soon spotted Bacon's way around this problem. Newbold deduced that when choosing which of the possible letter pairs to use to encrypt a plain-text letter, it was necessary to use a pair in which the first letter was the same as the last letter of the preceding pair. The doubled letters could then be combined and written once, drastically reducing the total number of letters in the cipher text. Although this sounds complicated it is in fact quite a simple process, and is easily demonstrated by the following example using English as opposed to Latin.

Supposing we wish to encrypt the word 'map', we would first choose from the biliteral alphabet one of the 22 letter pairs that represents 'm', in this case the letter pair BO. Next, we must obviously select a letter pair from the biliteral alphabet for 'a', but this time we must find a pair in the key table which begins with the letter O, as this is the last letter of the preceding pair (BO). So the pair we choose is OL. Now, to encrypt 'p' we use a pair beginning with L, hence LT. We are therefore able to encrypt the letters m-a-p using the biliteral pairs BO-OL-LT, which, once the doubled letters are combined, produces the recognisable English word BOLT.

Of course, this example reduces the length of the cipher text and produces a readable word without too much difficulty, but this is not always so. It seemed to Newbold that in most cases Bacon had also to rearrange the letter order to create sensible text; in effect creating anagrams, another of the processes employed in the Cabalistic tradition. This time, let us attempt to encrypt the word 'sun'; which could be written in the biliteral alphabet as RO-DR-OP, and then rearranged to produce DR-RO-OP, which in turn becomes DROP after the doubled letters are combined. When deciphering DROP we first double all but the first and last letters (producing DR-RO-OP again), then look up the plain-text equivalents to arrive at 'usn' which, after rearrangement, becomes 'sun'. In a letter to Professor John Manly, Newbold stated that Bacon seemed to anagrammatise letters in blocks of 55 or 110, and although this may seem a very large amount of letters through which to search for meaning, Newbold explained it thus:

> The element of doubt introduced by the necessity of recomposing the anagrams is not, I think, as great as it might seem to be. When I succeeded in hitting the clue early, the way it comes out is very impressive, to me at least. I keep on constructing new words and carrying over a residuum of unmanageable letters until I get near the end; then I discover that the last group of letters not only makes a word, but just *the* word needed to complete the sense.[13]

As Newbold further refined his understanding of the cipher system, he reached the conclusion that Bacon had used a shortened, eleven-letter alphabet to write the original text. This truncated alphabet, according to Newbold, relied on the combining of certain letters with similar phonetic values: hence 'p' could also represent 't', 'ph' and 'b'; 't' also stood for 'd'; 'r' for 'l', etc. This left Bacon with the following alphabet (A P C T E I R M N U S) with which to write his plain-text message. The phrase 'riddles and codes of Roger Bacon', once converted into the phonetic alphabet, would read 'RITTRES ANT CUTES UP RUCER PACUN'.

Already it is possible to see the fiendish complexity of the cipher that Bacon had devised, making it far in advance of other encryption systems of the Middle Ages, but there remained one mystery to be solved. While this cipher operated in the Latin alphabet, it gave no explanation of the use or meaning of the strange characters of the Voynichese alphabet. Still stumped by this problem, Newbold returned to what he believed to be the folio containing Bacon's key, where he was struck again by the odd shape of some of the recognisable Latin letters. He began to examine them more closely, and in doing so made the most important breakthrough in all his Voynich studies. Newbold discerned that each letter consisted of many minute, almost microscopic strokes and squiggles, so arranged as to look like a single letter to an untrained eye. These tiny characters were reminiscent of a form of Greek shorthand (which Newbold felt sure Bacon must have been familiar with), and each minuscule stroke could be transcribed into a Latin letter. Through careful examination of each Voynichese character under a magnifying glass, Newbold was able to identify the individual shorthand marks, translate them from Greek to Latin, and then apply the rules of decryption he had already uncovered. Starting work on the key page, Newbold identified 1300 shorthand strokes in the three lines of text, and at once began work on the decipherment. For the first time he believed he was seeing the words of the original text, written over six hundred years earlier. Most startlingly, the passage of text he deciphered began with the words 'Scripsi Rogerus Bacon...' ('I, Roger Bacon, have written this...'). At last Professor Newbold seemingly had the proof to back up Voynich's theory of authorship. (The rest of the text uncovered from the key page consisted of a description of the enciphering system, most of which Newbold had already deduced, but with the addition of another stage in the process, which Newbold termed 'commutation'. This extra level required the changing of letter pairs from the biliteral alphabet if either of the pair belonged to the 'commuting' set C, O, N, M, U, T, A, Q; the change being determined by a set of tables. The added complexity of the 'commutating' process need not, thankfully, detain us here.)

So, at last, Newbold felt he understood Bacon's multistage encryption system in its entirety. The first stage required the careful examination of each Voynichese character to identify the microscopic shorthand signs, copy them in the correct order, and convert them into Latin letters. In the second stage, each letter (except for the first and last) was doubled and the resulting string of letters divided into pairs, in order to produce the double-letter combinations of the biliteral alphabet; which in turn were altered again according to the complex set of rules of 'commutation', the third stage of the process. Next, in stage four, each letter pair was translated into its true alphabetic value, through the use of the key table, thus producing letters of the plain text. But these letters would not be in their correct order, and must undergo the final two stages before readable text appeared. The 11 letters of the 'phonetic' alphabet needed to be expanded to a 22-character alphabet (mirroring the 22 letters of the Hebrew alphabet), before, in the final stage, this string of letters had to be reordered or anagrammatised in blocks of 55 or 110, to produce the text of the original Baconian message.

Newbold then set to work on deciphering the Voynich manuscript itself, but his progress was painfully slow. His greatest problem was identifying the tiny shorthand characters which made up the Voynichese letters, and he soon found he could work only for a short time on this, as even with the aid of a powerful electric light and magnifying glass the effort produced painful eye-strain. This was somewhat alleviated when he replaced the reading glass with a microscope, but the decryption continued at a snail's pace. His work on the Voynich manuscript was further slowed when Newbold realised that he had uncovered not one, but two cipher systems. If the first and third stages of the process were ignored (the shorthand characters and the 'commutation'), one was left with a cipher system which Bacon could have used elsewhere in his writings. Newbold had already toyed with the idea, and we have seen with the 'map/BOLT' example how the biliteral alphabet allowed the composition of seemingly innocent words which in fact contained an inner, secret meaning. Although it would be difficult to produce long passages of coherent text in this way, Newbold thought that Bacon could have hidden information in alchemical writings, which were known for their obscure, almost impenetrable language. Following this hunch, he began to examine alchemical texts attributed to Bacon in the hope of uncovering other enciphered writings; the upshot being that he now divided his time between studying the Voynich manuscript, Bacon's alchemical works, and his own academic work at the University of Pennsylvania.

Naturally the first person to be informed of Newbold's breakthrough, and who was most interested by it, was Wilfrid Voynich. In a letter to English friends, dated 25 December 1920, we get a vivid picture of the excitement that Newbold's discoveries had caused, all captured in Voynich's stuttering English.

I received the best imaginable present for Christmas, and am still very excited over it. First came terribly trembling voice on the telephone from sheer excitement then letter explaining the whole matter – you can guess. It is Bacon – my professor finely [sic] reconstructed alphabet. It was fearfully difficult problem and the actual work can be done very slowly, but will be done.

It also becomes clear that Voynich was in no doubt about the importance of Newbold's work.

I am going to Philadelphia to…buck up my prof. From over-work and excitement over such victory he has collapsed with terrible headache. You see for him it means great name and career and most likely Nobel prize.

At 8.30 p.m. on Wednesday, 20 April 1921, Professor Newbold lectured to the College of Physicians of Philadelphia on the subject of 'The Voynich Roger Bacon Manuscript'. The evening had begun with a short address by Wilfrid Voynich, in which he presented his research into the history and prove-nance of the manuscript, after which Newbold revealed the secrets he had deciphered. Within moments the learned audi-ence would have been aware that Voynich's 'ugly duckling' manuscript was of utmost historical importance. If Newbold's theories were correct, the history of science would need to be rewritten.

Newbold began the lecture with a brief resumé of the life and works of Bacon, as understood by most historians, but soon moved on to the subject of his own discoveries. Bacon had, he claimed, constructed a telescope using a concave mirror, through which he had observed and recorded the spiral structure of the Great Nebula of Andromeda. In the second part of the lecture, Newbold gave a detailed description of the

manuscript, illustrated by almost sixty slides. In the presentation Newbold concentrated on the 'biological' section of the
manuscript, which he now believed demonstrated Bacon's
theory of how the soul becomes 'united' with the body. The
naked nymphs were in fact human souls, originally residing in
the heavens, before being brought to earth and achieving
physical form through the act of sexual intercourse, which
was also shown in the drawings, though in a highly stylised
and symbolic form. It was clear to Newbold that Bacon must
have had access to a compound microscope, as many of the
illustrations contained images of ovaries, ova, spermatozoa
and even the cellular structure of the testicle (for example,
Plates 16, 18, 30). The inescapable conclusion was that Bacon
had far surpassed his theoretical knowledge of optics, going as
far as to build powerful optical instruments which allowed
him to make scientific observations over two hundred and
fifty years earlier than was believed possible. Many figures
from history, such as Anthony Leeuwenhoek, the 'Father of
Microscopy', and even Galileo would lose their recognition as
innovators of science; all to be replaced by Bacon.

On the following day, Thursday, 21 April, at 2 o'clock in
the afternoon, Newbold spoke again, this time to the annual
meeting of the American Philosophical Society, at their hall
in Independence Square, Philadelphia. His lecture was entitled 'The Roger Bacon Cipher', and he went on to explain the
details of the cipher system used in the Voynich manuscript.
Newbold also demonstrated how the simplified cipher could
be applied to Bacon's alchemical works, in order to reveal
their true meanings. When he finished speaking on that spring
afternoon, Newbold could have been forgiven for wondering if
his name might not also achieve some academic fame, as the
man who uncovered one of the greatest secrets of science.
Perhaps he may even have allowed himself a fleeting moment
to consider Voynich's expectation of a Nobel prize.

Academics and the press, by and large, welcomed Newbold's
findings. Voynich, Newbold, Bacon and the Voynich manuscript itself were briefly front-page news in the Philadelphia
newspapers. Those present at Newbold's lectures seem to
have accepted his findings, even if some were left baffled by
the exact details of the cryptographic process. So it was that,

slightly over seven hundred years after his birth, Bacon was suddenly the flavour of the month.

Perhaps just as extraordinary as Newbold's claims regarding Bacon's use of advanced optical instruments was the fact that he had reached this startling conclusion having deciphered only three short passages of text, along with a few fragmentary lines. The three decipherments, each little more than a short paragraph, refer to an eclipse in 1290, a comet observed in 1274, and, most astonishingly of all, the description attached to one of the astral diagrams giving the location of the Great Nebula of Andromeda. It was from this deciphered text, and the accompanying illustration, which Newbold assumed to be of the nebula, that he deduced Bacon's invention and construction of a telescope. Without such a powerful instrument it would not have been possible for Bacon to have made out the spiral structure of the galaxy and recorded it in the diagram. As for Bacon's ownership of a compound microscope, Newbold seems to have reached this conclusion by examining the strange drawings of the 'biological' section of the manuscript, and interpreting these with the aid of the few other scraps of deciphered material. In his lecture, Newbold went into considerable detail as to the meaning of these otherwise obscure and unintelligible pictures, but his analysis is based on very little deciphered text to back up his theory.

Riding on the wave of popular interest, Voynich continued to push Newbold to produce more of Bacon's original text. This Newbold did, but not from the Voynich manuscript. Using the simplified cipher system he had begun to examine more alchemical documents linked to Bacon, and from these he had found more examples of Bacon's genius, including a method for smelting copper and a recipe for gunpowder. Startling as these discoveries may have been, they did not help Voynich in his attempt to sell his manuscript for the asking price of $160,000. To maintain the public's interest and, more importantly, prove the volume's worth, he knew that Newbold must produce more newsworthy decipherments, and it seems that Voynich hoped eventually for a complete decryption of the entire manuscript. This would have been an overwhelming task for almost anyone, especially when one considers the 200-odd pages of the manuscript, the long-winded process of decipherment, and the huge amount of information it must surely contain if every character was made up of many minute shorthand symbols. It certainly seems to have been too much for Professor Newbold. As Voynich pressed for further translations, which he hoped to publish in book form alongside a full explanation of Newbold's working method, so Newbold prevaricated and postponed. Voynich's letters from the mid-1920s suggest his barely contained exasperation towards the professor, as each promised delivery date for a finished decipherment was put further back. In fact, Voynich was never to receive his decryption. Returning from his summer home in Maine, Newbold was suddenly taken ill in September 1926, and within twenty-four hours was dead. He had made no more decipherments from the Voynich manuscript.

At this stage, the process by which Newbold had achieved his limited decipherments had not been made public in any detailed form. Luckily, Roland Grubb Kent, Professor of Comparative Philology at the University of Pennsylvania, and friend of Newbold, took up the task of sorting and publishing the late Professor's various writings on the Voynich manuscript. Kent appears to have been privy to Newbold's ongoing discoveries almost from the outset, and was familiar with the decryption system, so there could have been no one better qualified to take on the undoubtedly daunting task of sifting through the material, Augmenting the few chapters Newbold had prepared before his death with information gleaned from work notes, letters and personal conversations, Kent was able to publish *The Cipher of Roger Bacon* in 1928, with the credit of author going to Newbold.

Kent's achievement in presenting Newbold's somewhat abstruse and sketchy writings in a highly detailed and coherent form feels almost as impressive as Newbold's original work. In his introduction to the volume, Kent presents us with a delightfully eccentric image of Professor Newbold: 'half sitting, half lying on his bed, a powerful electric light over him as he examined the text with his reading glass and his microscope, the latter set in the right side of a pair of spectacles while the left was closed by an opaque disk. Such was his apparatus for study, and I sat at the foot of the bed and listened to the tale of his latest finds.'[14] It appears Newbold even encouraged Kent to examine the photostats of the manuscript himself, and see what he could make of the minuscule short-hand.

> I took his microscope or his reading glass, and after peering as long as my patience would permit I told him what I saw, or perhaps at his request I copied down on paper the tiny strokes. 'Wonderful!' he cried, 'I shouldn't have thought you could do so well.' But when I asked him what he had made of it, my pride fell: where I had seen eight strokes at most, he had seen twenty-five.[15]

Perhaps because of this, Kent contented himself with merely reproducing Newbold's findings, making no attempt to continue the decryption process, even though he understood its workings in great depth. Kent's great affection for Newbold is clear, as is his admiration for his work, and it is probably for this reason that his presentation of both method and results is totally uncritical. Kent accepts Newbold's efforts as accurate and the decipherments unquestionable. However, elsewhere and from other sources, sceptical voices were being raised.

Even before Newbold lectured to the College of Physicians in 1921, doubts had been expressed about some of the astronomical data he had uncovered (about which more later), but it was with the publication of Kent's book in 1928 that others were finally able to examine the working method in detail. What had been an almost inaudible murmur of dissent now began to build in volume, until one voice expressed, loud and clear, real uneasiness with Newbold's work. Somewhat surprisingly, that voice belonged to Professor John Mathews Manly, Professor of English at the University of Chicago, with whom Newbold had corresponded regarding the manuscript since 1921, discussing not only the process of decipherment, but also his tentative findings. At first glance, Professor Manly must have seemed the ideal sounding board for Newbold's ideas: he had worked as a cipher breaker during the First World War as part of the 'Black Chamber', the American military's cryptanalysis department, and admitted an initial eagerness to accept Newbold's results, due largely to a long-standing interest in Bacon and a sense of romance in the rediscovery of a forgotten scientific genius. As early as June 1921, in an article in *Harper's Magazine* entitled 'The Most Mysterious Manuscript in the World: Did Roger Bacon Write It and Has the Key Been Found?', we find Manly commenting on Newbold's work. The article is mildly sceptical, but still encouraging, and concludes: '...Despite the difficulties which attend every supposition in regard to the language, it does not seem possible to doubt that this is a real cipher, based upon a real language.'[16] However, in letters to Newbold, he began to voice real misgivings over the cipher (though it seems he would have been happy to let the subject remain a private academic debate), until his hand was forced by the publication of Kent's *The Cipher of Roger Bacon*. It was also, perhaps, because of his concern for Newbold's feelings that he waited until 1931, several years after the Professor's death, before he published in *Speculum* magazine his damning critique of the cipher system and its findings; a critique that Manly must have known would leave Newbold's reputation in tatters.

> ...Professor Newbold's decipherments have already been accepted by some eminent scientists and philosophers, and consequently threaten to falsify, to no unimportant degree, the history of human thought. One of the most eminent philosophers of France, Professor Gilson, though bewildered by the method, has accepted the results; Professor Raoul Carton, the well-known Baconian specialist, in two long articles accepts both method and results with enthusiasm; and American chemists and biologists have been similarly impressed The interests of scientific truth therefore demand a careful examination of the claims of the Newbold cipher.
>
> In my opinion, the Newbold claims are entirely baseless and should be definitely and absolutely rejected.[17]

Where had Newbold gone wrong? And more importantly, what inspired the seemingly sober academic to venture such a wild and barely credible hypothesis?

One of the most important attributes of any effective cipher, alongside its ability to conceal information from prying eyes, is the accuracy with which that information is conveyed. Whoever is sending a message needs to be sure that, once the processes of enciphering and deciphering have taken place, exactly the same message will be in the hands of the intended recipient, with no change having been introduced to the plain text. Any cipher which cannot guarantee the accurate transfer of information is not a good cipher. It may already have occurred to some readers of this book, having considered the cipher system described earlier in this chapter, that many of its elements are open to different translations, and therefore allow subjective interpretations to be introduced into the process. This is precisely the conclusion reached by Manly. It was clear to him that, at almost every stage, the cipher failed as a reliable means of carrying a message. Taking the individual steps of the cipher process, Manly pointed out the level of ambiguity and imprecision in each. Let us look once again at the cipher, step by step, this time from the point of view of someone attempting to encrypt information, in order to see exactly how fallible Newbold's system really is.

The first step in the enciphering process would be the conversion of the original message into the shortened, 11-letter, 'phonetic' alphabet. Here, at the very outset, Manly pointed out how the system introduced a level of ambiguity in the transmission of the message. As we have already seen, certain letters in the phonetic alphabet must stand for two or even three letters in the full alphabet; hence 'c' also represents 'g' and 'q'; 't' is also 'd'; and 'u' can also stand for 'o'. So, the words 'cut', 'cot', 'cud', 'cod', 'gut', 'got', and even 'God' in the plain text of the original message would all be represented by the three letters *cut* in the phonetic alphabet. Obviously the context in which the 'phonetically' spelled word was found would suggest which one of the possible 'full' alphabet words it was meant to represent, but there would still be an element of doubt. As we see from this example, and the one given earlier in the chapter, the use of the 'phonetic' alphabet produces confusing, often unreadable text, sometimes with a multiplicity of possible meanings.

The next stage, the translation of phonetic text into letter pairs of the biliteral alphabet, was the crucial stage of the enciphering process, and should also be the most straightforward. Taking one letter at a time from the original message, Bacon would have looked them up in a table and selected one of the 22 letter pairs assigned to each. Surely such a simple step, a purely mechanical process of checking each letter in a key table, was not open to the sort of vagaries that created such problems in other parts of the cipher. Unfortunately, Manly soon realised that it was. He noticed that for Newbold to make his decipherments produce intelligible text, he often allowed more than one letter in the plain text to be represented by the same letter pair in the biliteral alphabet. In this way, the letters 'p', 't', 'e', 'r', 'm' and 'n' could all be expressed by the letter pair AF (and let us not forget that because we are dealing with the shortened, phonetic alphabet, AF must also stand for 'f', 'd' and 'l' in the original message). The person enciphering a message would, of course, know which letter in the original text the pair AF stood for, but the recipient would have no way of knowing for sure which of the nine possible options (p, t, e, r, m, n, f, d or l) was correct. Once again, Newbold was bending the rules of the supposed Bacon cipher, in order to produce readable text in his decipherments.

The next two stages we need to examine, the so-called 'commutation', and the removal of all doubled letters to produce text of manageable length, also present us with problems, but of a different sort. Both Manly and Malcolm Bird expressed strong doubts as to whether these particular stages could ever have been carried out in the enciphering process. Yes, Newbold was able to apply these two techniques when deciphering, but could Bacon have used them in the original encryption? The answer, according to these two scholars, was almost certainly no. As David Kahn in his authoritative book *The Codebreakers* puts it: 'although the system might work in deciphering, it did not seem to work in the enciphering. Many one-way ciphers have been devised: it is possible to put messages into cipher, but not to get them back out. Newbold's seemed to be the only example extant of the reverse situation.'[18]

This section of the cipher system, centred around the use of the biliteral alphabet, seems logical and workable on paper, but the authors of this book can attest to the difficulty of putting it into practice. To prepare the two short examples above ('map/BOLT' and 'sun/DROP'), looking through Newbold's enciphering tables, took considerable time; and attempts to produce intelligible biliteral alphabet words from anything longer than three- or four-letter plain-text words proved impossible. We feel that Kahn is absolutely correct in his assumption that if Newbold had ever tried to *encipher* text using his system he would have found it almost impossible too.

But Manly concentrated most of his analysis on the two remaining elements of the supposed cipher system. The first of these that we must examine is the anagrammatising or re-arranging of the letters to produce the text of the original message. Anyone familiar with anagrams will be aware of the difficulty of solving even short ones of less than ten letters. Yet Newbold asserted that Bacon anagrammatised in the order of 55 or 110 letters, within which, Manly pointed out: 'The possibilities of anagrammising [sic] are greater than anyone without experience would readily believe.'[19] David Kahn demonstrates in his book how just four letters, E, L, I and V, can be used to produce five English words: LIVE, VEIL, EVIL, VILE and the proper noun LEVI. If the number were high enough, many perfectly intelligible, grammatically and syntactically correct phrases and sentences could be produced from the same group of letters. Manly gives the example of Frater Ambrosius who produced 1500 pentameters and the same number of hexameters from the angelic salutation, *Ave Maria, gratia plena, Dominus tecum*. If it is possible to create so many seemingly perfect anagrams from one phrase, how could anyone randomly rearranging the letters of the original message be certain that another person could ever recreate the true text? As David Kahn puts it: 'The answer is that he could not be certain at all.'[20]

The overwhelming task that faced anyone trying to deduce the correct arrangement of letters and hence the true message is amply demonstrated by the startling example given by Simon Singh in his excellent *The Code Book*.

> **For example, consider this short sentence.** It contains just 35 letters, and yet there are more than 50,000,000,000,000,000,000,000,000,000,000,000 distinct arrangements of them. If one person could check one arrangement per second, and if all the people in the world worked night and day, it would still take more than a thousand times the lifetime of the universe to check them all.[21]

But let us assume for the moment that Bacon did use just such an anagrammatising process (in a sense taking the risk that whoever the message was intended for would somehow, through luck or judgement, be able to recreate the correct arrangement), and look at the most important element of Newbold's work on the Voynich manuscript, the discovery of the minute Greek shorthand characters that he found within each letter of the Voynichese alphabet. It was for this part of Newbold's theory that Manly reserved his harshest criticism. The minute shorthand, that Newbold took such pains to identify, simply did not exist.

> To me, the scattered patches of 'shorthand signs' with which Professor Newbold operated seem merely the result of the action of time on the ink of the written characters. The vellum of the MS has a very rough surface, and the ink used was not a stain but a rather thick pigment. As the pigment dried out, the variations in sedimentary deposit and the cracking produced the phenomena which Professor Newbold has taken to be microscopic elements in the strokes.[22]

As we have seen earlier, Newbold's friend and colleague R. G. Kent was barely able to make out the signs upon which Newbold placed so much importance, and Manly went on to highlight Newbold's own admission that he found it nearly impossible to read a piece of Voynich text twice and produce the same results on both occasions 'The correct conclusion,' continued Manly, 'is that the microscopic shorthand signs have, as such, no objective existence, but are the creatures of Professor Newbold's imagination.'[23]

Of the cipher system, taken as a whole, Manly wrote, 'the Newbold system, whether in its Latin-text form or in the modified form of the microscopic shorthand system, is so vitiated by its flexibility and ambiguity that no confidence can be given to messages deciphered by it'.[24] Why, wondered Manly, would Bacon have employed such a complicated system, which gave no guarantee of accurate decipherment by the intended receiver, when just the correct use of the biliteral cipher would have been enough to outwit the most expert cipher breakers of the Middle Ages? Furthermore, to employ all six stages of the process, even if one ignores the possibility that two were unworkable, would be enormously time-consuming for such a large body of work. When one remembers that Newbold claimed to have found a 190-word message hidden in just the three short lines of the key page, the total amount of information contained in the whole manuscript would be huge. The feat of enciphering every letter through the first five steps, and then correctly transcribing them into microscopic shorthand, would have been an extremely arduous task for a whole monastery of scribes, let alone for one friar. A friar, moreover, who at the time of writing must have been elderly even by today's standards, but who would have been considered ancient in the medieval world.

Newbold believed he had uncovered text describing the annular eclipse of 1290, which therefore gives us the earliest date at which Bacon was working on the manuscript (considering he could not have recorded the eclipse before it happened). Although there is some doubt about Bacon's exact date of birth, it is known he died in the early summer of 1292, and could have been no younger than seventy-two years of age, with the upper estimate approaching eighty. It is almost inconceivable that a man of such considerable age could have written, enciphered and transcribed the entire Voynich manuscript, knowing as we do the painful eye-strain and headaches that Newbold suffered whilst studying it. It was clear to Manly that Newbold's system of decipherment was designed at every turn to allow multiple interpretations of the cipher text. More damaging still, he believed that Newbold was aware of the shortcomings, and so sought to emphasise the information he uncovered rather than the process itself.

> What the decipherer gets is not a message enciphered by a thirteenth-century scholar but the product of the subconsciousness of a twentieth-century scholar. A good cipher authenticates itself by its mode of operation, it does not need to be proved by the revelation of verifiable facts unknown to the decipherer; Professor Newbold recognised that his system was so flexible and ambiguous that it required authentication.[25]

Yet an explanation of the 'authentication', the actual deciphered text Newbold produced, remained to be found. Manly had demonstrated that the cipher system was at best almost unworkable, and in all probability never existed at all; but this left the problem of how Newbold produced what he believed were verifiable factual details. Manly's assertion that they were simply the product of Newbold's subconscious is not enough; other influences must have shaped the text he supposedly 'deciphered'. It seems likely that the polymath Professor had, in the course of his academic career, absorbed more information on many different subjects than even he himself realised, but this alone could not explain his findings. His own personality and his sometimes sloppy methodology also played a part, as the example of the Great Nebula of Andromeda will demonstrate.

On folio 68v3 of the Voynich manuscript is one of the more intriguing images of the book. Newbold himself described it thus: 'From a central circular space, within which is a legend, curved arms reach out towards a circular boundary, passing through masses of blue flocculi interspersed with yellow stars; here and there are irregular, greenish blotches.'[26] With some difficulty, Newbold deciphered the central legend, which gave the location of the object, when observed with the aid of a concave mirror, *'inter umbilicum Pegasi, cincturam Andromedae, et caput Cassiopeae'* ('between the navel of Pegasus, the girdle of Andromeda, and the head of Cassiopeia'). Sure enough, Newbold discovered that a spiral galaxy, of which he claimed no prior knowledge, does indeed lie within the triangulated co-ordinates he had uncovered. The existence of the Great Nebula of Andromeda seemed to confirm the veracity of his decipherment, whilst the obvious spiral arms in the illustration must, he thought, provide further evidence of Bacon's use of a telescope, as the spiral structure of the nebula is not apparent from observations with the naked eye. At first reading, this appears to be a convincing affirmation of the cipher system and Bacon's genius; but when one looks more closely at Newbold's story the gaps begin to appear, and the whole story begins to collapse like a house of cards.

From the outset, Newbold did not approach the decipherment of the legend with a completely open mind. It was suggested to him by Professor Eric Doolittle of the Flower Observatory that the illustration in his opinion was 'unquestionably' a spiral nebula observed through a telescope, and it was only after this thought was planted in his mind that Newbold began work deciphering the legend. As we have seen, with so many layers of the cipher system open to subjective interpretation, it is not at all surprising that Newbold should have discovered confirmation of Professor Doolittle's theory. Either consciously or unconsciously, Newbold could, in effect, manipulate the system so as to produce almost any text he wanted. But how, if he had never known of the Andromeda Nebula, could he possibly have 'created' the correct co-ordinates to locate it?

The Andromeda Nebula, or M (Messier) 31, is the nearest large galaxy to our own, and as such is one of the most famous and studied distant astronomical bodies. It was known to medieval Persian astronomers, but was 'discovered' in the West by the Bavarian astronomer Simon Marius (1573–1624), who described it as the 'Nebula in the Girdle of Andromeda'. It seems that somewhere in his wide-ranging reading, Newbold could have come across this nugget of information, and absorbed it almost without noticing. (This phenomenon, the unconscious storing of information that may later be retrieved without recollection of the original source material, is known as *cryptomnesia*, and will be discussed more fully in chapter 7.) However, the more one studies the image in the Voynich manuscript, the less likely it seems that the illustration has anything to do with the Andromeda Galaxy.

Manly was the first to point out that the location Newbold deciphered from the legend was imprecise. The Andromeda Nebula is described 'simply as in the girdle of Andromeda',[27] and does not require the additional information that Newbold uncovered. It seems possible that Newbold, perhaps with some unconscious input of astronomical information taken on board at an earlier date, came up with this triangular region of the heavens described in his translation, only to discover by happy accident that a spiral nebula *did* in fact inhabit this area of space. Even without the unconscious knowledge of the existence of a nebula in the girdle of Andromeda, it is not beyond the realm of possibility that he could simply have struck lucky and hit upon a part of the night sky that contained a spiral galaxy. But there were stronger objections still, and even before the publication of his work notes by Kent, there were doubts raised about Newbold's interpretation of the Voynich illustration as the Andromeda Nebula.

The Great Nebula of Andromeda is indeed a spiral galaxy, but its position relative to our viewpoint on earth means that it is 'tilted' away from us, and appears as an elliptical or cigar-shaped blur; in fact the earliest Persian astronomers referred to it as the 'Little Cloud'. The spiral structure was only discovered with the powerful telescopes and astrophotography of the twentieth century. The hard truth is that the illustration in the Voynich manuscript looks nothing like the Andromeda Nebula; a fact that was pointed out to Newbold, and to which he gave the somewhat lame reply that 'The nebula must have changed considerably in appearance in six hundred and fifty years.'[28] When he was further informed, in a letter from a professor at Yale Observatory, that for the galaxy to have changed so much in so relatively short a period of time was out of the question according to the laws of physics, Newbold refused to discuss the matter further, claiming he was simply 'not competent'.[29] And here, perhaps, we gain a slightly clearer picture of Newbold himself, a better understanding of his working methods, and a hint of the personality of the man.

It is obvious that Newbold often lacked the intellectual rigour necessary when confronting the intricacies of the Voynich manuscript. From the very beginning of his studies Newbold assumed the manuscript to be the work of Roger Bacon, and went looking for proof. Instead of rediscovering a long-forgotten cipher system, he had created a process with such in-built flexibility and open to such misinterpretation that he was able to produce whatever results he wanted; results that backed up his romantically inspired desire to prove the manuscript to be the work of Bacon. His supposed cipher could not possibly have worked to convey information with any accuracy, if it could have worked at all, and even Newbold's own working methods were described as 'a jumble of obscurely expressed ideas'.[30] When doubts were raised over the applicability of his system he hoped to justify the process by the results it produced; and when these were questioned he claimed ignorance of the evidence offered against his findings, or chose to ignore it. There emerges from all this the picture of a slightly credulous man, longing to believe that the astonishing facts he was uncovering were true, and somewhat childishly refusing to accept reality or the patent absurdity of his ideas when it was pointed out to him by others.

Newbold's unquestioning faith in his own findings may perhaps be in part explained if one looks more closely at his academic history. Although he started his academic career as a classicist, Newbold clearly had an intellectual attraction to the esoteric, and became known for his work on spiritualism and hypnosis. He seems to have been drawn to the world of the mystical, with an inclination to study the unknown, as demonstrated by two magazine articles he wrote on the subject of the Great Chalice of Antioch. Discovered at the beginning of the twentieth century, this silver bowl, elaborately decorated with gilded religious images, was thought by some to be the Holy Grail, the cup used by Christ during the Last Supper. Given the religious and mystical importance of such an object, it is no surprise to discover that Newbold should have given over his spare time to the study of such an artefact (and it is also, perhaps, not so surprising that this 'chalice' is no longer thought to be the Holy Grail, but more likely to be a Byzantine standing lamp). Here again we see the element of wishful thinking that creeps into Newbold's work, and which sometimes overrides more measured and objective investigation. Take, for example, his conclusion that Bacon invented a usable compound microscope. This assumption, at least in part, stems from the fact that Newbold was only able to detect the shorthand symbols clearly by using a microscope, therefore it follows that Bacon must have possessed a microscope himself in order to have created the shorthand in the first place. This is the sort of intuitive leap typical of Newbold, and he seems to have adopted the idea to the exclusion of the other, more plausible explanation, that Bacon could not have possessed a microscope, and so the microscopic images Newbold detected were not the product of design, but rather the chance action of the pigment on rough vellum. The creation was in Newbold's mind, not Bacon's.

Newbold was attracted to all manner of strange subjects, like a moth to many candles, but he seems never to have settled on one for very long. Continually distracted by the next intellectual challenge, he flitted from one topic to another, rarely completing his work on the last. Gradually the picture emerges of an eccentric, somewhat ingenuous man, who nonetheless must have been only too aware that his career had not lived up to its potential. His two colleagues in the philosophy department, E. A. Singer and Isaac Husik, both published widely and made important scholarly contributions. Comparing his own academic output with these two men, Newbold may have realised his failings. Then, after thirty-five years of university life, he is presented with a challenge that is not only ideally suited to his varied interests in medieval philosophy and spiritual arcana, but could at one stroke seal his academic reputation. To be the man who single-handedly uncovered one of the greatest secrets of science and rewrote history must surely have been a great attraction to Newbold.

Wilfrid Voynich, in another letter to his English friends, dated 15 April 1926, describes the scene as he and Newbold discussed the future publication of the deciphered manuscript.

> Now with no necessity to wait until whole [of] my MS will be translated and revealed in all its devilry and godliness, but we will start with publication of [its] history, and that will produce such a sensation that he will become famous, and I rich and half famous...But I wish you could see the excitement of Prof N and his wife. They danced, they embraced each other and me, they became ill, delirious, recovered, thanked God, thanked Bacon, thanked spirits. It was sight!

Manly's article instigated a backlash against Newbold's findings, and strange as it may seem, it is perhaps of some comfort to know that both Newbold and Voynich had passed away before its publication and so did not suffer from the ignominy resultant from the turn of the critical tide. Bacon, Newbold and the Voynich manuscript itself were all, unfairly, cast into the outer darkness of the academic world; a position from which none has subsequently fully recovered. It is the permanent damage done to Newbold's reputation that may explain why so few professional scholars have taken up the challenge of the manuscript since. But although Newbold's cipher system had been conclusively proven to be false, the question of whether Bacon could be the author of the manuscript remained unanswered. The letter of Marcus Marci found with the manuscript had suggested Bacon as a likely suspect, and Voynich's theoretical chronology created a plausible link with the thirteenth-century friar. Might it just be possible that, despite Newbold's bogus claims of decryption, the Voynich manuscript could still be the work of Roger Bacon?

THE MAGUS, THE SCRYER AND
THE EGYPTOLOGIST

It is now time to return to the second part of Wilfrid Voynich's hypothetical time-line, which states that John Dee might have sold a manuscript in his possession, the one we know today as the Voynich, to Rudolf II in the 1580s. This is not an unreasonable proposition.

In the 1921 lecture Voynich had exhibited considerable historical research into aspects of Dee's life. Whilst he is clearly wrong to state that 'Dee had no creative power nor a constructive mind',[1] he properly draws out the connection between Dee and Bacon, not by expounding their shared world-view, but by demonstrating Dee's respect for the friar evidenced by his bibliographical prominence in the large library at Mortlake. Like Voynich he was an obsessive collector, albeit from a thirst for knowledge rather than profit. In 1557 Dee published a document, a 'Supplication' to Queen Mary to establish a national collection of books to offset the destruction and dispersal of books following the Dissolution of the Monasteries in 1538. The playwright John Bale complained in 1546 that the resulting wastes of paper were used to 'serve their jakes, some to scour their candlesticks and some to rub their boots'.[2] When Dee's royal entreaty fell on deaf ears he set off to comb the country, buying up large quantities of books and manuscripts. Words in all their guises and contexts mattered supremely to him. Shortly before he left England in 1583 he drew up a catalogue of his acquisitions listing nearly four thousand items, many more than the Universities of Oxford and Cambridge combined, and covering a wide range of subjects – maths, magic, alchemy, medicine, mining, history and languages. According to Voynich, among the thirty-seven works of Roger Bacon bound in

John Dee

twenty-six volumes was the eponymous work that had been passed on to him by John Dudley, Duke of Northumberland. Could Dee have been the 'bearer' of the manuscript to Rudolf II during a visit to Prague in the 1580s?

Born in July 1527 in London, John Dee was allowed a privileged education as a son of a City merchant, progressing like Bacon to university – Cambridge not Oxford, where he, too, voraciously ate, slept and breathed his learning in liberal arts, strongly leaning towards mathematics. As with Bacon's formative years, it was an exciting time of fresh influences permeating the stolid world-view of Christianity. Although the Church itself was in turmoil as Protestantism levered itself away from the hegemonic power of Catholicism towards a new individualism, man's relation to the God-given universe had not significantly changed. The fresh Hellenistic breeze of Aristotle, allied to Arabic knowledge that had invigorated the thirteenth century, blew again with the influence of Plato, Pythagoras and Arab arithmetic in the sixteenth century. As ever, new ideas would ruffle the tidy feathers of orthodoxy and place wayward thinkers under suspicion. Like Bacon, Dee was a deeply religious man who sought to use his restless, inquiring intellect to better understand the natural world and hence to better serve man and God. This inevitably meant sailing close to heresy of thought, and the suspicion of magical practice.

Dee did not have to wait long to fall foul of authority. In

1547 at Trinity College, he built and flew a scarab-beetle prop to accompany Aristophanes' play *Peace*, and was accused of sorcery for his pains. Dee settled at Louvain University near Brussels in 1548, where he learnt practical and scientific skills of measurement under Gemma Frisius, facilitating a particular knowledge of astronomy, and through his great friendship with Gerard Mercator, the cartographer, a new rational model of a spherical rather than biblical world. As Benjamin Woolley notes, 'Dee must have felt himself at the centre of the intellectual and political firmament.'[3]

He returned to England during a period of intense turmoil following Henry VIII's death and the problem of succession – Protestant or Catholic? Dee seems to have been indifferent to matters of dogma. According to Benjamin Woolley, 'God's truth was … to be found in nature and learning', religion must be 'founded on ancient principles and confirmed by science'.[4] Such a philosophical hedging of bets did not keep him out of trouble, however, with the return to the 'true Church' under Mary. In 1555, three hundred Protestants were burned for their faith. This time Dee teetered on the edge of spurious yet highly dangerous accusations of conjuring and making enchantments against the Queen. Unlike Bacon, Dee survived his three months of detention, emerging penniless but intact.

In 1558 Queen Mary died childless, bringing Elizabeth to the throne. Dee's good favour with the new Queen marked a distinct turn for the better. Putting his learned astrological knowledge to good use, he began by choosing an appropriately propitious date, 15 January 1559, for her coronation, thereby becoming ex officio court astrologer. Over the following years Dee exercised his more down-to-earth skills ministering to Elizabeth over matters medical as well as celestial, and promoted a revision of the calendar and improvements in navigational practice. In 1570 he even drew up a State of the Nation report on the Tudor economy. As Gerald Suster avers, he was 'a polymathic giant of his era'.[5] For Dee, however, it was the realm of the spirits that held the greatest fascination, and his obsession with the acquisition of divine knowledge was to lead him into a strange world of his own.

Dee set out to write a major opus to examine the world about him, as N. Clulee puts it, 'as a path to divinity and moral regeneration',[6] but the *Propaedeumata Aphoristico*

John Dee's monad

(*Preliminary Aphoristic Teachings*) is not an encyclopedic work such as Bacon's Opus Majus. It does, however, show his hallmark. Dee seeks to examine the precise ways in which 'rays' from the heavenly bodies operate on the souls of those on earth using an analogy of magnetic influence (not unlike the loose term 'energy' used by modern astrological apologists), and speculates on the use of optics to focus, make visible and analyse these rays. Alongside the rationalism, however, he reveals a deep longing for an intuitive, visionary escape from the real world to a communion with the divine. On the title page, and more forcefully in the Monas Hieroglyphica of 1564, Dee exhibited the 'monad', an archetypal symbol revealed to him. This compounds elements of astrology and alchemy representing the earth, the sun, the moon and other planets, the cross, the four elements, and Aries, the signifier of fire, to help elicit the composite power the monad could evoke when meditated upon.

Dee is attempting no less, according to Suster, than 'to create a unifying symbol which embodies the entire cosmos',[7] in a similar fashion perhaps to the yin-yang icon. Dee the pragmatist, studier of tides, agent for his Queen, and proposer to her of a 'British Empire', is also a magus, a seeker of revelatory occult wisdom that borders on blasphemy in its turning away from knowledge dependent on scripture, and towards esoteric ritual not sanctioned by any Church.

Although the monad came intuitively, Dee had been travelling and acquiring a vast library to study and absorb a melange of influences relating to his quest for godly truth. Amongst these were the *Hermetic Tracts*, a group of writings composed by various authors between AD 100 and 300. They emphasised the mystical unity of all religions and the essential possibility of knowledge of God through the manipulation of symbols. This carried with it a dangerous notion of man's equality with, rather than subservience to, God. Jewish Cabala too was studied by Dee with its own esoteric search for keys to divine knowledge through interpretation of biblical Hebraic writing that could reveal numbers decodable, for example, to provide the names of angels. This mystical approach to numbers strongly echoes Bacon's own fascination with maths and scripture's ability to divulge a basic language of the mind of God. All sorts of intuited correspondences could be found to a seeker, such as the twelve apostles echoing the twelve constellations. Johannes Trithemius, a German Benedictine monk, had earlier in the sixteenth century produced three Cabala-influenced books listing enciphered names of angels and spirits that could be invoked to send etheric messages.

Despite the fact that Dee and others like him sought to universalise such teachings to bring harmony to mankind, there lay a strong emphasis on sophisticated dabblings with angelic hierarchies, words, numbers and symbols whose attraction in part must have been their elitist esotericism. Hardly surprisingly, those who usurped the role of the priest as interpreter of God's word and studied magical practices in private risked the obloquy of the powers-that-were and the rabble. Fortunately for Dee his secular position within Elizabeth's realm as adviser on state affairs and confidant allowed a certain protection and patronage. The Queen visited Dee twice at his home by the Thames at Mortlake, Dee being assured enough to amuse her with a trick mirror.

There was little systematic about John Dee's search for the transcendent; he seems to have absorbed many and all contexts on his quest. This is perhaps reminiscent of the great appetite in recent years exhibited by the 'New Age' for adepts ranging after truths found in concoctions of numerology, crystals, astrology and anything beyond the obviously rational. Dee's own restlessness eventually narrowed down to a fantastic, but focused exploration of the spirit world with direct relevance to the Voynich manuscript. The catalyst was the arrival at Mortlake in March 1582 of Edward Kelley.

Room 416, 'European Medieval', of the British Museum in

Diagram of one of Dee's seals

London exhibits a wealth of expensive finery from the houses of the rich of that period. Case 6, for example, holds a fine collection of English silver-plate and cutlery; incongruously alongside it are six objects made from more mundane materials that were, however, to their owner, completely special and beyond price. These are the 'Dee Relics', once belonging to John Dee, Queen Elizabeth I's 'conjuror', possible model for Shakespeare's

Edward Kelley

Prospero and alleged spy. Three of the objects are made from beeswax formed into 'cheeses', one 4cm thick, two of them about 15cm across, the third about 30cm. On one side of each are inscribed various interlocking geometric figures surrounded by strange writing. These 'seals' supported the legs of a small table covered in a red cloth upon which the 'scrying stones' or 'showstones' were placed and in whose bewitching depths revelatory images could be discerned. Adjacent to its leather carrying-case lies one of the 'stones', a densely black 'mirror', the size and shape of a table-tennis bat, made of obsidian, a natural form of volcanic glass that can be cut and polished. Its neighbour, a slightly smoky crystal ball, 9cm in diameter, was held in a small wooden cradle and similarly gave up countless visions to Edward Kelley which were faithfully transcribed by a credulous Dee over a period of five years.

Many stories surround the strange figure of Edward Kelley, mostly disreputable. Born in Worcester in 1555, he seems to have acquired enough education to become a lawyer, but squandered it with his criminal leanings. In Lancaster he was pilloried for forgery and had his ears cropped, a defect which he subsequently hid under a monk's cowl. Further south near Preston he was charged with digging up corpses; in Wales, still digging, he was rumoured to have uncovered ancient manuscripts and powders with which to make gold. Fleeing from London, having been accused of swindling, and travelling under the name of Talbot, he arrived at John Dee's house in the spring of 1582.

Dee had been experimenting before Kelley with 'scrying', as Deacon describes it, 'inducing visions by gazing into a clear depth',[8] but was unable to produce convincing results. Kelley lacked no such self-confidence. Dee was instantly impressed by his apparent ability to induce angelic visions, and took him into his household on a salary of £50 per annum plus bed and board. Many commentators would say that Dee too was 'taken in' over the period of their association during the 1580s.

Kelley wasted no time in conjuring up the archangel Uriel in one of his master's scrying devices, who, as set down in the *Heptarchia Mystica*, described in detail the apparatus for the seances or 'actions'. After mutual dutiful abstinence and prayers, Kelley would relate his received visions which Dee would write down diligently. Via an elaborate system of tables and squares painstakingly revealed by the angels letter by letter, rather like playing 'battleships', the names of forty-nine good angels were divined, plus the bewildering titles of heavenly royalty such as King Baligon, Bynepor and Butmona.

All this, however, was not as scattily complex as the revelations set down in 1583 in the *Book of Enoch*. The biblical prophet was of particular interest to Dee, who had read about him in Bacon's notes on the *Secretum Secretorum*, not only because Enoch reputedly knew the powerful God-given language spoken before the Fall, but also because of his prophesying the Day of Judgement. Dee took his role as prophet very seriously in a time of turmoil when astrological portents, comets and plagues seemed to point to an imminent reckoning for all mankind. As Clulee makes clear, Dee believed that divine knowledge should be acquired not just for its own sake, but for its earthly application in healing religious rifts and instituting worldly peace. The Monas Hieroglyphica and monad symbol, although obscure, were seen by Dee as contributions to healing, and were dedicated to Maximilian II, the Habsburg Holy Roman Emperor, secular head of the Catholic Church and potential agent of the changes Dee so earnestly wished for. Dee was also well-acquainted with the apocalyptic elements in hermetic texts and the search for harmony. Whilst the angels spent much time and effort laying out the names and ministries of celestial government, they also made many warnings about the woes of a wicked world that might be cataclysmically restructured into a new universal order. For example, from Meric Casaubon's *A True and Faithful Relation...*, a seventeenth-century compilation of Dee and Kelley's angelic conversations:

> This moneth in the 4th year shall Antichrist be known to the world. Then shall wo, wo dwell amongst the Kings of the earth for they shall be chosen all anew...the rivers become blood with the blood of men and beasts mixed together. In this time shall the Turkish State be rooted up and cast from the earth. And instead of him shall enter in that Devil, the father of liars, and such as dwell in the house of Vanity.[9]

It is difficult not to detect in all Dee and Kelley's concentrated and dazzling array of revelations a childlike devotion to babble in the belief that it gave them mystical power, later formalised in tables and grids. However pure and innocent it may have seemed, such magical dabblings ran the risk of accusations of devil-dealing. Dee himself was worried about the probity of some of the spirits. This climate of insecurity, and a timely warning from the child-spirit Maldini, hastened the Dee household to the continent in September 1583.

Maldini's kindred spirit Murifri had indicated that Count Albrecht Laski, an important Polish provincial lord, would make an excellent patron. Not only rich and powerful, he had an interest in alchemy and had participated in Dee's seances whilst on a state visit to Queen Elizabeth. He seemed to be a figure who might be a catalyst in any coming political reordering of Christendom. The association was short-lived, however, as Laski's political future became insecure, prompting Nalvage, another spirit like Maldini, to suggest they decamp from Cracow to Prague. They arrived in August 1584 – where our narrative finds a setting germane to the Marci letter.

Rudolf II, King of Bohemia and Holy Roman Emperor from 1576 to 1612, was ill-equipped to rule over the sprawling, polyglot Catholic empire that stretched northwards from Croatia to Holstein and eastwards from Holland to Hungary. Undermined by Protestantism, the rising power of a city-based merchant class and with the Turks ever threatening from the East, the Habsburg monarchy needed an absolute ruler to hold it together, not a dissolute. R. J. W. Evans describes Rudolf as 'Prince of the eccentrics',[10] and although proud and intelligent, given the times, he was perhaps understandably smitten with a deep vein of melancholy. Believing himself bewitched and likely to die before the age of fifty, he kept himself largely cooped up in the Hrad, the castle that towers high over the Vltava.

Perhaps to lighten his pessimism, shared by much of Europe as the baneful year 1600 loomed, Rudolf immersed himself in the diversions of art, including the Milanese Arcimbaldo who painted the Emperor sculpted out of fruits, some of which might have been grown in the palace gardens from the rare plants nurtured there. Rudolf was also an avid collector of the intriguing, such as automata and perpetual-motion machines, and had amassed a large and eclectic library consisting of rare books (including works by Bacon), and volumes relating to mysticism and alchemy. The angels seemed fated to direct Dee towards the Rudolfine court.

On 3 September 1584 Dee gained his only audience with Rudolf and bluntly rebuked him for his sins and offered his and the angels' services to help make 'your Seat...the greatest that ever was, and the Devil shall become your prisoner' (by which he meant the Ottoman threat). Surprisingly, such brazen conceit seems not to have ruffled the Emperor unduly, but neither was he so enamoured of Dee that he responded favourably to his request – in exchange for revealing the secrets of divine mysteries and alchemical transmutations – to appoint him as Imperial Philosopher and Mathematician. According to Clulee, Rudolf was not disposed to take on the mantle of activist in leading the Counter-Reformation, but preferred with his 'pessimistic resignation' a course of 'vacillation and indecision'.[11]

Despite both Kelley and Dee's apparent acknowledgement of Catholic, 'when in Rome' ritual, the continuation of their 'actions' prompted rumours once again of conjuring. Rudolf, according to Evans, acting 'on one of his abrupt moods',[12] and, avers Clulee 'motivated by a desire less of opposition to Dee than by a desire to pacify Catholic authorities',[13] expelled them from Prague. Fortunately for Dee and Kelley, and against the wish of the Papal Nuncio who demanded to have them actually sent to Rome for 'examination', they found another source of patronage.

Kelley and Dee left the city in June 1586 for Trebon and the estate of Vilem Rozmberk in southern Bohemia, but not before in April 1586 a weird episode occurred that is characteristic of the often wayward and unpredictable nature of their relationship. At the top of the tower of the medieval palace (now known as Faust's House), where they had taken up residence, Kelley, Dee and a priest named Father Pucci, suspicious of their activities, assembled for an action. Soon, 'A voice came down from on high...hard by the face of Edward Kelley'[14] that commanded Dee to burn in the room's furnace the precious twenty-eight volumes of revelation that they had established. This momentous sacrifice Dee stoically accepted as if he were Abraham offering the life of his son, whilst Kelley humbly concurred, 'afflicted by a pain he had never felt in his whole life'.[15] Pucci, a confidant of Dee, but bound to the Catholic hierarchy, was presumably led to believe that his friends had renounced their troublesome ways. The ploy clearly failed in the light of their subsequent expulsion, but the incineration must have bound Kelley and Dee closer together, especially as three weeks later, as if by magic, all the books were joyfully recovered under an almond tree in their garden.

Rozmberk's sheltering of the duo seems to have been largely mercenary; his interest lay in possible rewards from their knowledge of alchemy. Dee was well aware of the value of the practice having conducted experiments before meeting Kelley. It represented, says Evans, 'an aspect of his whole occult striving, the material demonstration of a superior power'.[16] Dee was not averse either (prompted by the spirits) to letting Rudolf know that he possessed the knowledge of gold transmutation. The pair conducted many experiments over the next two years in the laboratory set up by Rozmberk, but it was Kelley who drove the project forward, transmuting an ounce of gold from a speck of the red powder he had brought with him from England. Whilst Dee profited monetarily from this period, it was Edward Kelley's fame that spread widely; as Woolley puts it, Dee 'was now cast in the role of sorcerer's apprentice rather than sorcerer'.[17]

The angelic actions continued too, but took a decidedly non-spiritual turn. Kelley wished to be free of scrying and suggested, via the spirits, that Dee's seven-year-old son, Arthur, should take up his position as his father's amanuensis. Arthur, however, didn't seem able to make out much more in the crystal than a pair of lions, so Dee was relieved when Kelley resumed his post. But not for long, as Maldini, pronouncing that 'Nothing is unlawful which is lawful unto God', commanded that John and Jane Dee, Edward and Joan Kelley should swap marital partners for a night. After much wringing of hands, including even Kelley's, the union was consummated and the spirit Maldini appeared for what was to be the last time. Nine months later on 28 February Jane Dee gave birth to a baby boy.

Later that year Rozmberk asked Dee to leave. The fine style of his leaving in three coaches and three wagons plus an escort of soldiers attested to his current wealth, but this soon dissipated on his return in 1589 to his ransacked Mortlake home, most of his books and instruments having been stolen. Dee's reputation remained precarious, despite being on good terms with Elizabeth, but he never quite gave up his angelic exploration. The actions, now with another scryer, were still in progress as late as 1607, two years before his death.

Kelley meanwhile stayed on in Trebon to capitalise on his success as celebrity alchemist. Elizabeth, convinced of his powers, tried to woo him back to England, but now under Rudolf's patronage as a citizen and knight of Bohemia he had acquired a castle, estates and respectability. His nouveau richesse was short-lived, however. For some undetermined scurrilous activity he was arrested by Rudolf and held in jail until 1593. His last years are as murky as his first, according to Woolley, and reports varied as to his fate right up until 1598. None of them suggests a life of calm and respectability regained.

What then was the basis of their extraordinary double act? We need an assessment before relating it to the Voynich manuscript. Opinions vary, but not regarding the one half that was John Dee. An intensely religious man, although vain and prey to a worldly love of grandeur, he seems to have combined a huge, compendious intellect with an innocent sense of mission not only to realise his prophetic destiny but also to help heal the rifts in the Christian world. His dialogue with angels, unpredictable and exhaustive, was the outcome of his own depth of learning, culminating in a leap of faith to attain such elevated ends. A comparison with the earlier figure of Roger Bacon is apposite, save for Dee's final impetuous scramble up the ladder to the divine. A twentieth-century comparison might be found in Rudolf Steiner, another all-embracing philosopher attempting to combine the worlds of spirit and science.

Edward Kelley is at once more explicable and enigmatic. He appeared from obscure origins as a fully fledged opportunist and scoundrel; before he and his patron had set off on their continental mystery tour, Kelley had been up to his tricks from the outset. Advancing his knowledge of fairies to Dee at their first meeting, he changed his tack towards the scriptural world when Dee did not jump to employ him, and adroitly changed his name from Talbot in a bid to expunge his former dubious past. Treating Dee like a child on a treasure hunt, he planted a crystal ball by his study window for Dee to find, and clearly derived material from Dee's library that re-emerged from the mouths of the spirits; Kelley cheekily even cast doubts on their credibility. Helping himself to scans of Dee's private diary he was also able to stay abreast of his master's thinking. Kelley is both ventriloquist and dummy by turn, as Dee, in the front row, resolutely fails to realise that an act is being played out in front of him.

The direction of the script is not difficult to discern – the audience is led where its author wants it to go. Hence Kelley's faltering but determined self-serving progression from Dee to Laski to Rudolf to Rozmberk in search of his own goal of using divine gobbledygook and legerdemain to eventually make him rich. A keen and abnormal intelligence, almost equal to that of his employers, was at work. The hours spent scrying and inventing show a remarkable diligence and the angelic products a coherent, poetic, almost Blakeian imagination. Deacon suggests that the Enochian Kelley revealed has a grammar and syntax suggesting an authentic language. Certainly the Rosicrucian Order of the Golden Dawn, founded in England in 1887, of which occultist Aleister Crowley was a member, thought so, and still utilise it in their rituals. Deborah Harkness is less convinced, and notes how Dee was frustrated by the enormous variations contained in the Enochian tongue, 'suffering under the pressure of trying to learn a language on which the future of the world depended'.[18] Dee does not seem, however, to have queried some of the angels' lexicon that had more than a derivative tinge – Londoh meaning the Kingdom ('London' being the seat of Dee's monarch), or Madrid meaning Iniquity (that monarch's enemy).

Deacon, however, doubts Dee's motives with the notion that his spiritual quest may have been just a cover for his espionage activities on behalf of the Crown – Dee was in fact using Kelley. Other scholars, though noting the possible authenticity of religious experience, suggest various sources of Kelley's inspiration; for Head, the unconscious, for Suster, hallucination with perhaps neurological roots, but Woolley veers towards Frances Yates's opinion of Kelley as 'a fraudulent knave'. How strange that Dee, such an ardent disciple of his predecessor Bacon, never heeded his urgent advice to be wary of scoundrels and impostors.

Although Harkness suggests that the obsidian mirror in the British Museum was never used by Kelley, it is listed as such in Horace Walpole's catalogue of curiosities. Unable to be seen by today's museum visitor, on its underside is a piece of paper he pasted with a verse by Samuel Butler:

> Kelley did all his feats upon,
> The Devil's Looking-glass, a stone,
> Where playing with him at Bo-peep,
> He solved all problems ne'er so deep.

Even if the mysterious manuscript was not the work of Bacon it is reasonable to suppose that it might well have fitted in with Dee's interest and been worthy of collection. In 'John Dee's Library Catalogue' by R. J. Roberts and Andrew G. Watson[19] the Voynich manuscript is indeed enumerated as DM 93, one of a number of 'books and manuscripts which are known to have formed part of Dee's library which do not appear in his catalogues or lists', but 'can be ascertained by employing external evidence'. They add, however, that in the case of DM 93, 'evidence is in fact inconclusive'[20] although three aspects are significant.

Most importantly, as Professor Watson wrote in 1986 to Yale University, 'the foliation in the Voynich manuscript is Dee's...even allowing for the notorious difficulty in deciding that figures are or are not in one hand, I am sure as I can be'. He refers to comparisons made with two Dee documents in the Bodleian Library's Ashmole Collection.[21] There are no other Dee clues, despite the fact that he would often annotate and inscribe ownership symbols in his books – a ladder and the figure of Jupiter. Further, Roberts and Watson point out that although, of the several hundred books and manuscripts Dee took with him when he left England a significant proportion related to alchemy (perhaps suggesting that his motives for travel were not entirely pure), they do not believe that the Voynich manuscript was one of them. Rather they suggest it was 'surely acquired on the continent'.[22]

Rafal Prinke, in an elegant internet article, queries both Roberts' and Watson's assertions. Regarding the foliation he agrees that it is most likely sixteenth century in style, but then goes on to single out the number 8 as being constructed in a very different manner from Dee. Prinke remarks too that the serif on Dee's number 7 does not match those in the Voynich manuscript. Others have drawn attention to the differences in numbers 1 and 4.

This leads to a second oft-cited piece of 'external' evidence. Dee records in his diary on 17 October 1586 that he has 630 ducats in his possession, a lot of money. Could this be, more or less, the sum that the 'bearer' in Marci's letter received for passing on the manuscript to Rudolf II? However, in October 1586, as we have seen, Dee and Kelley were staying with Rozmberk at Trebon having been expelled from Prague. This makes it unlikely that any book transaction had taken place, but more importantly it is clear that the 630 ducats relates to a particular incident. According to Woolley, Francesco Pucci, who had witnessed the furnace-burning episode in Prague, was still hounding Dee and Kelley with his 'venomous and restless tongue'. They resolved to buy him off, and paid him, in front of witnesses, 630 ducats and a further 800 from 2000 ducats contained in 'two great bags of money'.[23]

Such relatively large sums of money were certainly not alien to the duo during their stay abroad and make it fairly unlikely that they would have needed to tout books. Both of them seem to have been doing well as a result of Rozmberk's patronage in return for alchemical services. Kelley, for example, had bought Jane Dee, the object of his lust, a gold

Foliation in VMS	John Dee's book catalogue (1583) [1582 from spiritual diaries]

Dee's foliation (courtesy Rafal Prinke)

necklace worth 300 ducats as a sweetener prior to the wife-swapping, and as we have noted, Dee, when he left Trebon, set off in luxurious style. Whilst in Prague too, Woolley suggests that they had 'enjoyed a dramatic improvement in their material circumstances'.[24] Might this have resulted in part from Dee selling on some of the new additions to his library that Roberts and Watson suggest might have included the Voynich manuscript?

Evans indeed declares that Rudolf, 'when he heard of a notable work, a rare gem, a manuscript or some object of superstition ... spared no pains to secure it'.[25] Certainly a work in cipher with tantalising drawings would fit the bill, although Evans adds that it is 'mere speculation that Rudolf could have acquired the manuscript from Dee'.[26] As far as is known Dee only had one audience with the Emperor, and although the Voynich manuscript could have been negotiated through an agent, it is much more likely that he would have given it to him in the hope of favour, in the same way that he actually donated his prized 'perspective glass' that had entertained Elizabeth at Mortlake, which he had brought over from England.

The third item of evidence relates less directly to Dee's ownership of the Voynich manuscript in so far as it originates from a letter written nearly a hundred years later. Sir Thomas Brown, a friend of Arthur, Dee's son, wrote in 1675 to Elias Ashmole that Arthur had told him some thirty years earlier that he had seen a book, 'containing nothing but hieroglyphics; which...his father [John Dee], bestowed much time upon, but I could not hear that he could make it out'. Prinke offers various reasons why this is unlikely to have been the Voynich manuscript, which is in an enciphered handwriting, rather than ideograms as the use of 'hieroglyphics' suggests. Furthermore, Arthur's story was related many years later from a youthful memory derived when he was only seven years of age.

As is so often the case with the Voynich manuscript, anything connected with it tends to be surrounded by wishful thinking, by stabbing at connections in a manner not unlike the medieval 'correspondences' that a pre-scientific age resorted to in making sense of the world around. Apart from the contested foliation, none of the evidence for Dee's ownership of the manuscript rises above a similar level of hearsay. Nothing like the Voynich manuscript was listed in Dee's 1583 catalogue of his books and neither the story of the 630 ducats nor Arthur Dee's recollection can be trusted as definite proof. Perhaps we must discard Wilfrid Voynich's confident assertion in the conclusion to his lecture, 'During one of his visits to Prague, Dee undoubtedly presented it to Emperor Rudolf II.'[27]

But what of the other people mentioned in the letter Voynich found with his manuscript? Apart from Roger Bacon and the Emperor Rudolf, four other names are mentioned in the letter:

Joannes Marcus Marci, the Rector of the University of Prague, who wrote the letter; Athanasius Kircher, Jesuit priest and scholar, and intended recipient of the manuscript; and 'Dr Raphael', described as a tutor to Emperor Ferdinand III. There is also a reference to a previous owner of the manuscript, frustratingly unnamed, who it appears was in correspondence with Kircher some years earlier, and who apparently sent him a partial transcription of it. It was these names which allowed Voynich, after some detective work, to deduce the probable location of the manuscript for a brief period in history. His investigation was also helped by a lucky accident that revealed the name of another, long-forgotten owner of the manuscript.

While preparing the photostats that were later to be of such importance to Professor Newbold, one of the plates was accidentally underexposed. This revealed, on the seemingly blank margin of the first page of the manuscript, a faded and hitherto unnoticed signature. After being treated with chemicals the autograph once more became legible, and the name Jacobus de Tepenecz appeared. Voynich then began to investigate this name, scouring biographical dictionaries and even contacting the director of the Bohemian State Archives, until he eventually discovered that de Tepenecz was in fact a Bohemian scientist originally known as Horcicky (or *Sinapius* in Latin). This was an important breakthrough for Voynich, as it gave a first, definite date in the manuscript's history. Horcicky was well known at the Bohemian court, and was probably close to the Emperor Rudolf himself. He had amassed a fortune through the invention of an elixir, a cure-all remedy known as *Aqua-Sinapius*; and was even wealthy enough to lend money to the Emperor. He was granted the title 'de Tepenecz' in 1608, reputedly as a reward for curing Rudolf of some serious illness. The discovery of the signature implied that the manuscript must have come into de Tepenecz's possession in the period between his ennoblement in 1608 and his death in 1622 (Voynich believed he must have received it either as a gift, or more likely as a loan from the Emperor's collection which was subsequently never returned).

Voynich's contact at the Bohemian Archives also provided him with the identity of 'Dr Raphael', who, according to the letter, had been a tutor to the children of Ferdinand II, and had originally suggested the link between the manuscript and Roger Bacon. The archives were able to give Dr Raphael the surname Missowsky. A lawyer and poet, Missowsky had joined the Bohemian Court during the reign of Rudolf II, and rose to eventually become Attorney-General under his old pupil Emperor Ferdinand III. But when it came to the unnamed 'former owner' of the manuscript, who had, according to the letter once again, bequeathed the manuscript to Marcus Marci, Voynich was unable to establish a name. It was many years later, after Voynich's death, that this shadowy figure finally emerged from the obscuring mists of time.

One of the most important names involved in Voynich manuscript research is Robert S. Brumbaugh, Professor of Medieval Philosophy at Yale University, who was able to devote much time to its study after it was donated to the Beinecke Library. Brumbaugh eventually developed his own theory of the manuscript's origin, and even claimed a partial decipherment. As well as holding the Voynich manuscript itself, the Beinecke has a number of cartons containing related material, such as scrapbooks of newspaper clippings, notebooks of Ethel Voynich, and correspondence and notes by Wilfrid Voynich himself. Here Brumbaugh takes up the story:

> In looking through cartons of material in the Beinecke Library files, I came across what seems an unaddressed and undated carbon of a translation of a note from Prague to Voynich. (Copies of translations of other letters from the Bohemian State Archives to Voynich, similarly undated and unaddressed, were in the same box.) This was apparently in response to an inquiry about the identity of the owner who had the manuscript between the death of de Tepenecz and its acquisition by Marci. This was the owner about whom Marci wrote, that he was determined to solve it. The note says that Marci probably inherited the manuscript from George Barschius, an alchemist, since 'Marci inherited Barschius' alchemical library.' Since the Bohemian Archives proved right in every other piece of information supplied – for example, the identity of 'Dr Raphael' – this is worth following up.[28]

As indeed it was, but neither Voynich nor Brumbaugh did so. Although he was in possession of this intriguing nugget of information, it seems Voynich was unable to discover any other information about this figure, and left out the name of 'Barschius' in his lecture to the College of Physicians of Philadelphia in 1921. Brumbaugh likewise did not follow up the lead; and so it was left to one of the modern Voynich experts, René Zandbergen, to finally confirm the mystery owner.

The clue to the necessary corroborative evidence lay within the letter addressed to Kircher, where it clearly stated that 'The former owner of this book once asked your opinion by letter, copying and sending you a portion of the book from which he believed you would be able to read the remainder...' To the immense luck of later Voynich researchers, Kircher's lasting legacy to posterity is the direct result of a profound hoarding instinct. His contemporary reputation as a great intellect allowed Kircher to amass a vast collection of scientific equipment and curiosities from the natural world, either sent to him or donated by visiting scholars. Even before his death, this collection had become so great that it was housed in a large hall and attracted many visitors, thus becoming one of the world's first public museums, named Museo Kircheriano. Along with his collection of strange artifacts, Kircher also kept much of the correspondence sent to him over the years, and this too was preserved. Catalogued, bound in volumes and held in the archives of the Pontifical Gregorian University in the Piazza Pilotta in Rome, the letters became known as the Carteggio Kircheriano. For many years access to this collection of letters was denied to all but a select few, until a new archivist, Father Marcel Chappin, allowed American scholar Michael John Gorman to publish them on the internet as part of the Kircher Correspondence Project.

Now it follows that if Barschius, or 'Baresch' as he is known in the non-Latinised version of his name, was the unnamed owner of the manuscript, and he had written to Kircher asking for his help in solving the riddle, his letter might just be part of the Carteggio Kircheriano. This was just the connection made by René Zandbergen, who began to search through Kircher's correspondence published on the internet. Zandbergen's detective work paid off. Although the first letter sent by the unnamed mystery man (presumably the one mentioned in the Marcus Marci letter) did not survive, Zandbergen found another, dated 27 April 1639, from George Baresch in Prague to Athanasius Kircher in Rome. In it, Baresch inquires about Kircher's progress in deciphering the transcribed pages he had sent sometime earlier. It appears that he had heard nothing back from Kircher, and was uncertain whether the first letter had even been delivered, until he checked with 'Father Moretus', to whom its delivery had been entrusted and who assured him it had arrived safely. Most importantly, Baresch gives a brief description of the strange codex in his possession, stating that it contains many pictures of herbs, and also illustrations of stars and chemical secrets. This brief description suggests that the document belonging to Baresch could be the one we know today as the Voynich manuscript.

So the combined efforts of Wilfrid Voynich, Robert Brumbaugh and René Zandbergen, over a period of eighty years, had identified the unnamed man – George Baresch. Unfortunately, we know very little about Baresch. Where and when he was born is not known, nor is the date of his death. We can be fairly certain of two facts: that at some point he was the owner of a book that bears many of the hallmarks of the Voynich manuscript, and that he was a friend of Joannes Marcus Marci. And what of Marci, the last confirmed owner of the manuscript before it disappears from historical sight? Wilfrid Voynich takes up the story:

Who was Marcus Marci? Today he is nearly forgotten, but among his contemporaries he was held in great repute as a physician, mathematician, physicist and orientalist, and he was rector of the University of Prague. That he was highly esteemed, not only on the continent, we know from the fact that the London Royal Society, through Edward Brown, son of Sir Thomas Brown, desired in 1667 to invite him to become a corresponding member of the society. The invitation, however, came too late, for he had just died. Marci died 10 April 1667, at the age of seventy-two years. A few months before his death he entered the Jesuit house at Prague. Before joining the Order he distributed his books among friends, and in August 1665 (or 1666), he sent this cipher manuscript to Kircher.[29]

The letter written by Marcus Marci gives us a brief window in time in which we can recap the probable movements of the manuscript, as it passes through the hands of a number of identifiable historical figures. First there is Jacobus Horcicky, who at some time after 1608 wrote his name on the first page of the manuscript – thus becoming its first confirmed owner. By the 1630s the codex is the property of the alchemist George Baresch (or Barschius), who, unable to decipher the volume, copies a number of pages and sends them to Athanasius Kircher in Rome. Receiving no reply from the Jesuit scholar, Baresch writes again in 1639, hoping for some explanation of the manuscript; but again it seems no decipherment is forthcoming. Baresch continues his own studies, wrestling with the problem until, upon his death, the manuscript is bequeathed to his friend Marcus Marci. At some point in the early 1640s, Marci discusses the book with Dr Raphael Missowsky, Attorney General to Ferdinand III, who it seems is already familiar with the manuscript and tells Marci what he knows of its history – the purchase of it by Rudolf II for 600 ducats and the possibility that it is the work of Roger Bacon. For the next twenty-odd years Marci holds on to the codex, until, as he prepares to enter the Jesuit order in the mid-1660s, he decides to distribute his library amongst his friends. With his strange manuscript still untranslated, he determines to finally entrust the whole volume, rather than just a few copied pages, to Kircher in Rome. With the manuscript he sends a letter, offering the book as a token of his affection and admiration, and hoping that Kircher will 'burst through its bars' and read the secrets hidden within.

It is from this letter that we have been able to glean the few facts listed here, and shed some rather dim shafts of light on to the murky history of the Voynich manuscript. But there is one figure we have yet to look at; the one to whom the other characters in our historical dramatis personae turn to, in the hope that he can solve the riddle of the manuscript. He is the 'Reverend and Distinguished Sir' to whom Marci addressed the letter, Athanasius Kircher.

He was born on the Feast of St Athanasius, 2 May 1602, near the modern German town of Fulda. The youngest of nine children, Kircher was born into a learned family and, according to his own account, seems to have been a gifted child whose inquisitive nature got him into a number of scrapes. Growing up during the period of religio-political turmoil that led eventually to the Thirty Years War, and apparently somewhat hindered by his own precocious nature, Kircher's education was continually interrupted. Hence his educational resumé reads somewhat like a tourist route around western Germany. His application to the Jesuit College in Mainz having been rejected, he subsequently studied at Paderborn, Cologne, Koblenz and Heiligenstadt before being summoned by the Elector of Mainz to teach at Aschauffenberg, from where he progressed to Speyer and then Wurzberg. In 1630, filled with an obvious wanderlust and Jesuitical zeal, Kircher applied to the Superior General of his order to be allowed to travel to China as a missionary; but when this was turned down he headed south to Avignon, and thence to Rome, where he was to spend the rest of his life as a professor of mathematics.

To attempt to define or categorise Kircher by a particular branch of learning or intellectual discipline is impossible. In an age of polymaths, Kircher cast his scholarly net particularly wide. In addition to the theological studies necessary to his training in the Jesuit order, Kircher applied himself to learning Greek, Hebrew and Syrian, as well as philosophy and the aforementioned mathematics. He borrowed a telescope and observed sunspots, wrote on the subjects of geology and magnetism, built a musical fountain, gave a detailed description of a magic lantern, and had himself lowered into the crater of Mount Vesuvius. He compiled reports of the Far East from the tales of returning Jesuit missionaries, catalogued early Baroque music, devised a system of logic, developed secret languages and wrote on the art of cryptography. But unlike many of his contemporaries, his brilliance, widely acknowledged in his own time, has faded over the subsequent three hundred and fifty years.

It almost seems as if Kircher was born too late – or too early – for such was the tide of the times that his holistic world view led even before his death to his rejection by the scientific world. He never made the kind of epoch-making discovery that assured the fame of Johannes Kepler, Robert Boyle, or Isaac Newton, and caused the modern world to forgive Kepler his interest in cosmic harmonies, and Boyle and Newton their serious concern with alchemy. Kircher, on the other hand, has been blamed for his atavistic beliefs in much that later ages were to regard as superstitious.[30]

So wrote Jocelyn Godwin on the nature of Kircher's particular brand of intellectualism. Here was a man who, whilst writing on the practical and scientific use of magnetism, could at the same time accept the existence of fabulous beasts and the spontaneous generation of insects. This contradictory nature allowed him the clarity of reason to denounce alchemy, yet maintain an absolute belief in the importance of the predictive power of astrology. Nor was he afraid to court publicity for himself and his ideas. Maurice Pope, in his book *The Story of Decipherment*, gives the following, less than flattering appraisal of Kircher's position in the history of ideas:

> Modesty was not … a part of his character. He was grandiose in all things, and wrote voluminously on a voluminous range of subjects, including Chinese, Universal Writing, and the Art of How to Think. Almost none of his work is reliable. Nevertheless, among his inaccuracies and his fantasies there is some brilliance and enough learning to make it unjust to label him a charlatan. He belongs to the category of the fashionable academic.[31]

It was his status as a 'fashionable academic' that explains Kircher's role in the story of the Voynich manuscript, because above all his other areas of learning, Kircher was famous in his own lifetime for unlocking the secrets of Egyptian hieroglyphics.

Rome in the mid-seventeenth century, the Rome of Kircher, was gripped by a fascination for all things Egyptian. The Renaissance, and the interest in classical learning that was its impetus and driving force, led scholars inexorably back, by way of ancient Rome and Greece, to Egypt. It was from the rediscovered texts of Graeco-Roman writers that men of the Renaissance learned of the greatness of Egyptian civilisation. 'They were learning daily, in almost all spheres of literature, science, and technology, from ancient Rome. Rome had learned from Greece; why should not Greece have in its turn learned from Egypt?'[32] In Kircher's Rome, this interest even took on a physical manifestation, as a craze for re-erecting fallen Egyptian obelisks swept the city. Unfortunately for Renaissance scholars wishing to unlock the wisdom of the pharaohs, the ability to read Egyptian hieroglyphics had been lost for well over twelve hundred years.

This form of writing, making use of symbols which vary from representational to highly stylised, first appeared in Egypt around the year 3000 BC, and was to adorn temple walls, tombs and obelisks for the next thirty-five centuries. Gradually another, simpler writing form was to emerge, known as demotic, which represented the same language but was easier and quicker to use. Both writing systems were to fall out of use relatively suddenly around the beginning of the fifth century AD thanks to the rise of Christianity, which aimed to break the ties with Egypt's pagan traditions. Hieroglyphics and demotic were replaced by the Coptic script, which itself was to be usurped by Arabic in the eleventh century. Even before the use of hieroglyphics had ended, their operation and meaning were becoming misunderstood, and many fanciful and incorrect interpretations were expounded. The most popular and persistent theory was that hieroglyphics represented an *ideographic* style of writing, where each symbol represented an idea rather than a phonetic syllable. As far back as the first century BC, the Greek historian Diodorus Siculus, who actually travelled in Egypt when hieroglyphics were still in use, reported that they worked 'by drawing objects whose metaphorical meaning is impressed on the memory': hence the image of a falcon represented 'anything that happens quickly', while a crocodile stood for evil. This kind of interpretation was still prevalent in the third century AD, when the philosopher Plotinus wrote: 'They [the Egyptians] did not employ devices to copy the sounds of a proposition and how it is pronounced. Instead in their sacred writings they drew signs, a separate sign for each idea, so as to express its whole meaning at once.'[33]

By the Renaissance, the belief that hieroglyphics were a form of picture-writing which expressed ideas had become firmly entrenched, and a number of books had been published on the subject. The first, *The Hieroglyphs, or a Commentary on the sacred letters of the Egyptians and other peoples*, had been published by Pierius Valerianus in 1556, and others were to follow; for example, in 1631 a priest named Nicolas Caussin produced *The Symbolic Wisdom of Egypt* in which his allegorical interpretations were greatly influenced by his own Jesuitical beliefs. Athanasius Kircher's first encounter with Egyptian civilisation seems to have occurred in the year 1628 when he saw illustrations of hieroglyphics in the *Thesaurus* of Horwart Von Hohenburg. Hohenburg seems to have strayed somewhat from the main body of opinion on Egyptian writing, claiming that hieroglyphics represented nothing more than pure decoration. Kircher felt instinctively that this theory was incorrect, and began his own study of hieroglyphics, with a desire to unlock their secrets.

In the 1630s Kircher produced a book on the Coptic language, *Prodromus Coptus* (the publication of which may well have prompted Baresch to write his first letter to Kircher), but it was an invitation from the family of Pope Innocent X to examine a fallen obelisk that afforded him his first opportunity to study hieroglyphics. This led to the publication in 1650 of his first work on the translation of hieroglyphics, *Obeliscus Pamphilius*, which was followed by Kircher's main work on the subject, *Oedipus Aegyptiacus*, published in three volumes between 1652 and 1654. This book was to focus attention on Kircher as the foremost authority on Egypt of his day, and was to influence the thinking on hieroglyphic translation for the next one hundred and fifty years. Kircher's theory seems to have been driven by twin obsessions that affected his whole career and influenced much of his writing: one was a passionate interest in the origins of ideas, the other, a need to unify disparate and varied areas of thought and belief. Nothing sums this up better than the inscription from the frontispiece of his *Ars Magna Sciendi* (*The Great Art of Knowledge*) which reads: 'Nothing is more beautiful than to know all.' This fascination with discovering the supposed original incarnation of human knowledge, coupled with his firmly held religious beliefs, was to lead Kircher to his particular interpretation of Egyptian hieroglyphics.

Kircher believed that it was impossible to know with any certainty the condition of the world before the Old Testament flood of Noah, which had been invoked by God to cleanse His creation. The original spark of divine wisdom present in Adam and Eve had been extinguished by the deluge; and it followed that Noah was the earliest possible root for human wisdom in the post-diluvian world, a wisdom that was subsequently disseminated by his sons. Egypt was colonised by Noah's son Ham, whose rebellious nature corrupted the knowledge of his father, which in turn led to the pagan practices of idolatry and the worshipping of many gods. Therefore all such 'corrupted', polytheistic religious systems, including those of the Chaldeans, the Greeks and the Romans, must have developed from the Egyptian original. So far, this theory seems quite in keeping with much of Renaissance thought, but Kircher was to go further in his ongoing quest to unify seemingly unrelated areas of learning. Not only had Egyptian beliefs led directly to the other pagan religions of the ancient world, but must also, Kircher reasoned, be the origin of non-Christian religions of his own time, including those of India, China, Japan and the Americas. Although he categorically dismissed Islam, Kircher felt some vestige of original truth could still exist in all these religions, and consequently he searched for correspondences in the varying belief systems which might in turn point to their original inspiration.

Employing the principle that later wisdom and belief derived from a beginning in Egypt, Kircher worked backwards from various other philosophical systems, including such diverse disciplines as the Cabala, Persian magic, Arabian alchemy and Greek philosophy, to arrive at his reading of hieroglyphics as a symbolic, rather than linguistic form of writing. His method of interpretation seemed to find corroboration when, in 1666, he provided a translation of the three visible sides of a fallen obelisk that had recently been uncovered by building work in Rome, and went on to predict what should be written on the hidden fourth side. When the obelisk was raised and erected in the Piazza della Minerva, and his prediction was shown to be correct, Kircher's theory seemed to be proven, and his reputation as the greatest solver of ancient linguistic riddles was firmly enshrined.

How exactly he arrived at his prediction, however, remains a mystery; because unfortunately for Kircher and his later place in the history of Egyptology, his reading of hieroglyphics was totally incorrect. Take, for instance, this example quoted by Maurice Pope of a translation of a cartouche on the Minervan obelisk. A cartouche is a set of hieroglyphics contained in a loop, and normally represents the name of an important person, often a pharaoh. Typical of his fanciful translations, Kircher believed the cartouches to be mystical spells for controlling magical spirits. His translation reads:

> The protection of Osiris against the violence of Typho must be elicited according to the proper rites and ceremonies by sacrifices and by appeal to the tutelory Genii of the triple world in order to ensure the enjoyment of the prosperity customarily given by the Nile against the violence of the enemy Typho.

In reality, the cartouche spells out nothing more than the name of the Pharaoh Pasammetichus.

The seventeenth-century assumption, championed by Kircher, that hieroglyphics were nothing more than picture-writing was utterly wrong. Each hieroglyph is in fact a phonogram – a symbol that represents a phonetic character. It was almost one hundred and fifty years after Kircher published his theories that the great breakthrough in the understanding of hieroglyphics was made; a breakthrough that was to allow scholars not only to read the words of ancient Egyptians, but to speak their language. This extraordinary achievement in the history of decipherment was made possible by that most famous relic of antiquity, the Rosetta Stone.

Discovered in 1799 by Napoleonic troops in the town of Rosetta in the Nile delta, this black basalt slab is inscribed with a decree from the council of Egyptian priests, written in the year 196 BC, which details the honours to be heaped upon the Pharaoh Ptolemy. The importance of this proclamation was that it had been inscribed on the tablet three times: once in hieroglyphics, once in demotic, and one final time in Greek. As scholars were already able to read the Greek inscription, they were soon able to find the hieroglyphic equivalents and translate them. For the first time in thirteen centuries it was possible to read the hieroglyphic symbols; but still no one knew how the language of the ancient Egyptians was spoken. This momentous advance in the understanding of ancient Egypt was made by a brilliant young French linguist, Jean-François Champollion. By the time he started work on the problem in the 1820s it was already known that the cartouches on the Rosetta Stone represented the name of the Pharaoh

Ptolemy, and so Champollion allocated phonetic values to the various symbols contained within the cartouche. He then began to look for other hieroglyphic inscriptions which incorporated the same symbols, to which he could then allocate the phonetic values he had already deduced from the 'Ptolemy' cartouche. By making educated guesses to fill in the phonetic values of unknown symbols, Champollion was eventually able to identify the cartouches of the Pharaoh Rameses, Alexander the Great and even Cleopatra. Champollion soon realised that the language of ancient Egypt was in fact Coptic, the language that had been spoken there right up to the eleventh century; it was only the ways of writing it that had changed – from hieroglyphics, to demotic and then to the Coptic alphabet. With this discovery, the concept of hieroglyphics as ideographic picture-writing was finally laid to rest, as was any last vestige of Kircher's reputation as an Egyptologist.

We must not, however, lose sight of the fact that in his own day Kircher was thought to be the greatest authority on Egyptian hieroglyphics; and it is for this reason that George Baresch and Joannes Marcus Marci sought his help in translating the Voynich manuscript. We can be confident in making this statement because of evidence contained in the two letters written to Kircher: in which both Baresch and Marci refer to the manuscript as a 'Sphinx', and Baresch even goes as far as to describe Kircher as 'the Egyptian Oedipus'. One would love to know what our misguided genius Athanasius Kircher made of the manuscript: perhaps applying his particular brand of inductive reasoning to produce another of his strange and fanciful translations, or whether he wrestled unsuccessfully with this conundrum until his death in 1680.

There is no mention in the catalogue of the Museo Kircheriano of a book resembling the Voynich manuscript, nor is there any mention of it in Kircher's surviving writing. One possible explanation for this is Kircher's inability to make any progress in understanding the strange Voynich script. Unlike the images used in hieroglyphic script, which lend themselves so easily to symbolic readings, the repetitive squiggles of the Voynichese alphabet could not be interpreted in the same imaginative way. Kircher, together with so many that were to follow him, was doubtless completely stumped by the Voynich manuscript, yet ever mindful of his reputation he was probably none too keen to let this failure become public knowledge. Another possibility is that Kircher may have suspected that the manuscript was a hoax, designed to expose him as an intellectual fraud. He may have feared that other scholars, jealous of his fame and reputation, might have deliberately constructed a test which he was bound to fail. If the codex was a fake, with a text consisting of nothing more than meaningless shapes and symbols, Kircher would have found himself in a no-win situation, a sort of scholarly 'catch-22'. If he produced a translation which was later shown to be incorrect, this would cast doubt over his work on Egyptian hieroglyphics; while if he failed to produce anything at all, his reputation as a great man of learning, one capable of seemingly impossible decipherments, would be brought into question. Both of these possibilities would, of course, explain why Kircher simply chose to ignore the problem, and the repeated requests for a progress report went unanswered. He would rather say nothing than admit defeat.

There is, however, a final, even more mysterious option which explains Kircher's silence, and that is that the manuscript never reached Rome at all. When Marcus Marci signed and dated his letter, and dispatched his gift to Kircher, the Voynich manuscript slipped out of sight and out of verifiable history. For a relatively brief period of just under sixty years, between 1608 and 1666, we are able to identify its probable whereabouts and likely owners. Before and after this time everything is supposition. Whether the manuscript reached Kircher, only to frustrate him to the point where he suppressed knowledge of its existence, or whether its journey between Prague and Rome was interrupted, is impossible to know.

Wilfrid Voynich's research, which has been continued and added to over the following decades by many other interested parties, has furnished us with some sense of the probable historical melee from which the manuscript could have emerged. What it failed to do, however, was provide any plausible or verifiable explanation as to what the codex actually *meant*. This task, first attempted by Professor Newbold, has also been taken up in the intervening years by an entirely new cast of characters, united by one seemingly simple aim: to discover what truth lies beneath the ambiguous swirls of the Voynichese script.

⇥ 4 ⇤

THE CRYPTOLOGICAL MAZE
Part I

If one were to suggest the single most enduring legacy of
William Newbold's work on the Voynich manuscript, it
would probably be the unwillingness of other medieval historians to investigate the inscrutable codex. Professor
Newbold's extravagant and misguided claims of decipherment, or, to be more accurate, the subsequent refutation of his
theories by Professor Manly, has left the manuscript largely
outside the mainstream academic world, in a sort of intellectual wilderness. The critical backlash that followed the publication of Manly's article no doubt deterred other academics
from risking their reputations in the way Newbold did, and
has led to the current situation where many scholars of the
medieval and Renaissance worlds, whose skills might shed
light on the enigma, are unaware of the manuscript's very
existence. Over the eighty-odd years since Professor
Newbold's death it has largely fallen to cryptanalysts or professional academics working in their spare time to continue
Voynich research, with little support or interest from the academic establishment. Indeed, when American military cryptanalyst William F. Friedman applied for a research grant to
continue his work on the manuscript, it was refused because
the learned society he applied to thought that 'the result
would simply be some familiar textbook of botany'.[1]

However, the publication of Professor Newbold's work
notes in 1928 had another, perhaps more important effect on
subsequent study of the Voynich manuscript. Included in the
Newbold book were a number of photographic plates of
various pages of the manuscript, and it was these illustrations
that gave many members of the public their first glimpse of
the Voynichese script. As Wilfrid Voynich's widow Ethel

continued to ration out photostat copies of the manuscript to academics whom she hoped might produce the much sought-after decryption, a number of enthusiastic amateurs also began to take up the challenge, basing their efforts on the photographs in Newbold's book. A friendly, though undoubtedly competitive race had started between professional and amateur cryptanalysts around the world: a race to be the first to solve the riddle of the Voynich manuscript. First to emerge was an American lawyer named James Martin Feely, who in 1945 published a book entitled *Roger Bacon's Cypher: the Right Key Found.*

Before we can look at Feely's attempted decryption of the Voynich manuscript, and indeed the other significant claims of decipherment that have followed over the years, it will be useful to take a look at the history of cryptology, or the science of secret writing, as it developed during the centuries in which the manuscript was probably written. By studying the advances made in codes and ciphers over this period, we will be better able to understand the problems facing any would-be decipherer of the manuscript; and this excursion into the vast field of cryptology will also provide a better insight into just how unique the Voynichese 'language' really is when placed in the context of other early modern systems of secret writing. What follows is a necessarily brief introduction to some of the broader concepts of this vast and fascinating subject. (Anyone wishing to delve deeper into this area will find a list of recommended books in the bibliography.)

We have already touched on the world of cryptology and encountered a number of commonly used terms (such as plain text and cipher text), but now we must examine the various branches of this science (or 'art', as the more romantically inclined might prefer), and define some of the terminology that we will be using in the rest of this chapter. An ancient form of secret writing is known as steganography, which aims not to hide the meaning of a message, but the message itself, and covers such techniques as the use of invisible inks and, more recently, microdots. The use of steganography has largely been discounted in the Voynich manuscript, for as Robert Brumbaugh says: 'the Voynich manuscript makes no attempt to disguise the fact that there is a hidden text; and so there is no reason to expect any elaborate *additional* methods

such as secret inks'.[2] However, the most important definition
we must establish is the difference between the two most
commonly used (and misused) terms in cryptology: a *cipher*
and a *code*. Although both are techniques for hiding the
meaning of a message or text from prying eyes, there is a
simple and fundamental difference: a cipher is the replacement of *letters* in a text with other letters, numbers or
symbols, whilst a code requires the replacement of whole
words or *phrases* with other words, letters, numbers or
symbols. A cipher, therefore, changes the component parts of
words, rather than the words themselves; whereas a code acts
as a form of secret language, where each word in the original
message must have an equivalent in the code language. The
major drawback with a code is that for it to operate successfully, both the sender and receiver of a message would need to
possess a codebook, a dictionary-like work in which every
word in the plain-text language would be listed alongside the
code equivalent: so for example, to compile a codebook we
could allocate the word **the** the number 20, the word **attack**
the number 47, the word **town** the number 163, and so on,
giving every possible word we might need to use a code
number or symbol. To encode the message **attack the town**,
we simply write 47 20 163, which could be decoded by anyone
possessing a copy of the same codebook. However, the huge
task of creating a usable code now becomes apparent. The
task is almost equivalent to creating a new, secret language.
(The possibility that the Voynich manuscript is written in a
form of code will be discussed in the next chapter; for now we
will focus on the use of ciphers, as it is in this area that most
Voynich researchers have concentrated their efforts.)

Ciphers fall into two broad categories; transposition and substitution. A transposition cipher, as the name suggests, trans-
poses or rearranges the letters of the original text, in effect
anagrammatising the message. As we saw in chapter 2 with the
work of Newbold, a transposition cipher can offer a relatively
high level of security, but unless there is an agreed method for
unscrambling the cipher text, the receiver can never guarantee
that they are correctly reproducing the original message. In a
substitution cipher, the letters of the plain-text message remain
in their correct order, but are substituted or replaced by other
letters, numbers or symbols. One of the simplest and oldest

1. Folio 100r

2. Bramble, Julian Anicia Codex, Vienna med.gr.1, f83

3. Wood sorrel, sorrel, strawberry-tree and balsam,
Egerton ms 747, f12, British Library

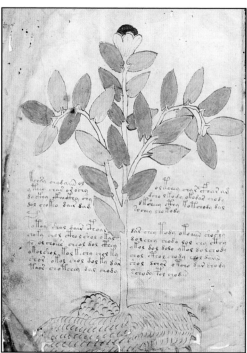

4. Folio 1v

5. Folio 15v

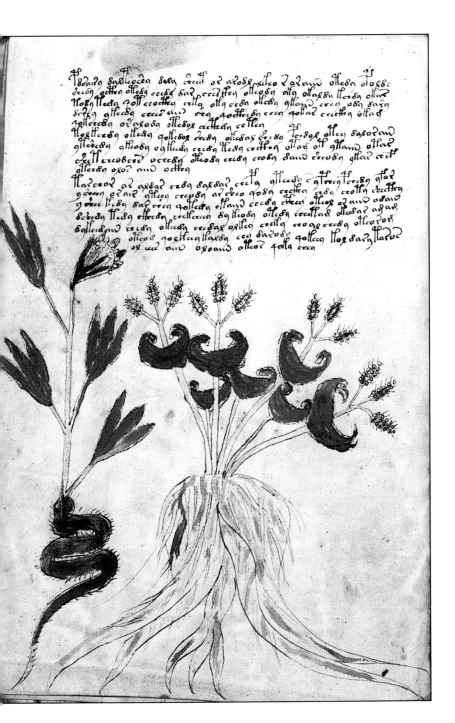

6. Folio 43v

7. Folio 44r

8. O'Neill's 'sunflower', folio 93r

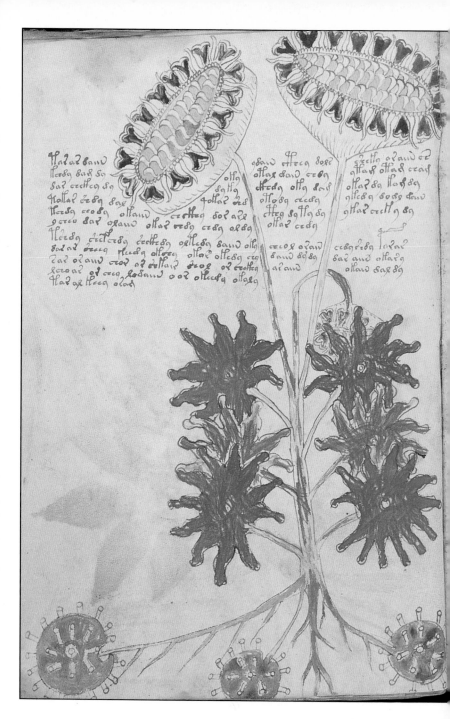

9. 'Sunflower', folio 33v

forms of substitution cipher was used by Julius Caesar, recorded by the Roman historian Suetonius, and is still used today by
school children around the world. It is known as the Caesar
shift cipher. To encrypt a message using this form of cipher,
one replaces each letter in the original message with a letter
that is an agreed number of places further along the alphabet. If
this description sounds complicated, it is in fact an extremely
simple process to put into practice, as the diagram below will
demonstrate. The top row (in lower case) is the alphabet representing the letters of our original message, which we already
know as the plain alphabet from our look at Newbold. The row
below (in capitals) is the cipher alphabet from which we would
construct our encrypted message.

Plain alphabet a b c d e f g h i j k l m n o p q r s t u v w x y z
Cipher alphabet F G H I J K L M N O P Q R S T U V W X Y Z A B C D E

Here we have a 'shift' of five, as the letters of the two alphabets have been shifted five places relative to each other. To
encipher, take each letter of your message, find it on the top,
or plain alphabet, and replace it with the corresponding letter
in the cipher alphabet below. For example, the message **The
Elegant Enigma**, once encrypted, would read:

YMJ JQJLFSY JSNLRF

To decipher the message, the recipient would simply reverse
the process, assuming of course that they knew the value of
the 'shift' used in the encryption. Knowing the value of the
shift is the *key* for this type of cipher. If the key – in this case
the value of the shift – falls into enemy hands, the cipher is
breakable and so no longer secure. Unfortunately, even if the
key is unknown to the enemy, the Caesar shift cipher does
not afford the sender of the message much security. There are
only twenty-five 'shifts' available to the encryptor, twenty-
five positionings of the two alphabets relative to each other;
and so if the message were to be intercepted, it would not take
long for a cryptanalyst to try out all the possible shifts and discover the plain text. (The term *cryptanalyst* is used to denote
a code or cipher breaker, whilst someone who develops codes
and ciphers is known as a *cryptographer*.)

Much greater security is provided if the cipher alphabet is a random rearrangement of the plain alphabet rather than just a shift, as shown below:

Plain alphabet   a b c d e f g h i j k l m n o p q r s t u v w x y z
Cipher alphabet J Z O N D H Q L B W S M G A E V U K Y I C X R P F T

Now, rather than being one of only twenty-five possible cipher alphabets, the arrangement of letters which we could use to encrypt a message is one of over four hundred million, million, million, million possible combinations of the twenty-six letters of the alphabet. It would now be impossible for even a vast team of cryptanalysts to try out every permutation. This level of security ensured that the monoalphabetic substitution cipher, as it is known because it uses only one cipher alphabet, was believed to be virtually unbreakable. With the exception of a few, minor refinements (for example, the addition of a small number of *code* equivalents, whereby commonly occurring words in the plain text could be allocated numbers or symbols in the cipher alphabet), little advance was made in the use of ciphers throughout Europe until the Renaissance.

Roger Bacon, writing in around the year 1250, listed seven techniques for hiding a message, stating that: 'A man is insane who writes a secret unless he conceals it from the crowd and leaves it so that it can be understood only by the studious and wise.' By examining Bacon's suggestions, we will gain some idea of the state of cryptology in the thirteenth century; a good starting point, perhaps, for investigating the sort of cryptographic forces that may have been brought to bear on the writing of the Voynich manuscript. Bacon's first two methods involved disguising the meaning of a message through the use of 'characters and symbols' or 'mysterious and symbolic words', in effect using such complex language so as to make the text unintelligible to all but the initiated. Bacon used the example of writings on alchemy, but the best modern analogy might be the use of technical or scientific jargon. Imagine trying to read an advanced guide to particle physics or computer programming if one had no previous knowledge of the subject: within a few sentences the inexperienced reader would be totally lost. This is effectively the use of a code or secret language, known only to a select few who understand the technical terms involved. The third technique suggests using only consonants in writing a message, 'thgh jst hw sccssfl ths frm f wrtng cld b fr sndng mssgs s nt ntrly clr'; whilst the fourth relies on the 'commingling' of letters in a transposition cipher. The fifth and sixth techniques detail simple substitution ciphers, one using letters, the other employing specially devised 'geometric figures', and the seventh describes the use of shorthand, which again is essentially a type of code.

These seven techniques (with the exception of the rather dubious writing without vowels) all fall within the broad definitions of medieval cryptography as outlined earlier. (They also, coincidentally, give us a good idea of where Professor Newbold may have found inspiration for his elaborate Baconian cipher system!) If one ignores the use of codes due to the difficulty of creating complete secret languages, and also transposition ciphers because of the uncertainty of ever recovering the original message in its correct form, one is left with only one viable option. Throughout Europe in the Middle Ages, simple substitution ciphers were the only secure way of encrypting a message available, and, in fact, the only means necessary, as no one had devised a way of breaking them.

However, by the beginning of the fifteenth century, new types of cipher had to be developed in response to a breakthrough in the skill of cryptanalysis. This need for more complex ciphers was prompted by the adoption from the Arabic world of frequency analysis, and its development by cryptanalysts as a powerful new weapon in their armoury. The power of frequency analysis comes from one simple fact: not all letters in a given language appear as often as others. For example, in English the most commonly occurring letter is **e**, followed by **t, a, o, i, n** and so on until **q** and **z**, the least frequent. If the cryptanalyst has an idea in what language the original message was written (and this would most likely have been Latin in medieval times), he can easily establish the frequency of letters by sampling just a few pages of text from that language. By comparing the frequency with which different characters appear in the cipher text with the known frequency of letters in the original language, one can begin to crack the cipher. This form of analysis is of little use on short cipher messages, but if the sample of cipher text is big enough, and the cryptanalyst persistent, the simple mono-alphabetic cipher is no longer safe. In the following example, a piece of text has been encrypted using a simple substitution cipher, which we will attempt to break using frequency analysis:

MFNPGJ DGX DA VK ZXNPDMPE TPWPLW LD LIX EDGLPGXGL DA XFNDZX PG HFXWL DA NONX DUM QDDCW OGW VOGFWENPZLW P EOVX OENDWW O VDWL NXVONCOQUX EDUUXELPDG DA ZNXEPDFW PUUFVPGOLXM VOGFWENPZLW ADN VOGK MXEOMXW LIXWX TDUFVXW IOM UOPG QFNPXM PG LIX EIXWLW PG YIPEI P ADFGM LIXV PG OG OGEPXGL EOWLUX PG WDFLIXNG XFNDZX YIXNX LIX EDUUXELPDG IOM OZZONXGLUK QXXG WLDNXM PG EDGWXHFXGEX DA LIX MPWLFNQXM ZDUPLPEOU EDGMPLPDG DA XFNDZX MFNPGJ LIX XONUK ZONL DA LIX GPGXLXXGLI EXGLFNK

The first stage in our attempted decryption entails the careful examination of the cipher text to establish which letters occur most frequently. After counting the various letters, it turns out that the most commonly occurring is X, with fifty appearances, then D with thirty-three, followed by L and P, both with thirty-two. We know that e is the most frequently used letter in the English language, and with X being the most frequent letter in the cipher text by a considerable margin, we can make a tentative assumption that X=e.

MFNPGJ DGe DA VK ZeNPDMPE TPWPLW LD LIe EDGLPGeGL DA eFNDZe PG HFeWL DA NONe DUM QDDCW OGM VOGFWENPZLW P EOVe OENDWW O VDWL NeVONCOQUe EDUUeELPDG DA ZNePDFW PUUFVPGOLeM VOGFWENPZLW ADN VOGK MeEOMeW LIeWeTDUFVeW IOM UOPG QFNPeM PG LIe EIeWLW PG YIPEI P ADFGM LIeV PG OG OGEPeGL EOWLUe PG WDFLIeNG eFNDZe YIeNe LIe EDUUeELPDG IOM OZZONeGLUK QeeG WLDNeM PG EDGWeHFeGEe DA LIe MPWLFNQeM ZDUPLPEOU EDGMPLPDG DA eFNDZe MFNPGJ LIeONUK ZONL DA LIe GPGXLXXGLI EXGLFNK

Of the other three cipher letters that appear most often in the cipher text (D,L and P), it is probable that one of them represents the letter **t**, which is the second most commonly occurring letter in English. Back to the cipher message, and we find that the three-letter combination LIX occurs nine times, six times on its own, and three times within other words. The most commonly occurring three-letter words in English are 'and' and 'the', but our allocation X=**e** suggests that LIX cannot be 'and', so we can try L=**t** and I=**h**, and add this to our decryption.

MFNPGJ DGe DA VK ZeNPDMPE TPWPtW tD the
EDGtPGeGt DA eFNDZe PG HFeWt DA NONeDUM
QDDCW OGM VOGFWENPZtW P EOVe OENDWW O
VDWt NeVONCOQUe EDUUeEtPDG DA ZNeEPDFW
PUUFVPGOteM VOGFWENPZtW ADN VOGK MeEOMeW
theWe TDUFVeW hOM UOPG QFNPeM PG the EheWtW PG
YhPEh P ADFGM theV PG OG OGEPeGt EOWtUe PG
WDFtheNG eFNDZe YheNe the EDUUeEtPDG hOM
OZZONeGtUK QeeG WtDNeM PG EDGWeHFeGEe DA the
MPWtFNQeM ZDUPtEOU EDGMPtPDG DA eFNDZe
MFNPGJ the eONUK ZONt DA the GPGeteeGth EeGtFNK

According to frequency analysis, it is probable that the remaining three highest occurring cipher letters, P, D and O, could represent **i**, **o** and **a**, the next three most common letters in English. Only P and O appear on their own in the cipher text, and as letters **i** and **a** are the only letters in standard English grammar to occur singularly, it therefore follows that P=**i** or **a**, and O=**i** or **a**, and D *might* represent **o**. Let's make these assumptions and see if we can deduce more from the text.

Look at the seventh word in the cipher text, tD. This must be **to**, and so confirms our hunch that D=**o**. The two-letter word PG occurs five times, and the word OG once. We now suspect that both words begin with either **a** or **i**, and must end with the same letter, represented in the cipher alphabet by G. The only letters that can follow both **a** and **i** in two-letter words are **n**, **t** and **s**: we can discount **t** as we have already established its cipher equivalent, leaving us with G=**n** or **s**. Look at the second word of the cipher text, DGX. We can confidently replace X with **e**, and D with **o**, giving us **oGe**. Of our two possible equivalents for G, only **n** fits, giving us **one**, therefore G=**n**. Having uncovered the plain-text letters **e**, **n**, **t** and **h**, the second to last word now reads **nPneteenth**, allowing us to deduce that P must be **i**, to give us the only possible word that fits the already decrypted letters: **nineteenth**. With our discovery that P=**i**, we are left with the inevitable conclusion that O=**a**.

There are one or two other conclusions we can reach before we see how far our decipherment has progressed. The eighteenth word of our text originally read OGM, but we now know it must read **anM**. With the letter **t** already discovered, this must mean that M=**d**, giving us **and**. Another clue is the occurrence of the word **oA** five times in the text. This could be **or**, **on** or **of**; however, we can discount **on** as we already know G=**n**, which leaves us with A=**n** or **f**. **Of** is the more commonly occurring word, so we can hazard a guess that A=**f**.

We have thus worked out that D=**o**, G=**n**, P=**i**, O=**a**, M=**d**, and A *probably* represents **f**. Now we can add these deciphered letters to our text.

dFNinJ **one** of VK ZeNiodiE TiWitW **to the E**ontinent of
eFNoZe **in** HFeWt of NaNe oUd QooCW **and** VanFWENiZtW
i EaVe aENoWW a VoWt NeVaNCaQUe EoUUeEtion of
ZNeEioFW iUUFVinated VanFWENiZtW foN VanK deEadeW
theWe ToUFVeW **had** Uain QFNied **in** the EheWtW **in** YhiEh i
foFnd **theV in an** anEient EaWtUe **in** WoFtheNn eFNoZe
YheNe **the** EoUUeEtion **had** aZZaNentUK Qeen WtoNed **in**
EonWeHFenEe of **the** diWtFNQed ZoUitiEaU Eondition of
eFNoZe dFNinJ **the** eaNUK ZaNt of **the nineteenth** EentFNK

We are progressing quickly towards a complete decipherment, using the clues provided through frequency analysis, some educated guesswork and linguistic common sense. The eighth word now reads **E**ontinent, which must surely be **continent**. Taking this with the following two words we have the phrase **continent of eFNoZe**: the only possible word that would make sense here is **Europe**. So now we have E=**c**, F=**u**, N=**r** and Z=**p**. Once these deciphered letters have been added, the most common cipher letter left is W, which frequency analysis suggests is likely to be the most common plain alphabet letter yet to be uncovered, **s**. When we add these breakthroughs, a clear text begins to appear.

> **durinJ one of VK periodic Tisits to the continent of europe in Huest of rare oUd QooCs and Vanuscripts i caVe across a Vost reVarCaQUe coUUection of precious iUUuVinated Vanuscripts for VanK decades these ToUuVes had Uain Quried in the chests in Yhich i found theV in an ancient castUe in southern europe Yhere the coUUection had aZZarentUK Qeen stored in conseHuence of the disturQed poUiticaU condition of europe durinJ the earUK part of the nineteenth centurK**

There is no need to detail the final few decipherments, though the reader might like to fill in the final gaps on their own. The decrypted text is the opening of Wilfrid Voynich's speech to the College of Physicians in 1921, and should read:

> ... during one of my periodic visits to the continent of Europe in quest of rare old books and manuscripts, I came across a most remarkable collection of precious illuminated manu-scripts. For many decades these volumes had lain buried in the chests in which I found them in an ancient castle in Southern Europe where the collection had apparently been stored in consequence of the disturbed political condition of Europe during the early part of the nineteenth century.

So, as we have now demonstrated, simple substitution ciphers are not safe from the cryptanalyst skilled in the use of frequency analysis; and cryptographers of the late Middle Ages began to search for new ways of providing security in their ciphers. These early attempts to counteract frequency analysis were a type of cipher that was later to be known as a homophonic cipher, and the earliest surviving example dates from the Duchy of Mantua in 1401.

The cryptographer, knowing the frequency with which characters appear in the language of the plain text, allocates proportionally more substitutes in the cipher for the most commonly occurring plain alphabet letters. For example, knowing that **e** is the most frequently used letter in English, our hypothetical cryptographer would allocate a number of cipher equivalents for **e**. On the other hand, **k** being used relatively rarely, would be represented by only one substitute. The upshot of this is to 'even out' the frequency with which the cipher symbols appear, so that each symbol appears roughly the same amount of times as every other one, thus making frequency analysis virtually impossible. In the early years of such ciphers, only vowels were allocated homophones, as these multiple symbols are known, and it was not until the mid-sixteenth century that full homophonic ciphers, with equivalents even for consonants, began to appear.

However, a homophonic cipher is not unbreakable (for the purpose of the following examples, we shall use the early form of homophonic ciphers in which only vowels had homophones). Although there may be many different cipher symbols for the letter **e**, these symbols will *always* represent **e**, and it is because of this seemingly insignificant fact that the first signs of weakness in the cipher begin to appear. The letter **u**, being a vowel and thus frequently occurring, would normally be allocated several equivalents in a homophonic cipher; for the purpose of this demonstration, for example, **u**=13, 42 and 56. The letter **q**, being a consonant, would be represented by one cipher equivalent, so we can allocate the number 25. However, to the great benefit of the cryptanalyst, the letter **q** is always followed by the letter **u**, so if we search the cipher text for a particular cipher symbol (in this case 25) that is *only* followed by one of three others (13, 42 or 56), we will have identified the letters **q** and **u**. Admittedly, this is not an enormous breakthrough, but it is still a small advance in the favour of the cryptanalyst.

There are other such patterns that occur in English, subtler maybe, but patterns nonetheless, and it is these tantalising relationships between different letters that create the chinks in the armour of this cipher. Take the letters **e** and **h**, which have a particular partnership in English. Although **h** directly precedes **e** in many English words, it hardly ever directly follows it. No matter how many equivalents you allocate to the plain-text **e**, this strange relationship will remain, and could be detected through careful analysis. Take also this example: a studious cryptanalyst spots the following 'word' in the cipher text: 18 36 23 10, and then a little further on: 18 36 45 10. What does this mean? It is likely that these two patterns of numbers represent the same word in the plain text, and the change in the third number (from 23 in the first 'word', to 45 in the second) shows that these two numbers are homophones for the same vowel. A patient cryptographer can identify such patterns as these, making the homophonic cipher not nearly as secure as it may at first have appeared.

The introduction of frequency analysis, and then homophonic ciphers, set in motion the cryptological arms race that took place in Europe during the Renaissance, with cryptographers always trying to stay one step ahead of the cryptanalysts. The names of some of these cipher innovators have come down to us through the years, and one such is Matteo Argenti. Matteo, along with his brother Marcello, had learned his trade from his uncle Giovanni Batista, and wrote a manual on cryptography in the early seventeenth century in which he pointed out the weaknesses of homophonic ciphers. He suggested a number of countermeasures to improve the security of ciphers; one such device being the introduction of nulls to a cipher alphabet. Nulls are symbols or numbers used in the cipher that have no equivalents in the plain alphabet, and are essentially meaningless; their implementation is explained here by Simon Singh.

> For example, one could substitute each plain letter with a number between 1 and 99, which would leave 73 numbers that represent nothing, and these could be randomly sprinkled throughout the cipher text with varying frequencies. The nulls would pose no problem to the intended recipient, who would know that they were to be ignored. However, the nulls would baffle an enemy interceptor because they would confuse an attack by frequency analysis.[3]

The Argentis were also responsible for the introduction of what David Kahn describes as a 'mnemonic key' to create the cipher alphabet. It is obvious that for a cipher to work successfully, both the encipherer and the receiver must be in possession of the same cipher alphabet; however, should a copy of the cipher alphabet fall into enemy hands, the cipher is rendered useless in terms of security. This is the age-old problem that has faced all cryptographers: how to keep the key safe. The Argenti brothers' breakthrough was to develop a method whereby the key could be easily memorised, and once it had been used to encipher a message, all physical trace of it could be destroyed. For the mnemonic key to operate, the sender and receiver simply had to agree on an easily memorisable word or phrase, known only to themselves, which would become the main element in creating the cipher alphabet. For the purpose of our example, let us take the name **MARCELLO ARGENTI**. The first step is to remove all repeated letters and spaces from the phrase, leaving us with the following string of letters: **MARCELOGNTI**. We now add all the remaining letters of the alphabet, in their usual order, following on from the last letter of our mnemonic key phrase:

Plain alphabet   a b c d e f g h i j k l m n o p q r s t u v w x y z
Cipher alphabet M A R C E L O G N T I H J K P Q S U V W X Y Z B D F

Thus we have a substitution cipher that we can create and use whenever we need it, but which relies only on us remembering the name Marcello Argenti, and not the whole cipher alphabet

Of these early cryptographers, it was Leon Battista Alberti, a brilliant scholar born in 1404, who made the leap towards modern cipher systems, and so earned himself the epithet 'The Father of Modern Cryptology'.[4] His great advance, which was subsequently to be taken up and developed by others, was to introduce *a number* of cipher alphabets into the encryption process, thus creating what have become known as poly- or multialphabetic substitution ciphers. His ideas, apparently inspired by a conversation with the pontifical secretary Leonardo Dato whilst strolling in the Vatican gardens, were explained in a short treatise written in 1467; and it is this essay that constitutes the oldest surviving Western text devoted solely to the science of cryptography. Alberti's lasting achievement was to suggest that the cipher alphabet could shift during the process of encryption, in effect creating multiple, changing equivalents for each plain-text letter. Alberti's method of carrying out this operation relied on the use of a cipher disc or cipher wheel, which consists of two circular metal plates, one smaller than the other. Placed on top of each other, they are attached by a pin through their shared axes, allowing them to rotate relative to one another. Around the circumference of the larger, bottom plate are etched the letters of the plain alphabet, while on the smaller, inner plate is the cipher alphabet. As the discs are turned, different letters of the cipher alphabet can be aligned with the letters of the plain alphabet. The operation of the system is shown below in a linear arrangement of the alphabets, but the process is the same. (Note that the letters in the cipher text are jumbled. This fact will become relevant later when we look at the work of another cryptographer by the name of Porta.)

For the system to work, in addition to identical cipher wheels, the sender and recipient of the cipher message must also have a prearranged key or index letter; for our example, let us use **T**. The sender randomly aligns the cipher and plain alphabets on their cipher wheel by rotating the discs, and notes the plain alphabet equivalent to the index letter **T**, in this case the letter **q**, which becomes the first letter of the message.

Plain alphabet a b c d e f g h i j k l m n o p **q** r s t u v w x y z
Cipher alphabet W S M G A E V U K Y I C X R P F **T** J Z O N D H Q L B

The recipient, receiving **q** at the beginning of the message, now knows with which letter of the plain alphabet to align the index letter **T**. Now both sender and receiver have the same alignment of the discs on their cipher wheels, and the encryption process can begin. At this stage it should be noted that we are dealing with nothing more than a simple substitution cipher. However, after a few words the encipherer rotates the discs on his cipher wheel, shifting the two alphabets relative to each other and producing a new alignment; in our example so that cipher letter **T** has shifted five places and now corresponds with **v** in the plain alphabet, as shown below:

Plain alphabet a b c d e f g h i j k l m n o p q r s t u **v** w x y z
Cipher alphabet D H Q L B W S M G A E V U K Y I C X R P F **T** J Z O N

The encipherer now adds the single letter **v** to the message, indicating that the receiver should realign their cipher and plain alphabets in order to continue decryption. After a few more words the alphabets can be shifted again, so now **T** aligns with **c**, and so **c** is sent to the receiver as the signal to change the relative positions of the two alphabets once more.

Plain alphabet a b c d e f g h i j k l m n o p q r s t u v w x y z
Cipher alphabet P F T J Z O N D H Q L B W S M G A E V U K Y I C X R

And so on; thus creating a polyalphabetic cipher, because now each plain-text letter can be represented by many different letters from the cipher alphabet during the course of the message. And now we see why Alberti's system was such a huge leap forward in cryptographic terms. In a simple or monoalphabetic substitution cipher, a letter in the plain text will always be represented by the same letter in the cipher text, so leaving the cipher open to frequency analysis, and hence decipherment by cryptanalysts. Even in a homophonic cipher, where there are a number of equivalents for the most commonly occurring letters, these letters will always be represented by the *same* equivalents. However, in a polyalphabetic cipher, a plain-text letter can now be represented in the enciphered message by many changing cipher substitutes. This can be observed in the example given above, in which, for the first alignment, the plain alphabet letter **e** (always the weak link for a cryptographer because of its frequency of use), corresponds with **A** in the cipher alphabet. If the relative positions of the two alphabets were to remain the same for the encryption of the whole message, then **A** would become the most frequently occurring letter in the cipher text, thus giving a hefty clue to the cryptanalyst of its likely plain-text equivalent, and thus a way of cracking the cipher. But now, in our polyalphabetic cipher, the alignment of the two alphabets changes after a few words and **e** becomes **B**, and then a few words later, **Z**. Suddenly the cryptanalyst's weapon of frequency analysis seems much less fearsome.

Although Alberti claimed his cipher was unbreakable, the introduction of polyalphabeticity did not have the revolutionising impact on cryptography that one might have anticipated. The Argenti brothers incorporated elements of Alberti's theories into their works, but it required the efforts of a number of others to bring his ideas to their logical conclusion. The next step was taken by the extraordinary figure of Johannes Trithemius, a devout monk and bibliophile, who at the same time achieved infamy in his own lifetime as an occultist and dabbler in the magical black arts. His contribution to the advancement of cryptography comes from his book *Polygraphia*, published in 1518, a year after his death, and which represents the first *printed* book on the subject. Among the various secret-writing systems he discusses, many of which consist of hiding the plain text within magical incantations in much the same way as Bacon favoured, is a system which takes Alberti's cipher to another level of complexity. In book V of *Polygraphia*, the following table appears:

```
a b c d e f g h i j k l m n o p q r s t u v w x y z
B C D E F G H I J K L M N O P Q R S T U V W X Y Z A
C D E F G H I J K L M N O P Q R S T U V W X Y Z A B
D E F G H I J K L M N O P Q R S T U V W X Y Z A B C
E F G H I J K L M N O P Q R S T U V W X Y Z A B C D
F G H I J K L M N O P Q R S T U V W X Y Z A B C D E
G H I J K L M N O P Q R S T U V W X Y Z A B C D E F
H I J K L M N O P Q R S T U V W X Y Z A B C D E F G
I J K L M N O P Q R S T U V W X Y Z A B C D E F G H
J K L M N O P Q R S T U V W X Y Z A B C D E F G H I
K L M N O P Q R S T U V W X Y Z A B C D E F G H I J
L M N O P Q R S T U V W X Y Z A B C D E F G H I J K
M N O P Q R S T U V W X Y Z A B C D E F G H I J K L
N O P Q R S T U V W X Y Z A B C D E F G H I J K L M
O P Q R S T U V W X Y Z A B C D E F G H I J K L M N
P Q R S T U V W X Y Z A B C D E F G H I J K L M N O
Q R S T U V W X Y Z A B C D E F G H I J K L M N O P
R S T U V W X Y Z A B C D E F G H I J K L M N O P Q
S T U V W X Y Z A B C D E F G H I J K L M N O P Q R
T U V W X Y Z A B C D E F G H I J K L M N O P Q R S
U V W X Y Z A B C D E F G H I J K L M N O P Q R S T
V W X Y Z A B C D E F G H I J K L M N O P Q R S T U
W X Y Z A B C D E F G H I J K L M N O P Q R S T U V
X Y Z A B C D E F G H I J K L M N O P Q R S T U V W
Y Z A B C D E F G H I J K L M N O P Q R S T U V W X
Z A B C D E F G H I J K L M N O P Q R S T U V W X Y
```

Each row of the table is a simple Caesar shift cipher, with a progressively larger shift in each successive line, so that there are a total of twenty-five ciphers in the whole table. Using the top row as the plain alphabet, one would encrypt the first letter of a message by using the cipher equivalent from the row directly below; so **e** would be enciphered as **F**. However, to encrypt the second letter in our message we would use the equivalent from the next row down (the third row of the table); so this time **e** would be enciphered by **G**. For the next plain-text letter we would encrypt using row four, then row five, and so on. Thus the word **keeper**, when encrypted using this system, would read **LGHTJX**, as shown in the diagram below:

```
a b c d e f g h i j k l m n o p q r s t u v w x y z
B C D E F G H I J K L M N O P Q R S T U V W X Y Z A
C D E F G H I J K L M N O P Q R S T U V W X Y Z A B
D E F G H I J K L M N O P Q R S T U V W X Y Z A B C
E F G H I J K L M N O P Q R S T U V W X Y Z A B C D
F G H I J K L M N O P Q R S T U V W X Y Z A B C D E
G H I J K L M N O P Q R S T U V W X Y Z A B C D E F
```

The great advantage of this encryption process is that a new cipher alphabet is brought into use with every *letter* of the plain text, not every three or four words as it does in Alberti's system. If we had enciphered the word **keeper** using the Alberti method shown above, we would arrive at the encryption **IAAFAJ**. Notice that the three occurrences of letter **e** are all enciphered using the letter **A**, which shows how the cipher is still, despite Alberti's claims, vulnerable and breakable. In Trithemius's system, with the cipher alphabets changing much more frequently, the letter **e** is encrypted with three different letters (**G**, **H** and **J**) within the same *word*. However, the Trithemian cipher suffered from the huge weakness that the order in which the successive cipher alphabets was used was sequential and unvarying. Simply working down the table, row by row, with each cipher alphabet shifted one letter on from the last, was too rigid a system for the cipher to be truly secure.

This problem was overcome by Giovan Batista Belaso, about whom, unlike his contemporaries in the pantheon of Renaissance cryptography, we know very little. In 1553 he published *La cifra del. Sig. Giovan Batista Belaso*, in which he suggested the use of words or phrases as a key – or 'countersign' as he referred to them – which would ensure the non-sequential use of the cipher alphabet. The idea is similar to the mnemonic key system suggested years later by the Argenti brothers, and employs a simple key that can be memorised by both sender and receiver, with all the concomitant protection this supplied. As so often in the world of ciphers and codes, this sounds far more daunting and impenetrable than it is in practice, and the process can easily be demonstrated by the example below.

To encipher the phrase **The manuscript retains its cryptic secrets** we first need to choose a key word or countersign, which, as usual, must be known to both the sender and receiver of the message; let's use the name **Bacon**. Now we write out our message, with the key word written above it.

y word

A C O N B A C O N B A C O N B A C O N B A C O N B A C O N B A C O N B A

ain text

h e m a n u s c r i p t r e t a i n s i t s c r y p t i c s e c r e t s

Now we can begin to encrypt the message, using a table of alphabets similar to the one used in Trithemius's cipher system, only this time, rather than using each row in sequential order, we will just use the five rows that begin with the letters of our key word (which are underlined in the diagram below).

a	b	c	d	e	f	g	h	i	j	k	l	m	n	o	p	q	r	s	t	u	v	w	x	y	z
B	C	D	E	F	G	H	I	J	K	L	M	N	O	P	Q	R	S	T	U	V	W	X	Y	Z	A
C	D	E	F	G	H	I	J	K	L	M	N	O	P	Q	R	S	T	U	V	W	X	Y	Z	A	B
D	E	F	G	H	I	J	K	L	M	N	O	P	Q	R	S	T	U	V	W	X	Y	Z	A	B	C
E	F	G	H	I	J	K	L	M	N	O	P	Q	R	S	T	U	V	W	X	Y	Z	A	B	C	D
F	G	H	I	J	K	L	M	N	O	P	Q	R	S	T	U	V	W	X	Y	Z	A	B	C	D	E
G	H	I	J	K	L	M	N	O	P	Q	R	S	T	U	V	W	X	Y	Z	A	B	C	D	E	F
H	I	J	K	L	M	N	O	P	Q	R	S	T	U	V	W	X	Y	Z	A	B	C	D	E	F	G
I	J	K	L	M	N	O	P	Q	R	S	T	U	V	W	X	Y	Z	A	B	C	D	E	F	G	H
J	K	L	M	N	O	P	Q	R	S	T	U	V	W	X	Y	Z	A	B	C	D	E	F	G	H	I
K	L	M	N	O	P	Q	R	S	T	U	V	W	X	Y	Z	A	B	C	D	E	F	G	H	I	J
L	M	N	O	P	Q	R	S	T	U	V	W	X	Y	Z	A	B	C	D	E	F	G	H	I	J	K
M	N	O	P	Q	R	S	T	U	V	W	X	Y	Z	A	B	C	D	E	F	G	H	I	J	K	L
N	O	P	Q	R	S	T	U	V	W	X	Y	Z	A	B	C	D	E	F	G	H	I	J	K	L	M

<u>O</u> P Q R S T U V W X Y Z A B C D E F G H I J K L M N
P Q R S T U V W X Y Z A B C D E F G H I J K L M N O
Q R S T U V W X Y Z A B C D E F G H I J K L M N O P
R S T U V W X Y Z A B C D E F G H I J K L M N O P Q
S T U V W X Y Z A B C D E F G H I J K L M N O P Q R
T U V W X Y Z A B C D E F G H I J K L M N O P Q R S
U V W X Y Z A B C D E F G H I J K L M N O P Q R S T
V W X Y Z A B C D E F G H I J K L M N O P Q R S T U
W X Y Z A B C D E F G H I J K L M N O P Q R S T U V
X Y Z A B C D E F G H I J K L M N O P Q R S T U V W
Y Z A B C D E F G H I J K L M N O P Q R S T U V W X
Z A B C D E F G H I J K L M N O P Q R S T U V W X Y
<u>A</u> B C D E F G H I J K L M N O P Q R S T U V W X Y Z

To encipher the first letter of our plain text, **t**, we will use the cipher alphabet from the row that begins with the first letter of our key word **Bacon**, so we use row **B**. To find the cipher equivalent we look along the plain-text alphabet at the top of the table until we reach the letter **t**, then we look down the column until we reach the **B** row, which happens to be the row directly underneath, where we find the cipher equivalent is **U**. For the second letter of the message, **h**, we encrypt using the row beginning with **A**, as this is the second letter of our key word, giving us the cipher substitute letter **H**. For the letter **e** we encrypt using row **C**, giving us the cipher letter **G**. And so on, using the letters of the key word to dictate which cipher alphabets encrypt which plain-text letters. The reader might wish to try encrypting a few more words of the original message to test the cipher before looking at the complete enciphered message below.

Key word
B A C O N B A C O N B A C O N B A C O N B A C O N B A C O N B A C O N B
Plain text
t h e m a n u s c r i p t r e t a i n s i t s c r y p t i c s e c r e t
Cipher text
U A G A N O U U Q E J P V F R U A K B F J T U Q E Z P V W P T E E F R U

The next star to appear on the cryptographic stage was Giovanni Battista Porta, yet another remarkable Renaissance polymath, who, at the age of twenty-eight, published *De*

Furtivis Literarum Notis in 1563. The volume is divided into four books, in which Porta examined the history of ancient ciphers, ciphers of his own time, the science of cryptanalysis, and a list of linguistic traits that could be used as 'cribs' to help solve a cipher (for example, if one knows the subject of a message it is possible to deduce likely words that it may contain; so words such as 'soldiers', 'generals' and 'weapons' might be hidden in an enciphered military order). He also discussed the use of cipher wheels and made the earliest known distinction between transposition and substitution ciphers. Porta's main contribution to the advancement of polyalphabetic ciphers, which is what concerns us here, was to bring together the ideas of those who preceded him, and unify them into one, improved cipher system. Firstly, he suggested one could use a jumbled arrangement of letters for the cipher alphabets, as had been used by Alberti on his cipher discs. Secondly, one could employ the letter-by-letter switching of cipher alphabets as described by Trithemius, but this should be carried out according to the keyword or countersign system as specified by Belaso, which in turn constituted the third element of Porta's new cipher. However, as David Kahn puts it when summing up his place in the history of cryptography: 'Unfortunately for Porta...he illustrated the system only with standard alphabets, and a lazy posterity, while naming this trivial system for him, cheated him of full recognition of his contribution.'

The honour of recognition for producing this polyalphabetic cipher goes to a French diplomat by the name of Blaise de Vigenère, who slotted the final piece of the cryptological jigsaw into place in his 1585 book *Traicté des Chiffres*. However, before we look at the complete cipher system (which includes the ideas of Alberti, Trithemius, Belaso, Porta and Vigenère combined), it is important to make clear that the Vigenère cipher, or *Le Chiffre Indéchiffrable* as it became known, is somewhat erroneously named. The system that has been attributed to Vigenère for over four hundred years is in fact merely the Trithemian multialphabet table combined with Belaso's keyword system, and is thus a much simplified form of the complete cipher. How this misunderstanding first occurred is not clear, but it has certainly stuck. Even today, when the Vigenère cipher is mentioned, it is the Trithemius/

Belaso method that is normally being referred to. Let us for once give credit to the additional work of Alberti and Porta, and use Vigenère's full cipher in all its cryptographic glory.

Vigenère's breakthrough was the replacement of Belaso's key word with what Kahn refers to as an 'autokey'. The keyword system, although far superior to the sequential use of cipher alphabets suggested by Trithemius, still has a number of weaknesses. The first and most obvious is that if the key word were to fall into enemy hands, the encryption system would be compromised – but if the key to any cipher becomes known the cipher is no longer secure, so in this respect the key-word system is not unique. The main flaw was that the *length* of the key word becomes vitally important, and provides the cryptanalyst with a method of attacking the cipher. Porta almost stumbled upon this defect, but it was not until the nineteenth century that this weakness was fully exploited to break the cipher that had seemed so impenetrable. Let's look again at the example from earlier; our encryption of the phrase **the manuscript retains its cryptic secrets**, using the key word **Bacon**.

The encipherment produced the cipher text:

UAGANOUUQEJPVFRUAKBFJTUQEZPVWPTEEFRUT

which we know, because it uses multiple cipher alphabets, is invulnerable to frequency analysis. Or is it? If we look more closely at this seemingly random string of letters, we begin to see patterns emerging. The three-letter combination **UQE** appears twice in the cipher text, as does the combination **FRU**.

UAGANOU<u>UQE</u>JPV<u>FRU</u>AKBFJT<u>UQE</u>ZPVWPTEE<u>FRU</u>T

If we compare this with the original message, we see that these repetitions in the cipher text represent repeating three-letter combinations in the original message: **UQE=scr**, and **FRU=ret**.

themanu**SCR**ipt**RET**ainsit**SCR**yptic**sec**RET
UAGANOU<u>UQE</u> J PV<u>FRU</u>AKBF J T<u>UQE</u>ZPVWPTEE<u>FRU</u>

How has this happened? It all comes down to the length of the key word. If we add our key word **Bacon** to the example we will begin to see how the repeated encipherments occurred.

```
A CONBACONBACONBACONBACONBACONBACONBACONBA
h e m a n u S C R i p t R E T a i n s i t S C R y p t i c s e c R E T s
A G A N O U U Q E  J  P V F R U A K B F  J  T U Q E Z P VW P T E E F R U T
```

On both occasions the letters **scr** appeared in the plain text, they were in the same relative position to the key word, lining up with the letters CON in **Bacon**, and were therefore encrypted using the same three cipher alphabets, the ones beginning with **C**, **O** and **N** in the cipher table. Likewise with the plain-text letters **ret**, which corresponded both times with the key letters ONB and so were encrypted using the cipher alphabets beginning with **O**, **N** and **B**. This may at first seem like a strange but unimportant anomaly, but it is actually a flaw in the cipher system that could allow a careful cryptanalyst to break the cipher.

If our cryptanalyst counts the space between the two occurrences of **UQE** in the cipher text, he or she discovers that they are 15 letters apart. From this piece of information the cryptanalyst can deduce that the length of the key word or phrase must be a factor of the number 15 (that means a number by which 15 is divisible). So the key word must be either 1, 3, 5 or 15 letters long. The cryptanalyst now counts the number of letters between the two appearances of **FRU**, only to discover they are 20 letters apart. The factors of 20 are 1, 2, 4, 5, 10 and 20. The cryptanalyst can discount the number 1, as a single letter used as a key word would have produced a simple monoalphabetic cipher, with only one row of the cipher table being used to encrypt the message. The only other factor common to both sets of numbers is 5, which tells our cryptanalyst that the key word is 5 letters long (which indeed it is). This is significant because we now know that the sequence of cipher alphabets used to encrypt the message repeats itself after every five letters of cipher text. It therefore follows that the first, sixth, eleventh, sixteenth, twenty-first, twenty-sixth, thirty-first and thirty-sixth letters of our cipher text (**U**, **O**, **J**, **U**, **J**, **Z**, **T** and **U**) were all encrypted using the cipher alphabet indicated by the first letter of our key word (**B**); whilst the second, seventh, twelfth, seventeenth, twenty-second, twenty-seventh, thirty-second and thirty-seventh letters (**A**, **U**, **P**, **A**, **T**, **P**, **E** and **T**) were encrypted using another cipher alphabet beginning with the second letter of the key word (**A**); and so on. These five sets of letters, each one encrypted by a single letter of the key word, can be separated out from the main cipher text, thus: **UOJUJZTU**, **AUPATPET**, **GUVKUVE**, **AQFBQWF**, **NERFERPR**. Our clever cryptanalyst now realises that each of these five strings of letters represents a simple, monoalphabetic Caesar shift cipher, and as such they are vulnerable to frequency analysis. (In our example, frequency analysis would be a problem because the cipher text is so short, but when we remember that there are only twenty-five possible shifts of the cipher alphabet, plus one, non-shifted alphabet, it would still be a relatively easy task for a team of cryptanalysts to test each possible shift and break the cipher.)

What has been demonstrated here is that a polyalphabetic cipher can be broken, and the weakness lies in the use of a key word. Once a cryptanalyst, through examination of repeated letter combinations in the cipher text, has deduced the length of the key word, it is possible to use frequency analysis even on complex multialphabetic ciphers. One way around this problem would be to use a key *phrase* that is the same length as the original plain-text message, for example, taking a text from a book:

Key phrase
NOWI S THEWI NTE RO FOURD I S CONTENTMADEGLO
Plain text
t h e m a n u s c r i p t r e t a i n s i t s c r y p t i c s e c r e t

The difficulty, as always, is how to convey the key to the intended recipient of the message. If the message to be enciphered is long, it would be impractical to try and memorise large passages of text, and though one might send a copy of the book containing the key text with the message, if this falls into enemy hands the cipher is immediately rendered useless. A key that can be easily remembered by both the sender and recipient is still the best guarantee of security.

Vigenère's autokey system solved the problem of having a key that could be easily memorised, whilst at the same time being the same length as the plain-text message. He achieved this seemingly impossible task through a brilliantly simple idea – he let the plain-text message itself become the key. For this system to work, the sender and recipient need only to agree upon, and remember, a single letter, known as the priming key; for the example below, we shall use the letter **P**. Now we will once again encrypt the message **the manuscript retains its cryptic secrets**, this time using the full Vigenère cipher (note that now we have incorporated jumbled cipher alphabets into the cipher table, rather than the shifted alphabets used in the earlier examples, which would mean that both sender and recipient of the message would need to be in possession of the same cipher table).

Plain-text alphabet

	a	b	c	d	e	f	g	h	i	j	k	l	m	n	o	p	q	r	s	t	u	v	w	x	y	z
A	F	B	I	N	L	S	A	Z	G	D	U	P	T	H	Y	E	X	K	W	C	R	O	V	Q	J	M
B	P	X	B	Y	R	I	L	M	Z	A	V	E	F	H	G	D	W	Q	C	U	O	K	J	T	N	S
C	S	A	P	I	T	G	J	M	H	K	F	O	Y	D	R	X	B	E	V	W	N	Z	U	L	Q	C
D	R	G	S	J	C	U	D	B	E	Y	T	O	I	X	F	M	P	Z	K	A	L	N	V	H	W	Q
E	Z	F	W	E	G	V	N	U	J	P	M	B	C	L	Y	D	I	S	A	R	T	H	Q	X	O	K
F	K	Q	H	C	U	F	B	P	A	L	G	I	S	R	J	T	E	W	Y	O	U	D	Z	M	X	N
G	T	C	N	U	R	L	S	F	I	V	B	Q	H	Z	D	X	P	O	E	J	Y	W	M	K	G	A
H	D	L	U	O	I	A	Z	E	M	B	H	N	Y	C	X	G	Q	S	T	J	F	W	P	V	K	R
I	W	T	L	S	Z	C	N	X	Q	B	A	M	Y	J	E	V	K	U	R	H	D	P	O	I	G	F
J	J	M	E	L	K	T	Q	C	N	G	X	F	Z	B	Y	W	I	A	R	V	P	U	H	D	S	O
K	O	S	Q	B	F	J	T	K	Z	U	C	Y	L	G	A	P	R	M	X	E	W	N	I	V	H	D
L	A	I	K	G	Q	C	O	P	M	R	S	B	F	Y	U	L	T	E	Z	D	X	W	V	H	N	J
M	I	S	G	W	M	V	R	J	F	X	N	O	D	T	Q	A	Z	P	U	C	K	L	B	Y	E	H
N	X	F	O	Q	J	P	I	G	A	W	L	D	N	Y	C	Z	K	H	U	B	T	M	V	R	E	S
O	M	P	V	N	A	W	U	B	L	H	O	K	C	F	I	S	R	T	G	Q	E	Y	D	J	Z	X
P	L	J	B	P	V	H	N	U	Z	C	K	Y	R	M	X	G	D	T	W	A	F	Q	S	O	I	E
Q	C	U	N	R	L	Z	F	J	B	P	Y	S	T	E	M	I	X	O	W	K	H	Q	A	D	V	G
R	R	D	C	S	E	O	M	V	P	W	G	Q	F	I	K	T	H	B	X	U	J	A	Z	N	Y	L
S	Q	E	A	N	T	D	O	I	G	F	J	R	V	H	Y	U	C	L	Z	W	B	S	X	M	K	P
T	H	K	P	S	N	B	U	A	T	M	Y	G	W	L	E	D	Q	X	C	R	O	Z	V	J	F	I
U	V	R	G	F	H	M	K	Z	W	D	B	T	E	S	Y	J	N	Q	O	P	X	I	L	N	A	C
V	T	Z	K	D	N	V	C	Q	P	I	W	F	A	O	H	X	J	G	Y	E	U	M	S	R	L	B
W	G	W	X	A	Q	P	J	H	C	M	R	K	T	D	B	Z	L	F	I	Y	U	E	V	O	N	S
X	N	J	M	S	B	L	E	V	R	D	I	P	X	W	Y	C	Q	Z	G	O	H	U	F	A	K	T
Y	E	W	D	R	X	K	F	N	Z	Q	J	M	I	S	L	Y	A	G	B	H	T	O	U	P	C	V
Z	Y	K	F	X	Z	J	Q	L	H	E	W	O	V	A	U	T	G	B	P	I	D	C	N	M	S	R

The enciphering process operates in much the same way as described before, only this time, to encrypt the first letter of our message (**t**) we use the cipher alphabet indicated by the priming key letter **P**. We find the letter **t** in the plain alphabet which runs along the top of the table, and then drop down the column to the point where it intersects with the cipher alphabet signified by the letter **P**, which provides us with the cipher equivalent **A**. This can be seen in the diagram below:

Plain-text alphabet

	a	b	c	d	e	f	g	h	i	j	k	l	m	n	o	p	q	r	s	t	u	v	w	x	y	z
A	F	B	I	N	L	S	A	Z	G	D	U	P	T	H	Y	E	X	K	W	C	R	O	V	Q	J	M
B	P	X	B	Y	R	I	L	M	Z	A	V	E	F	H	G	D	W	Q	C	U	O	K	J	T	N	S
C	S	A	P	I	T	G	J	M	H	K	F	O	Y	D	R	X	B	E	V	W	N	Z	U	L	Q	C
D	R	G	S	J	C	U	D	B	E	Y	T	O	I	X	F	M	P	Z	K	A	L	N	V	H	W	Q
E	Z	F	W	E	G	V	N	U	J	P	M	B	C	L	Y	D	I	S	A	R	T	H	Q	X	O	K
F	K	Q	H	C	U	F	B	P	A	L	G	I	S	R	J	T	E	W	Y	O	U	D	Z	M	X	N
G	T	C	N	U	R	L	S	F	I	V	B	Q	H	Z	D	X	P	O	E	J	Y	W	M	K	G	A
H	D	L	U	O	I	A	Z	E	M	B	H	N	Y	C	X	G	Q	S	T	J	F	W	P	V	K	R
I	W	T	L	S	Z	C	N	X	Q	B	A	M	Y	J	E	V	K	U	R	H	D	P	O	I	G	F
J	J	M	E	L	K	T	Q	C	N	G	X	F	Z	B	Y	W	I	A	R	V	P	U	H	D	S	O
K	O	S	Q	B	F	J	T	K	Z	U	C	Y	L	G	A	P	R	M	X	E	W	N	I	V	H	D
L	A	I	K	G	Q	C	O	P	M	R	S	B	F	Y	U	L	T	E	Z	D	X	W	V	H	N	J
M	I	S	G	W	M	V	R	J	F	X	N	O	D	T	Q	A	Z	P	U	C	K	L	B	Y	E	H
N	X	F	O	Q	J	P	I	G	A	W	L	D	N	Y	C	Z	K	H	U	B	T	M	V	R	E	S
O	M	P	V	N	A	W	U	B	L	H	O	K	C	F	I	S	R	T	G	Q	E	Y	D	J	Z	X
P	L	J	B	P	V	H	N	U	Z	C	K	Y	R	M	X	G	D	T	W	**A**	F	Q	S	O	I	E
Q	C	U	N	R	L	Z	F	J	B	P	Y	S	T	E	M	I	X	O	W	K	H	Q	A	D	V	G
R	R	D	C	S	E	O	M	V	P	W	G	Q	F	I	K	T	H	B	X	U	J	A	Z	N	Y	L
S	Q	E	A	N	T	D	O	I	G	F	J	R	V	H	Y	U	C	L	Z	W	B	S	X	M	K	P
T	H	K	P	S	N	B	U	A	T	M	Y	G	W	L	E	D	Q	X	C	R	O	Z	V	J	F	I
U	V	R	G	F	H	M	K	Z	W	D	B	T	E	S	Y	J	N	Q	O	P	X	I	L	N	A	C
V	T	Z	K	D	N	V	C	Q	P	I	W	F	A	O	H	X	J	G	Y	E	U	M	S	R	L	B
W	G	W	X	A	Q	P	J	H	C	M	R	K	T	D	B	Z	L	F	I	Y	U	E	V	O	N	S
X	N	J	M	S	B	L	E	V	R	D	I	P	X	W	Y	C	Q	Z	G	O	H	U	F	A	K	T
Y	E	W	D	R	X	K	F	N	Z	Q	J	M	I	S	L	Y	A	G	B	H	T	O	U	P	C	V
Z	Y	K	F	X	Z	J	Q	L	H	E	W	O	V	A	U	T	G	B	P	I	D	C	N	M	S	R

So far, so familiar; we are simply using the system described by Porta. However, it is at this point that Vigenère's brilliant

idea comes into play. To encrypt the second letter of our original message, **h**, we now use the first letter of the message, **t**,
as the key letter to determine which cipher alphabet to use.
To encrypt the third letter, **e**, we now use the second letter, **h**,
as the key letter. This is shown more clearly in the diagram
below:

word

THEMANUSCRIPTRETAINSITSCRYPTICSECRET

in text

hemanuscriptretainsitscrypticsecrets

her text

AICIHTOAEPVAXERHGJUGHCAEYYATLVTWEERC

Vigenère's autokey system overcomes the need for a key
word, with all its inherent security weaknesses, but still
allows both the sender and receiver to memorise the simple
priming key, which consists of a single, prearranged letter.
The key phrase will always be as long as the message, because
the key phrase *is* the message. The recipient of the message,
knowing the priming key, would use that to decrypt the first
letter of the cipher message. The resulting decipherment
would not only be the first letter of the plain text, but also the
key for decrypting the second letter of the cipher text, the
second decrypted letter becomes the key for deciphering the
third, which in turn deciphers the fourth, and so on; until the
whole message is revealed.

Vigenère's final adjustment to the polyalphabetic ciphers
that developed during the Renaissance produced an encryption system that remained secure until the twentieth century.
Indeed, so advanced was Vigenère's cipher that few cryptographers adopted its methods in their entirety, preferring the
simpler versions of Trithemius and Belaso. This reticence is
understandable when we remember that even the basic
polyalphabetic systems were thought to be indecipherable
until the nineteenth century, and Renaissance cryptographers
felt that the added complexities of jumbled cipher alphabets
and autokeys were unnecessary. The easier the cipher was to
operate, the less likelihood that mistakes would creep into
the encryption or decryption processes. In effect, Vigenère had
produced the Rolls Royce of Renaissance ciphers, a system so

advanced and highly tuned that its use was deemed beyond the needs of most. If we stretch this analogy further, the simple substitution ciphers of the ancients, combined with Bacon's seven forms of secret writing, look like the Model-T Fords of the cryptographic world: sturdy, easy to use and available to many, but eventually surpassed by more advanced and highly crafted models. If the Voynich manuscript is written in a form of cipher, it must logically be one that falls between these two extremes.

If the Voynich manuscript is a product of the thirteenth century, the century of Roger Bacon, then it is highly unlikely that it constitutes anything much more complicated than a simple substitution cipher. The latest possible date for creation of the manuscript falls in the years leading up to 1608, the earliest confirmed date in its history thanks to the signature of Jacobus de Tepencz; which would place it firmly in the era of polyalphabetic ciphers of the type described by Vigenère. The three and a half centuries between these two extremes offer us a sliding scale of cryptological complexity – the earlier the manuscript, the easier the cipher should be to crack: from simple substitution ciphers in the thirteenth century, to homophonic ciphers with the addition of code words and nulls by the beginning of the fifteenth century, and then on to the elaborate multialphabetic ciphers of the Renaissance.

This period has already been described as one in which a cryptological arms race took place, with cipher makers and breakers each trying to stay one step ahead of the other. (By the end of the Renaissance it was the cipher makers who were clearly in the ascendant through the development of the supposedly unbreakable multialphabetic ciphers, a situation that was to remain unchanged until the Victorian age.) Such advances in the sciences of cryptography and cryptanalysis were not seen again until the twentieth century, when the need for the secure transfer of information took on new importance due to the cataclysmic events of two world wars. It was as a direct result of the need to combat mechanised encryption, through such equipment as the German Enigma cipher machines of the Second World War, that led to the construction of the world's first programmable computer. Today, even home computers can encrypt messages to a level which would have been unimaginable to the great names of Renaissance cryptology. Surely, with the skills of modern cryptanalysis and the advantage of computing power to draw upon, the Voynich manuscript must be ready to give up its secrets. Over the last ninety years, many people have reached just this conclusion; some even claiming to have broken the cipher and read the mysteries contained within the manuscript. Armed with our knowledge of ciphers and codes, we can now examine the main claims of decipherment, starting with the decryptions of the lawyer from Rochester, Maine: James Martin Feely.

A copy of Feely's slim book, *Roger Bacon's Cypher: the Right Key Found*, apparently printed at his own expense, resides today in the British Library in London. Probably the most remarkable aspect of this little book is that the information contained within its somewhat forbidding black covers was gleaned from only a few photographs of the Voynich manuscript. In fact, Feely claimed to have decrypted the Voynichese cipher by examining only plate V from Professor Newbold's book, which reproduces just one page of the original manuscript. Folio 78r (plate 16) comes from the balneological section, and was interpreted by Feely as showing two ovaries in the top left and right corners of the page, from which a 'stream of ova' flow down and join before passing through two short lengths of tube 'into a sacklike container; whence they drop still lower into a like receptacle, which may be rather another stage of their performance in the first container'.[5] Each 'sacklike' receptacle holds the usual band of cavorting naked nymphs. Forty-one lines of Voynichese script fill the left-hand side of the page, the end of each line of text running up to the illustrations which proceed down the right-hand side.

Feely was a keen amateur cryptologist, and had already published on the then fashionable topic of secret ciphers hidden within the works of Shakespeare. It is no surprise, then, that he should have been lured into the world of the Voynich manuscript. Feely opened his book with a flat dismissal of Newbold's decryption process. He did, however, keep an open mind as to the creator of the manuscript, and finding no reason to immediately discount Bacon as the author of the manuscript, Feely began his study with the innate assumption that it was a product of the thirteenth century, rather than a Renaissance artifact. Clearly knowing something of the history of cryptography, his tentative dating led Feely to conclude that the cipher was most likely to be of the monoalphabetic substitution variety. Having reached this deduction there was, therefore, one logical avenue of attack for Feely to take – frequency analysis.

As always with this form of cryptanalysis, the cipher breaker needs to know the frequency with which letters occur in the language of the original, unencrypted message; and to this end Feely carried out a frequency analysis on a number of Bacon's works. Concentrating mainly on the second, third and fourth chapters of *Communia Naturalium*, he identified that E, I, T, A, N, U and S were the most frequently occurring letters in Bacon's Latin lexicon. The next stage was for Feely to carry out a similar analysis on the Voynichese text of folio 78r, and compare this with the Baconian frequency table, in the hope of deducing Latin alphabet equivalents for the Voynich symbols. Such a process makes good cryptanalytical sense, and certainly seems a good deal more sensible than the confused mishmash of deciphering techniques employed by Professor Newbold. However, Feely immediately ran into a problem that has hampered many other would-be decipherers of the Voynich manuscript: just how many Voynichese characters are there? Without knowing exactly which are individual symbols and which are 'ligatured' or 'compounded' characters, it is impossible to build up a Voynichese alphabet; and if one cannot identify the individual symbols that make up the alphabet, it is likewise impossible to carry out an accurate frequency analysis. The kind of difficulties faced when trying to identify different characters in an unknown alphabet are eloquently demonstrated by American Voynich expert Jim Reeds:

> The kind of mistakes that the wrong choice leads to can be imagined by supposing a future race of beings trying to decode our writing system. If they mistakenly assume that 'm' and 'n' are the same letter (because they don't believe the exact number of humps is important) or that 'h' and 'n' are the same (because they differ only in the length of a single stroke), or

that 'n' and 'u' are the same (because they are rotated versions of each other), their analysis will be made harder. On the other hand, if they think that 'm' and '𝑚' are genuinely different letters, or that 'A' is fundamentally different from 'a', their analysis might become bogged down with irrelevant minutiae.[6]

Feely, rather than getting tied up with just such a problem of character identification, neatly sidestepped the issue by taking another approach. Having failed in his first attempt to produce the Voynichese alphabet, Feely ignored the main body of text and focused exclusively on the six labels which accompany the illustrations running down the right side of the folio. Two labels apparently refer to the 'ovaries' in the top corners, two are next to the length of 'tubing' where the ova streams join, and the final two appear alongside the pair of 'sacklike' containers housing the naked nymphs. In Feely's own words: 'The choice of this gambit lay along the line of the assumption that had proved successful in the case of the Rosetta Stone and also in the case of the cuneiform inscriptions, wherein the repetition of the same symbol or outline is matched with the position of the letters in a word that the drawings naturally suggests was used...' In other words, Feely hoped he had identified a possible crib. The word 'crib', when used in cryptological terms, refers to a direct, identifiable link between a piece of cipher text and a known plain-text word; for example, if we are somehow able to deduce what a particular cipher-text word (**ERRN**) means in the plain text (book), we can work out the key to the cipher that encrypted the word (in this case a simple Caesar shift cipher of three places). Feely hoped that if he could identify the objects in the illustrations, he would have a reasonable chance of working out what the label for each object must be when written in Latin, and from this he would be able to discover by what process the plain text had been encrypted. Throughout his book, Feely referred to these cribs as clews, a rather delightful archaic usage that refers to a ball of thread, such as was used by Theseus to navigate his way around the Cretan labyrinth.

Starting with the drawings that he took to represent ovaries, Feely transcribed the accompanying labels thus:

oℳ𝔠𝔠8℥8℥o and oℳ𝔠𝔠89

Following his hunch that these words must refer to the illustration, he allocated the symbols 'δ' and 'ϱ' with the Latin equivalents **i** and **n**, as he believed the plain-text word encrypted here might be **femminino**. It follows from this that the Voynichese 'c' symbol must be **m** in Latin, and so on, until he produced the following translation:

o M c c 8 Q 8 Q o
f e mm i n i n o

(The second label is just a shortened form of the same, **femmin**, the only difference being that the Latin letter **n** was represented by the symbol '**9**', which Feely took to be the same as '**Q**', except that '**9**' was used at the end of words.)

Moving down the diagram, to the labels relating to the strange tubing, Feely continued to allocate Latin equivalents to the Voynichese characters in ways which he felt gave likely meaning to the illustrations. For the next label he produced the following translation: **ISTSNFUNDUNTR**. This seems a much less successful decryption than the first two labels, but Feely was undeterred. He felt sure that the author was following the medieval custom of abbreviating the Latin text, and so he expanded the text to produce the following (Feely's added letters are in parenthesis): **IST(I)(I)NFUNDUNT(U)R**, which Feely translated into modern English as 'they are poured into each other', a seemingly appropriate description of the two streams of green liquid flowing into the same tube.

For the next label, Feely produced the decryption **IMM-CISTNNTR**, which he expanded to **IMMCIS(TI)N(A)NT(U)R**, or, in English, 'they are mixed together'. The final two labels, accompanying the naked ladies bathing in their green pools, translated as 'they make a festive beginning' and 'they are festive'; again, not unreasonable decipherments given the drawings. As further proof that he was on the right track, Feely was pleased to note that of the ten Latin equivalents he was sure he had identified correctly, eight of them corresponded with the most commonly occurring letters in Bacon's other writings according to his own frequency analysis.

Armed with these breakthroughs, Feely returned to the problem of distinguishing the number of symbols in the Voynichese alphabet. He soon identified fourteen basic characters, augmented by a further nineteen compound symbols, and immediately began work on deciphering the main body of text on folio 78r. Feely was by now sure he had uncovered a rather simple, two-stage cipher process: firstly, the use of an abbreviated Latin plain text, which, in the second stage was translated into Voynichese characters via a straightforward substitution cipher. Hence, in his decipherment, the substitution of Latin equivalents for Voynichese symbols in the first four lines of text on folio 78r produced the following:

PERHUMMIFT RMIN PODERUMIN POEMIN IN PVESL VEN. PVESIN POEMIN RUMMIN PERUMIN VEST VNEMIN. ISTNC PEMMIN MMVEN IFN MMMIN PRVEDINT PRVESCIS VNEMIN. NPERMMIN PVERSN IFN RMMIN PFEMIST MMMERMN OPERVT IUT FT PVESN FEMIN.

Feely was able to expand this string of letters into full Latin, thus:

Perhumifactum raminat; post-derumpitur minus; posteminus in prae-vesiculam venit. Pervesiculinatum, posteminus ruminatur; peruminatum vestitur veneminis. Istinc posteminus movent inferne; mamminas provediunt pervesiculus veneminarum. Inpermmiantur: perversuntur inferne; ruminantur; perfemiscitur mammerminis; operavitur itant fit praevestinntur feminas.

Which is all well and good, until one translates this into English:

Well humidified, it ramifies; afterward it is broken down smaller; afterwards, at a distance, into the fore bladder it comes. Then vesselled, it is awhile-after ruminated; well humidified it is clothed with veinlets. Thence after-a-bit they move down below; tiny teats they provide in the outpimpling of the veinlets. They are impermiated; are thrown down below; they are ruminated; they are feminised with tiny teats. It is operated so that it happens that they are fully vested with femininity.[7]

And so it goes on, repetitive and almost unintelligible, for forty-one lines. In a situation that was almost a perfect reverse of that which Newbold had found himself in, Feely had described a workable and credible cipher system; a cipher system, however, that produced unbelievable and unreadable results.

So how did Feely explain this bizarre decipherment? He saw it as the jottings of a medieval scientist, scribbling down the observed results of an ongoing experiment. Feely had already concluded that the cipher system was simple enough to be memorised by the user, and would not have required the use of look-up tables to find the cipher equivalents; allowing it to be used as a form of secret shorthand. The Voynich manuscript was therefore a scientific notebook, in which observations were recorded at speed and without due care and attention to correct grammatical and syntactical rules. Furthermore, our 'proto-scientist' recording his experiments would have lacked the exact scientific vocabulary of a modern experimenter, and so was struggling to record all the phenomena he was witnessing; thus explaining the strange repetitive nature of the deciphered text.

As to the question of Bacon's possible authorship of the manuscript, Feely remained undecided. Whilst he now felt totally confident in refuting Newbold's cipher system (Feely translated the legend accompanying the famous 'Andromeda Nebula' diagram as a reference to a statue of Memnon 'in the wooded glade, beyond the Ionian Sea'), he did not rule out all of Newbold's assumptions. Feely agreed that the drawings in the biological section of the manuscript, and the text from folio 78r, all suggested the use of a microscope of some sort in order to make such detailed observations. Furthermore, he pointed out that the cipher system he had uncovered was similar to certain methods of encryption as described by Bacon himself. In Bacon's list of seven techniques of secret writing mentioned earlier in this chapter, the third suggested omitting vowels from the text, which is similar to the abbreviated Latin Feely had uncovered. The sixth technique is the use of fabricated geometric figures in a substitution cipher, which could conceivably explain the Voynichese characters. However, in spite of these congruences, Feely stopped short of making a definite pronouncement on who the author of the Voynich manuscript might be.

If Feely's cipher system seems logical, and his explanation of the unusual plain text just about believable, there are a number of objections to the actual execution of the encryption process which cast a shadow of doubt over Feely's theory. For a medieval scholar to have created such a simple cipher and committed its operation to memory is not beyond the realm of the possible; but for the system to have been used to record the observed changes in microscopic material during an ongoing experiment becomes less likely when one examines folio 78r as a whole. Nowhere on this page, or in fact anywhere in the Voynich manuscript, is there a single correction to the text. With no apparent erasures or amendments to the script in any form, the inevitable conclusion is that the text was at least written with great care, perhaps even copied from a rough version. To imagine Feely's medieval scholar hastily making his scientific observations and then scribbling them down in a notebook without making one mistake seems highly unlikely; if not totally improbable when one takes into account the mental agility required to simultaneously translate the text into cipher. And if the Voynich manuscript were a *proper* version, reproduced from an earlier set of rough notes, why then did our proto-scientist not correct the grammatical and syntactical mistakes in the text during the copying process, thereby avoiding any later confusion due to the scrappy nature of the original writing? Another problem is posed by the spatial relationship between the text and the illustrations in the manuscript; because, as many Voynich researchers have pointed out, the drawings in the manuscript appear to have been created *before* the text was written. This can be seen by the way in which the lines of Voynichese script begin or end irregularly, demonstrating that the illustrations were produced first and the text then had to 'fit in' to the remaining space on each page. How could the author have been writing down the details of an experiment, supposedly as it happened, whose outcome they had already carefully recorded in illustrations? Feely's hypothesis of a set of work notes only functions if the text comes before the pictures, but it is clear from even a cursory examination that the Voynich manuscript was created in the reverse order.

So, with Feely's theory of the manuscript as a rough scientific notebook written in a substitution cipher looking less and less likely, we are left without any credible explanation of the bizarre stream of plain text he deciphered; and it is the quality of the plain text that finally puts paid to Feely's theories. Consequently his work has been almost totally dismissed, and his findings discounted, despite the employment of solid cryptographic methods. As David Kahn puts it: 'James Martin Feely recklessly exposed to the world – and to its ridicule – a solution that makes little sense in Latin and not much more in English.'[8] We must remember, however, that Feely had no access to the Voynich manuscript itself, that he had worked entirely from the plates in Newbold's book to produce his cryptanalytical theories, and for this endeavour at least Feely must be due some recognition. If his decipherments can be dismissed out of hand, his position as the first in a long line of enthusiastic amateurs to take on the challenge of the manuscript cannot be overlooked, and it is for this that James Martin Feely should be best remembered.

Pasted inside the back cover of the British Library copy of Feely's book is a typed and clearly carbon-copied addendum. Obviously produced by the author, with corrections to typing mistakes rather touchingly still evident, this single sheet apprises the reader of recent developments in Voynich manuscript research. Between finishing the book and its publication, Feely became aware of two new theories relating to the codex, and clearly unable to afford a reprint was forced to stick his hastily prepared appendix into every copy of his book. The first disclosure was that respected botanist Dr Hugh O'Neill had managed to identify a number of plants from the herbal illustrations, and in so doing had produced new evidence on the dating of the manuscript. The second, more startling announcement was that a further new decipherment of the manuscript had been claimed by another amateur cryptanalyst, the renowned cancer specialist Leonell C. Strong.

In 1931, continuing her husband's attempts to identify the author of the manuscript, Ethel Voynich delivered a complete set of photostats to Father Theodore C. Petersen, a teacher at St Paul's College and the Catholic University of America. Petersen, at his own expense, made a further set of copies from the Voynich originals and passed them in turn to Dr

Hugh O'Neill, at the same university. But it was not until 1944 that Dr O'Neill published his findings in a brief article in *Speculum* magazine. He considered that most of the illustrations in the botanical section of the manuscript had been drawn in such a way, probably deliberately, so as to make a definite identification of the plants almost impossible. He did, however, make tentative suggestions as to the possible plants represented in a few of the more plausible Voynich images.

Most importantly, he made a positive identification of two plants that, if correct, added a date in the chronology of the manuscript that had not been considered before. On folio 93r (plate 8), O'Neill recognised *Helianthus annus L*, otherwise known as the Common Sunflower; and on folio 101v a fruit that he thought likely to be some sort of Capsicum. What made these particular illustrations so important is that both these plants are native to the Americas, and were introduced into Europe by Columbus on his return from his second voyage. These identifications, if O'Neill was right, placed the creation of the Voynich manuscript sometime after 1493, and would lay to rest once and for all the possibility that it was written by Roger Bacon. (A full discussion of the botanical illustrations, their relationship to real plants, and whether O'Neill's identification is likely, follows in chapter 6.)

O'Neill's post-1493 dating of the manuscript threw the historical cat among the pigeons. Although Newbold's decryption of the Voynich manuscript had been rubbished, other researchers and the ever-hopeful Ethel Voynich had not discounted the possibility that Bacon was still the author. If O'Neill were right, then Bacon, who had died at the end of the thirteenth century, was clearly out of the running. The first person to offer another contender for authorship of the manuscript was Leonell Strong, the medical scientist from Yale University. His interest stemmed from reading O'Neill's article, and following the same 'unofficial' route as James Feely, his study of the manuscript was restricted to the few folios reproduced in other published works. (Strong's copious correspondence, recording his failed attempts to gain access to the manuscript itself, is published on the internet.) In 1945, just before the publication of Feely's book, Strong produced an article claiming the author to be a sixteenth-century English astrologer and physician, Anthony Ascham. According to

Strong, the Voynich manuscript was enciphered using a 'Double reverse system of arithmetical progressions of a multiple alphabet',[9] from which David Kahn deduces Strong's meaning to be 'some form of polyalphabeticity'.[10] This most likely refers to the kind of multialphabetic ciphers created by Trithemius et al, which were discussed earlier in the chapter. However, it is impossible to be certain of this, or to test Strong's cryptanalytical reasoning, because he never published the exact details of the cipher system. His reason for not disclosing his discoveries? With the Second World War still raging, he feared the cipher, if fully explained, might fall into enemy hands and be used against America and her allies.

Unfortunately for Strong's theory, the quality of his decrypted plain text quickly put paid to any serious discussion of his claims for Anthony Ascham. Although his translation included a recipe for a herbal contraceptive potion (which, when tested in a laboratory, apparently caused sperm to lose their motility), the other examples he produced stretched credibility to breaking point. The best example, and clearest summing up, of Strong's work is provided by Mary D'Imperio:

> Strong's plain text, of which he provides several examples in his articles, has been rejected by other scholars as completely unacceptable for medieval English. The reader may arrive at his own conclusions from the following sample: 'When skuge of tun'e-bag rip, seo uogon kum sli of se mosure-issue pedstans sku-bent, stokked kimbo-elbow crawknot.' This astonishing string of letters is translated by Strong thus: 'When the contents of the veins rip (or tear the membranes), the child comes slyly from the mother issuing with the leg-stance skewed and bent while the arms, bent at the elbow, are knotted (above the head) like the legs of a crawfish.' To my mind, at least, this seems a highly unlikely thing for any writer of any age to have said, whether in cipher or not.[11]

Strong's claim that the cipher system he had discovered might be of use to America's world war enemies amply demonstrates his lack of real cryptographic knowledge; as the kind of cipher he was describing was primitive compared to the actual encryption systems of his day. But we cannot entirely blame him for this, as the advances made in the science of cryptology during the war were of course top secret, and were to remain so for many years to come. Nor was Strong to know that military cryptanalysts were already taking an interest in the Voynich manuscript.

THE CRYPTOLOGICAL MAZE
Part II

One of the most important figures in the history of twentieth-century cryptology is William Frederick Friedman: America's chief cryptanalyst during the Second World War, breaker of the infamous Japanese 'Purple' cipher, and later the special assistant to the director of the ultra-secret National Security Agency. He was a studious, somewhat introverted man, though well liked and much admired by his colleagues, with a penchant for bow ties and golf. Friedman, along with his wife Elizebeth, first developed an interest in the Voynich manuscript in the 1920s. William attended both of the initial lectures given on the subject by Professor Newbold, and it was whilst in Philadelphia that he met Professor John Manly, with whom he subsequently worked to help disprove Newbold's claimed decipherment. Over the next forty years, the Friedmans initiated two study groups to examine the manuscript, and, though never producing a decipherment of their own, merit mention in this book not only for the theories they *did* produce, but also for the unusual manner in which they presented them, typical of their playful natures and their love of word games.

William Friedman, or Wolfe as he was originally named, was born in Kishinev, Russia, on 24 September 1891. Forced to leave their home due to a rising tide of anti-Semitism, the young Wolfe and his family emigrated to America in 1892, where they settled in Pittsburgh. Having studied genetics at Cornell University, attracted to the subject partly because of a general interest in science, but mostly because the course was free, by 1915 Friedman found himself in Geneva, Illinois, working at the three-hundred-acre Riverbank estate owned by wealthy textile merchant George Fabyan. Fabyan was a man of little formal education who tried to cultivate the airs of an intellectual, and so, at his own expense, maintained laboratories and researchers in the fields of chemistry, acoustics and genetics, and was in the habit of signing his own name at the bottom of scientific papers that had been prepared by his staff. This appears to be but one example of his eccentricity and obsession with somewhat peculiar displays of his wealth: he styled himself 'Colonel' Fabyan, though he had never been in the Army, and paraded around his estate in a knickerbocker riding suit though he had never ridden a horse. He could, however, drive a carriage, and was often seen collecting guests from the local railway station, himself at the reins of a team of trained zebra. He also kept vegetarian bears, and a pet gorilla that was allowed free range of the villa that stood at the heart of the estate.

Another of his fixations, rather surprisingly, was cryptology. Fabyan was apparently gripped by the belief that the works of Shakespeare were in fact written by Francis Bacon (no relation to the thirteenth-century friar), and in his attempts to prove this theory, he kept a permanent team of fifteen cryptanalysts on staff, all poring over Shakespeare's plays in the hope of finding evidence of Bacon's influence. William Friedman, although employed by Fabyan as a geneticist to improve the quality of grain and livestock on the estate, soon found himself, thanks to an aptitude for photography, helping the cryptology department to produce prints of the Elizabethan texts they were studying. It was during this period that Friedman was to discover the two passions that were to dominate the rest of his life: one for cryptology, and another for the co-ordinator of the cipher-breaking team, a young woman by the name of Elizebeth Smith. By 1917, Friedman was head of both the genetics and cryptology departments at the Riverbank estate, and husband of Elizebeth. William and Elizebeth were destined to become, in David Kahn's words, 'the most famous husband-and-wife team in the history of cryptology'.[1]

In April 1917, a month before the Friedmans' wedding, America had entered the First World War. At that time the Riverbank housed the only permanent cryptological department in the country, so the Friedmans soon found themselves working on decryptions for the Government. William

Friedman's success, not only in breaking enemy ciphers, but also in proving the fallibility of Allied encryption systems, meant that he was soon instructing Army officers in the science of cryptanalysis. To complement his teaching, Friedman produced a series of cryptanalytical manuals which were to prove a watershed in the history of cryptology. One of these short pamphlets, entitled 'The Index of Coincidence and Its Applications in Cryptology', described the use of various new statistical techniques to break two complex ciphers, and has been called 'the most important single publication in cryptology'.[2] By 1922 Friedman had become the Chief Cryptanalyst of the Army Signal Corps, which, despite the job title, meant he was in charge of military cryptography; developing and testing new ciphers and cipher machines. By the late 1920s the Army Signal Corps decided to combine its cryptographic and cryptanalytical branches into one body, and so in 1929, William Friedman became the director of the Signal Intelligence Service. Meanwhile his wife Elizebeth had been utilising her cryptanalytical skills to help the US coastguard break the ciphers used by rumrunners and bootleggers during the years of prohibition.

In 1925, whilst in his position as head of cryptanalysis for the Signal Corps, Friedman employed his recently developed statistical deciphering techniques to test a new encryption machine which had been developed for the American Army. Friedman's success in breaking the cipher, thereby demonstrating the weakness of the machine, was to lay the foundation for his most famous exploit. In the late 1930s the Japanese government and military introduced a new cipher machine for their secret communications: the 97-*shiki O-bun In-ji-ki* or Alphabetical Typewriter '97, or simply The Machine; known to the Americans as 'Purple'. Based on the German Enigma machine, Purple consisted of a fiendish combination of revolving rotors and a plugboard of interchangeable cables, attached to a pair of electrically operated typewriters. A plain-text letter typed into the first keyboard sent an electric current through the ever-changing maze of internal wiring, until it produced a corresponding cipher letter on the output keyboard. Friedman, armed with his statistical expertise and a familiarity with similar mechanical polyalphabetic ciphers he had encountered before the war, led a team of cryptanalysts in a concerted attack on Purple. Within months their dedicated efforts had produced a 'pencil-and-paper analog' of the machine,[3] which was then, with the aid of old telephone switches and household hardware, turned into a gear-grinding, spark-spewing contraption that could nonetheless exactly reproduce the workings of the Japanese machine. By August 1940, Friedman and his team were able to present a complete solution to the Purple cipher.

As if all his official cryptanalytical duties were not enough, towards the end of the war Friedman decided to turn his attentions towards the Voynich manuscript once again, and founded an 'after-hours informal club of Army cryptanalysts'.[4] The first meeting of this Voynich study group took place on 26 May 1944, though unfortunately, apart from William and Elizebeth Friedman, the identities of the other fourteen people who attended are unknown. The group based their studies on a photocopy of the manuscript they had obtained from Father Petersen, and began the arduous process of producing a machine-readable transcription of the Voynichese text on a set of punch cards, with the aim of using these on IBM accounting equipment. The group continued this laborious task sporadically throughout 1945 and 1946; but with the war over, and many of the team being demobilised and returning to their civilian homes and occupations, the transcription was left incomplete by the time the group finally disbanded. Although the group never published any results, it was during this period that Friedman undoubtedly began to develop his own ideas of what the inscrutable Voynichese script might represent in cryptological terms.

In 1958, the Friedmans were approached by Curt Zimansky of the *Philological Quarterly* to write an article on the application of cryptanalysis in the study of literature. The article would discuss the various (spurious) attempts by amateur cryptanalysts to uncover the *real* authors of a number of literary classics, whose identities had supposedly been concealed within the texts through various ciphers. The Friedmans were only too happy to produce a critique of these rather foolish and cryptologically unsound ideas, and it no doubt must have brought back many memories of their days at the Riverbank estate, where they had toiled away in a vain attempt to prove Fabyan's theory that Francis Bacon had written *Hamlet*. For William and Elizebeth, it was not only a return to the beginning of their cipher-breaking careers, but also provided an opportunity to indulge themselves in the sort of cryptographic game-playing that they enjoyed.

The first draft submitted by the Friedmans contained a long and, to Zimansky's mind, irrelevant section regarding Newbold's fallacious analysis of the Voynich manuscript, its debunking by Manly, and a brief explanation of Friedman's own interpretation of the manuscript. Bowing to Zimansky's criticism, Friedman agreed that the Voynich/Newbold story should be relegated to a footnote in the article, but on one condition: Friedman would still present his own theory on the Voynich manuscript, but in the form of a sixty- to sixty-five-letter anagram. Friedman suggested that, as his theory was not fully prepared for presentation, this was the ideal way of making it public; and as corroboration of this argument he quoted the example of just such an anagram created by the famous astronomer Galileo. Unwilling to announce his theories on the phases of the planet Venus due to a lack of observational data, yet still hoping to gain the rightful recognition for his work should his hypothesis later be proved correct, Galileo transposed a precis of his ideas into a thirty-five-letter anagram, which he delivered under seal to Giuliano de Medici. In 1611, once he had carried out the necessary astronomical observations, Galileo was able to reveal the true message hidden within the anagram, thus demonstrating that he had long suspected what his studies now proved.

Apparently delighted by Friedman's idea, no doubt because of the historical precedent and its playfulness, which was in keeping with the spirit of the article, Zimansky agreed to the inclusion of the hidden message. Thus, when the article was published in 1959, it included the following puzzle from Friedman:

I put no trust in annagrammatic acrostic cyphers, for they are of little real value – a waste – and may prove nothing. – Finis.

In the true spirit of the intellectual challenge, Zimansky was presented with a sealed and dated envelope containing the correct solution to the anagram, which he was to keep safe until such time that either the puzzle was solved or Friedman was prepared to go public with his hypothesis.

As we have seen during the examination of Newbold's attempted decryption, the odds of correctly rearranging an anagram of even moderate length are stacked against the would-be solver. The almost impossible task of finding the original message in a transposition of ninety-six letters such as Friedman's did not, however, deter several people from having a go. A number of (incorrect) solutions were sent to Friedman, including the following:

William F. Friedman in a feature article arranges to use crypt-analysis to prove he got at that Volynich manuscript. No?

Or the pessimistic:

This is a trap, not a trot. Actually I can see no apt way of unravelling the rare Voynich manuscript. For me, defeat is grim.

Or even:

To arrive at a solution of the Voynich manuscript, try these general tactics: a song, a punt, a prayer. William F. Friedman.

As this playful battle of cryptanalytical wits continued, the Friedmans continued their more serious research into the Voynich manuscript, and in the later months of 1962 inaugurated a second study group to tackle the problem. On this occasion the team had 'after hours' access to a 301 computer at the Radio Corporation of America, and with the aid of specialist programmers offering assistance in their spare time, the Friedmans again planned to create an entire transcript of the manuscript. The first meeting was held on 25 September 1962, and the work continued on the project until the late summer of 1963. Unfortunately, once again the task was never completed. As the complex set of charts, graphs and programme specifications was still being prepared, the management at RCA decided that the unofficial use of its computer equipment could not be sanctioned. Before the project had really begun, it was over; and the study group was disbanded its transcription still incomplete. However, Friedman's views on the manuscript remained unchanged, and his anagram unsolved. During the years following the publication of the original article, the Friedmans did let slip a few clues as to what their theory might be; or rather, they hinted at what they believed the Voynich manuscript *was not*. In an article for the *Washington Post* in 1962, Elizebeth Friedman stated that the manuscript's resistance to cryptographic attack suggested it was not a simple substitution cipher of the type Feely proposed. William Friedman also ruled out the possibility that Roger Bacon was the author of the Voynich manuscript when he announced that it was probably written sometime between 1480 and 1520.

However, it was not until 1970, after William Friedman's death, that the solution to the anagram was finally revealed in another article in *Philological Quarterly*. With the correct rearrangement of letters, the message reads:

The Voynich MSS was an early attempt to construct an artificial or universal language of the a priori type. – Friedman.

Artificial or 'synthetic' languages can be divided into two broad categories. The kind with which most people will be familiar is termed 'posterior', and is based on existing languages and language structure, the most famous example being Esperanto. The 'priori' type, of which Friedman believed the Voynichese language was an example, is founded on entirely different principles. In these languages, human experience is divided into sets of logical categories, in much the same way as Dr Roget classified words when creating his famous thesaurus. A number of priori-style languages were devised during the seventeenth century, the impetus being the decline in the use of Latin as the universal language of scholars. In addition, interest in new forms of communication had been sparked by missionaries returning from the Far East with reports of ideographic writing systems in which whole concepts and ideas could be contained in a single symbol. (It was just such tales as these that had no doubt partially inspired Athanasius Kircher in his fanciful interpretation of Egyptian hieroglyphs.)

One of the earliest attempts to create an artificial language was made by Scotsman George Dalgarno. In his system, ideas and experience were divided into twenty-two classes, each of which was represented by a single letter from the Latin alphabet – hence **H** stood for all things spiritual, **N** for natural objects, and **K** for 'political matters'. Each category could be subdivided by the addition of further consonants or vowels to produce more precise subclasses: hence **Ke** was 'judicial affairs' and **Ku** 'war'. Another priori language was created by John Wilkins, the Bishop of Chester. The brother-in-law of Oliver Cromwell, Wilkins was the first secretary of the Royal Society and wrote the first book on cryptology in the English language. In Wilkins' language, which he called Real Character, there were forty-two basic philosophical categories, each denoted by a sign. Further subcategories could be produced by the attachment of vertical or oblique lines to the basic symbol. An even more bizarre system was created by Jean-François Sudre, based around seven musical notes; which meant that the language could therefore be sung or played on musical instruments, and, if the notes were converted into seven colours, even painted!

In 1950, William Friedman introduced the British cryptologist Brigadier John H. Tiltman to the puzzle of the Voynich manuscript, and Tiltman had soon reached the same conclusions as Friedman regarding its cryptological basis. Tiltman's own studies had uncovered a still earlier synthetic language devised in the 1650s by Cave Beck, known as the Universal Character. This used a basic vocabulary of four thousand English words, each of which was allocated a four-digit number. Further detail and expressiveness could be obtained by adding extra digits to the original code-number, in the form of prefixes or suffixes. It struck both Friedman and Tiltman that some form of synthetic writing system broadly along these lines might explain the more unusual aspects of the Voynichese language. Tiltman had already identified certain 'behavioural characteristics' displayed by Voynichese symbols, with some characters tending to appear at the beginning of words, others at the end; perhaps indicating that 'words' in the manuscript all possessed a root, a core group of symbols to which others were added as prefixes or suffixes to create more precise meaning (such as case, tense or plurality). This seemed a good central hypothesis, but Tiltman and the Friedmans were unable to advance this theory further. Although the language of the manuscript certainly seemed to share some traits that could be found in other artificial languages, none was an exact match, and despite the attempts of his two study groups, Friedman was never able to complete the detailed analysis of Voynichese linguistic characteristics that his theory demanded.

Friedman's later life was plagued by ill health of various kinds. As early as 1940 he suffered a serious nervous breakdown which hospitalised him for over three months, no doubt brought on by the stress of cracking the Purple cipher; and he was to be haunted by the recurrent spectre of depression for the rest of his days. His variable state of mental health could not have been helped by a long-drawn-out legal battle with the American Government over the issue of compensation for the 'immeasurable stress of his work',[6] and the loss of earnings from the various cipher machines he had invented for the US Army, which, if he had been able to sell them on the commercial market, would have netted Friedman considerable sums. William F. Friedman died on 2 December 1969, after a massive coronary. Amongst all his other great achievements in the world of cryptology, the Voynich manuscript remained unconquered.

Asked why he persevered [with the Voynich manuscript] he replied simply: 'Because it hasn't been read': a parallel with George Mallory's explanation of why he wished to climb Mount Everest – 'Because it is there.'[7]

Robert Brumbaugh first came across the Voynich manuscript in the late 1930s, when, as an undergraduate at Yale University, he read Newbold's book, followed quickly by Manly's critique. The manuscript took on a fascination for Brumbaugh, as it had done for so many others before, and its study took up much of his spare time. However, unlike all those other Voynich researchers who had gone before, Brumbaugh had one distinct advantage: he had access to the manuscript itself. Based at Yale in his capacity as Professor of Medieval Philosophy, Brumbaugh was able to visit the Voynich manuscript in its post-1969 resting place in the Beinecke Library, and in the early 1970s was even able to gain two research grants to continue his studies. The amount and quality of time Brumbaugh was able to give to his research led to him becoming a major figure in the history of Voynich study. He published a number of articles on the subject throughout the 1970s, and edited a book, *The Most Mysterious Manuscript*, which dealt with Voynich research up to that date, as well as explaining Brumbaugh's own theories and partial decryption.

Brumbaugh's first and most important breakthrough came in the spring of 1972, when he noticed that some of the Voynichese symbols were similar to others he had seen on a visit to Milan, scribbled on the back of another old manuscript. In the Milanese document, the symbols had been used in an astrological diagram to represent *numbers*. Brumbaugh began to wonder if the cipher system used in the Voynich manuscript, assuming it was a 'remote cousin' of the Italian manuscript, might also be based on a numerical system, outside the mainstream of Renaissance cryptography.

Following his hunch, Brumbaugh examined a set of what he described as 'marginal doodles' on folio 66r of the Voynich manuscript, and from these was able to deduce numerical values for the Voynichese symbols. Put another way, this meant that every character in the Voynichese alphabet actually represented a number between 1 and 9. Many Voynichese symbols closely resemble the Arabic numerals we use today, and so it seemed logical to Brumbaugh that they must represent those numbers, with the addition of other, less obvious equivalents. So, the number 4 was represented by the Voynichese character that looks most like the Arabic numeral (𝟺), as well as symbols that look like both a Latin and Italian cursive *d*. Brumbaugh's explanation of how he determined which Voynichese character represented which number is not totally clear, and even Mary D'Imperio, the doyenne of Voynich scholars, is forced to admit that 'while those he explains are convincing enough, the rest of the "formulae" remain somewhat mysterious to me in the absence of further clarification'.[8]

It took Brumbaugh until 1975 to finally identify the numerical equivalents for all the Voynichese symbols (though annoyingly, after all the detailed study, he fails to provide the list in his book published on the subject). To complete what he described as a 'numerological box cipher', Brumbaugh then wrote out the letters of the normal Latin alphabet underneath the numbers 1 to 9, producing the following table:

1	2	3	4	5	6	7	8	9
A	B	C	D	E	F	G	H	I
J	K	L	M	N	O	P	Q	US
	R		S		T		U	
V		W		X		Y		Z

And now we can begin to see the cipher in operation. For this example, let us take the commonly occurring Voynichese symbol ℴ, which Brumbaugh presumed had the numerical value 7. We can therefore look up the number 7 in our table and see which letters appear in the column beneath, in this case G, P and Y. Hence ℴ =7=G, P or Y. Obviously there is a level of ambiguity in such a cipher system, as each Voynichese character can represent any one of three plain-text letters; a fact that Brumbaugh was quick to acknowledge. He felt the system was not precise enough to be used for military or diplomatic purposes, but he was convinced that the cipher was easy to use and was probably more accurate in conveying messages than it might at first appear.

Using the system, Brumbaugh set to work on a series of labels accompanying plant illustrations on folio 100r (plate 1) in the pharmaceutical section of the manuscript. Taking the label:

Brumbaugh derived the number equivalents:

7 1 7 5 2 (7+3) 9

The '(7+3)' appears because ⚭ is a compound symbol, in which ℴ =7 and ƒ=3; therefore ⚭ can represent six Latin plain alphabet letters in total (G, P and Y which are the equivalents for 7, plus C, L and W, the equivalents for 3). The number sequence in turn gives us the following plain-alphabet options:

7	1	7	5	2	(7+3)	9
G	A	G	E	B	GC	I
P	J	P	N	K	PL	US
Y	V	Y	X	R	YW	Z

from which Brumbaugh selected:

G **A** G **E** B G**C** I
P J **P** N K PL **US**
Y V Y X **R** **Y** W Z

to give the plain-text word **paperycus**, which Brumbaugh took
to be *paprika*, as the label for a (vaguely) pepper-like plant. At
this stage the cipher system seemed to operate reasonably
well, and Brumbaugh was able to produce similar, though less
completely successful translations for other labels on the
same page. (The authors of this book must confess that their
attempts to follow Brumbaugh's decryption process on the
same sample of Voynichese text were less straightforward,
and it appears that on a few occasions Brumbaugh might have
been somewhat 'loose' in his identification of the original
Voynichese symbol, thus allowing a more subjective element
to creep into the decipherment.)

Brumbaugh went on to translate a set of star names in the
astrological section, as well as some large passages of text. He
explained the rather scrappy and sometimes almost unfath-
omable nature of the decrypted plain text in a number of
ways. Firstly, Brumbaugh felt the original author was using a
simplified form of Latin, 'in which inflections have been
replaced',[9] allowing the writer to ignore the usual grammatical niceties of conjugation and declensions. Furthermore, he
suggested that the 'eccentric and impressionistic' spelling,
which meant the same 'word' was often spelled in many different ways, was 'typical of the early stages of modern
European language'.[10] Brumbaugh's efforts to translate more
of the manuscript were hampered by the fact that the cipher
alphabet/number/plain alphabet relationship appeared to shift
or change from one section of the manuscript to another;
which meant that the cipher system which seemed to work
well on one page might fail totally on the next. In fact,
Brumbaugh was unable to read *anything* from the whole of
the botanical section.

And what kind of decipherments did he produce? The following is a transcription of the plain text deciphered by
Brumbaugh (and subsequently translated into English from
the abbreviated Latin), from folio 75r:

LIQUID SYRIAN MATTER LIQUID MATTER PLUS
SYRIAN SICILIAN PLUS SYRIAN SALT EUROPEAN
SWEDISH...SICILIAN PLUS SYRIAN PLUS RUSSIAN
ASIAN SICILIAN SALT LIQUID...ASIAN ITALIAN SICIL-
IAN SALT LIQUID SICILIAN ITALIAN PLUS SICILIAN
PLUS SALT...SALT PHYSICAL SALT...SICILIAN SALT...
SALT ASIAN...MATTER PLUS SALT... ITALIAN... SICIL-
IAN SALT ASIAN SICILIAN SALT AFRICAN EUROPEAN
SALT ASIAN RUSSIAN PLUS PLUS ASIAN SALT LIQUID...
SALT SALT SALT SALT SALT...etc.[11]

What could this possibly mean? Brumbaugh thought it had
the appearance of a formula, but with no guide to the quantities of the various substances to be used, or any clue as to the
process by which the materials were to be mixed, the recipe, if
that is what it is, would be next to useless.

In spite of the small amount of decrypted text, its very
dubious quality and uncertain meaning, Brumbaugh gradually
developed a theory for the provenance and content of each
section of the manuscript. The botanical section, with its
strange drawings of unrecognisable plants, he felt was little
more than 'some arbitrary set of illustrations adapted from
large Herbals'; though Brumbaugh did admit that the lack of
any deciphered text from this section limited his analysis to
an examination of the diagrams. The second section, in which
he had decrypted the names of 'classical statesmen and Arab
sages assigned to stars', Brumbaugh again thought to be a copy
from an earlier, possibly thirteenth-century text, which must
have consisted of material of both English and Spanish origin.
Next, following surprisingly closely to Newbold, Brumbaugh
interpreted the biological drawings as showing the immortal
human soul, freed from the body, both before and after death.
Once again, he felt the look of the naked nymphs in their
pools of green liquid owed more to the works of antiquity,
particularly Galen, than the more accurate, realistic illustrations of Renaissance medicine. The pharmaceutical pages,
with their plants from the New World identified by the deciphered pages, were taken to be a purely sixteenth-century
invention, and Brumbaugh's assessment of the author's creative skills deserves to be quoted verbatim. 'His ability to see
plants as animate verges on the mentally deranged; his

attempts to apply numerology to pharmacy verges on the absurd.' Brumbaugh is hardly less scathing in his views of the final, unillustrated section, which he concludes to be a deliberate parody, again from the sixteenth century, designed to emulate 'indices, contents, summaries and the like', which would have been present in genuine reference books.[12]

Brumbaugh therefore seems to be suggesting that the Voynich manuscript as a whole was constructed from several distinct and varied sources: some sections copied (apparently without much care and attention) from earlier documents, whilst others were the product of a sixteenth-century author attempting to give the manuscript the appearance of an obscure work of scholarship. But how then to explain the unusual nature of the decrypted plain text? To his great credit, and unlike many of his Voynich-deciphering predecessors, Brumbaugh was quick to accept that the quality of the plain text did not stand up to close scrutiny, and so offered a number of explanations for it. Firstly, he postulated that his 'numerological box cipher' was only one stage in the encryption process, and that the uncovered 'plain text' might have to undergo a further stage of decipherment before the true message would appear. Brumbaugh suggested that such extra concealment might use a coded alphabet, wherein each word in his decrypted 'plain text' represented a single letter in the inner, final plain-text message. Or maybe, wondered Brumbaugh in his second explanation, there was no further level of concealment; the true plain text had been discovered, but there was a special way of reading it. Perhaps only certain words were relevant, and these could be detected by placing a grille (a perforated sheet of metal or cardboard) over the pages of the manuscript to reveal only those words that were supposed to be read. Or was some form of word or letter 'pattern' to be employed, in which the reader, knowing the correct spacing of the true plain-text words (for example, concentrating on the third word or letter, then the sixth, then the ninth, etc.), would read only them, and ignore the remaining meaningless, filler text. Another possibility was that the deciphered plain text actually did make sense to an initiate who knew the correct way to read it. Brumbaugh used the example of his decrypted 'formulae', proposing that the information describing the quantities of each substance to be used was conveyed in some obscure, non-literal manner; for example, through counting words in the text (this use of jargon, a language known only to a select few, reminds us once again of Bacon's seven methods of secret writing).

These explanations are all plausible enough, though whether Brumbaugh's numerological cipher was the correct deciphering system in the first place is still open to question. Brumbaugh does, however, give one final justification for the garbled plain text; a justification that has much wider implications for the Voynich manuscript and all those who study it. On the last page of his book, Brumbaugh wrote the following: 'Suppose, however, that there is meant to be no hidden message and all that is there is simply text as our alphabet reads it.' Brumbaugh's final hypothesis is that the deciphered plain text is *intended* to be mostly nonsensical, with just enough recognisable and intelligible text to keep a decipherer intrigued. The Voynich manuscript was therefore constructed to appear as if it contained a hidden yet accessible meaning, when in fact there is no secret message contained within its pages at all. The Voynich manuscript could be entirely without meaning.

On 10 March 1208, the somewhat ironically named Pope Innocent III called upon the lords and princes of Christendom to undertake a crusade. This act of combined military duty and religious penance was not, however, to be directed at the Islamic Middle East, but rather the Christian towns and communities lying between the Pyrenees and the Mediterranean in what is today southern France. The target of the papal ire was a heretical sect known to history as the Cathars. Although the crusade was nominally instigated in direct response to the murder of the papal legate Peter of Castelnau, it was in reality the inevitable outcome of simmering tension between the Catholic Church and the Cathars that had been building towards this bloody climax for over half a century. The Albigensian Crusade, as it became known, was to ravage Languedoc from 1209 to 1229, and in those twenty years the region was to experience innumerable atrocities, most notably the sack of Béziers and the annihilation of its inhabitants, as noblemen from northern Europe seized the lands of the Languedocian princes under the pretence of Holy War.

The period of crusade was followed by years of persecution, as the remaining Cathars were crushed in the steely grip of the Dominican-led Inquisition. This time of zealous oppression reached its zenith, or nadir depending upon one's religious viewpoint, with the year-long siege of the mountain bastion of Montsegur, and the subsequent immolation of its Cathar defenders in 1244. The last recorded execution of a Cathar heretic occurred at the village of Villerouge Termenès in 1321.

Whence had the Cathars come, and what were their beliefs, so troubling to the Catholic authorities they caused thirty years of bloodshed and misery? Both these questions are still hotly debated. What is known is that the first Cathars appeared in Languedoc in the mid-twelfth century, and in 1167 a conclave was held in the town of St Felix en Lauragais, with heretics arriving from as far afield as Lombardy and the Byzantine Empire. The origins of this strange offshoot of Christianity are uncertain, but it seems likely that their beginnings lie in the east, with the Bogomil heretics of Bulgaria and Bosnia, themselves probably descended from the Paulicians, an Armenian sect persecuted by the Byzantines in the ninth century. Indeed, one of those attending the conference of 1167 was Nicetas, in all probability a Bogomil bishop from Constantinople.

Catharism was a dualist faith, espousing a belief in the two opposing principles of good and evil. To the Cathars, the realm of good was the spiritual, invisible world of God. All that was visible and material was entirely the product of the devil and, by its very nature, evil. The physical world around them was, therefore, corrupt and worthy of little or no consideration in relation to the achievement of spiritual salvation. Neither did the Cathars believe in the existence of hell, for this world, being the creation of darkness, was literally a hell on earth. Upon death, the soul was reborn – reincarnated – to suffer another turn on the rack of this world. Only by living a pure, spiritual existence, immune to the trappings of the physical, could the soul be released from the continual round of death and rebirth, and regain its true, angelic status with God.

To the Cathars, the material path would simply doom one to return to earth in a future life. It was this *personal* choice, the choice of the spiritual over the physical, that mattered; not the living of one's life by the doctrines of the temporal, and therefore corrupt, Catholic Church. It therefore followed that it mattered not one iota if a person chose to keep the company of Jews, sleep with someone before marriage, or treat male and female with equality; all things proscribed by the medieval Church. Those who expressed a belief in these Cathar doctrines were known as *credentes*, but the true Cathars were the small band of the *Perfect* who had received, and could therefore confer, the Cathar sacrament of the *consolamentum*. Having been thus 'consoled', the *Perfect* lived their final pure and ascetic life on earth, before attaining their rightful angelic existence after death. They referred to themselves simply as 'Good Christians', the term Cathar being coined by their enemies in reference to the fallacious belief that their practice of worship included the kissing of a cat's behind.

The region of Languedoc was well known for its religious tolerance. Jews traded and ran businesses with relative impunity there, and it was in this corner of the Mediterranean that the mystical investigations which were to become the basis of the Cabala first began. It was therefore not surprising that the Cathars should flourish in Languedoc, with local noblemen and their families either turning a blind eye to the heretical practices, or on occasion actively supporting them. Such a situation, and such a set of beliefs, could not be overlooked by the Catholic Church, challenging, as they did, the very tenets of religious doctrine that held the fabric of the medieval world together. Papal legates were hastily dispatched, instructed to enter into doctrinal debates with the Cathar *Perfect* in an attempt to win back the wayward flock of Languedoc. But when this missionary work failed, and the legate Peter of Castelnau was mysteriously murdered, the Pope set in motion the bloody chain of events that was to lead to the eventual obliteration of the Cathar faith.

Our knowledge of the Cathars comes to us from a handful of contemporary chroniclers, mostly siding with the Catholic orthodoxy, and records of the Inquisition that followed the years of the crusade. So complete was the suppression of the heresy that no Cathar text survived, if indeed any had existed in the first place. Or so it seemed. In 1987 a book was published that claimed not only a solution of the Voynich manuscript, but also proof that it was the only example of a document written by the Cathars themselves.

Solution of the Voynich Manuscript: a Liturgical Manual for the Endura Rite of the Cathari Heresy, the Cult of Isis by Dr Leo Levitov is a strange book, being filled as it is with assumptions and assertions, but with little verifiable historical fact to back up its startling pronouncements. It does not even contain a bibliography which would allow a curious scholar to examine how Dr Levitov reached some of his more far-fetched conclusions. What the book does contain, however, is a wholly new take on the mysterious Voynich script.

Dr Levitov, a doctor of medicine and amateur cryptologist, first became aware of the Voynich manuscript having read about it in David Kahn's *The Codebreakers*, and subsequently obtained a photocopy of the entire manuscript so that he could carry out his own investigation. Having exhausted the usual cryptological approaches, and like so many before him, having nothing to show for his efforts, Dr Levitov cast the manuscript aside for several months. Then, inspired by the story of Michael Ventris, the scholar who uncovered the secrets of the forgotten Minoan B script of ancient Crete, Dr Levitov returned to the problem with an entirely different approach. Rather than the Voynich script being a cipher or code, he assumed it was a real, though hitherto unknown language, that could be read directly from the page by those familiar with it, without any need for a system of decryption. Within twenty-four hours Dr Levitov had allocated phonetic values to the Voynich symbols from which he could 'transliterate' the Voynichese into equivalent-*sounding* Latin letters, and then 'translate' the resultant text into readable modern English. (Although Dr Levitov goes into great length in his descriptions of the uncovered text and its meaning, he is sparing with the details of how he obtained the phonetic values in the first place.)

Dr Levitov claimed that the language his 'transliteration' process uncovered was a 'polyglot oral tongue',[13] a garbled mixture of the other languages spoken by Cathar *credentes* from northern Europe, especially the German dialects of 'Flanders, the Rheinland, and the River Maas'.[14] There was little grammatical structure to the language, and a very limited vocabulary, with only twenty-three 'roots' (infinitives) from which all other words, both nouns and verbs, were derived. The structure was highly repetitious, as one would expect from a direct transliteration from Voynichese, and Dr Levitov's translation of the 'Cathari' language roots into modern English showed a preponderance of words relating to illness and death. From this fact he deduced the Voynich manuscript to be a liturgical manual of the *Endura*, or Cathar suicide rite.

As mentioned earlier, for the Cathar *credente* to escape the continual cycle of death and rebirth, they must receive the *consolamentum* sacrament to attain the status of *Perfect*, and then maintain their newfound spiritual purity through a life of strict asceticism. Even a minor infringement of the rules governing the life of a *Perfect* meant the immediate loss of this exalted status and the promise of a joyous afterlife, not only for the lapsed *Perfect*, but for all those others to whom they had in turn conferred the *consolamentum*. However, in the years of persecution and suppression that followed the Albigensian Crusade, the strict regime that denoted a *Perfect* made them an easy target for the Inquisition, and the secrecy necessary for the practice of Catharism meant great danger and difficulty in readministering the *consolamentum* to a lapsed *Perfect*. It therefore became standard Cathar ritual to receive the *consolamentum* at the last possible moment before death.

This feat of exact timing was easier said than done. The *Perfect* who was to administer the sacrament might have to travel a large distance, and then find an opportunity to deliver the *consolamentum* to the ailing *credente* away from the prying eyes of nosy neighbours and suspicious priests. However, once the sacrament had been received, it was then best for the newly exalted *Perfect* to pass away as quickly as possible, before some inadvertent act such as a kiss from a weeping relative or a spoonful of meat from a well-meaning carer instantly undid their chance of salvation. So it was that the *Endura*, or suicide rite, became a standard part of Cathar ritual.

Dr Levitov's translations appeared to produce ample evidence to support his theory that the Voynich manuscript was a manual to accompany the religiously justified suicide of the

The prone figure, folio 66r

Endura. In the bottom left-hand corner of folio 66r, a page from the end of the botanical section of the manuscript, there is an illustration of a small prone figure with a swollen belly, lying next to what appear to be two small cakes or loaves. Above the figure is the following legend:

which Levitov transliterated into his 'Cathari' polyglot language to give:

AILIVIA TEM VILETH THEDEESVISETH

giving us the modern English translation (according to Levitov):

When one is as sick as he is, he wants to know death.[15]

Dr Levitov also provided an explanation for the naked nymphs of the balneological or bathing section of the manuscript, who were, according to his theory, engaged in suicidal vein-opening whilst in their green baths. Furthermore, and possibly most startling of all, dotted throughout the manuscript Dr Levitov found numerous references to the Egyptian goddess Isis, thereby placing the mysterious beginnings of the Cathar heresy not with the Bogomils of Byzantium, but as a mystical cult descended from the religions of Ancient Egypt. Levitov claimed to have identified symbols representing this cult of Isis on almost every page of the botanical section (though he gave no explanation as to what these symbols were), and also identified allusions to the Egyptian deity in the cosmological diagrams. And how had this unique document survived the purging of the Inquisition? According to Dr Levitov, it had been carried to England by fleeing Cathars, where it was confiscated 'and given to some monastic order',[16] whence it progressed to the Duke of Northumberland after the Dissolution of the Monasteries, and then on to John Dee.

Unfortunately for Dr Levitov, his theory and translation have been attacked, very convincingly, on almost every level by modern Voynich scholars. Linguist and Voynich expert Jacques Guy has expressed grave doubts regarding Levitov's 'polyglot oral tongue', citing the extremely low number of consonant sounds in the language (a mere twelve as compared to twenty in Dutch), the ungrammatical construction and usage of compound words, and even the 'meaningless babble' of the phrase 'polyglot oral tongue' itself.

Far more damaging, however, are the criticisms of Dennis Stallings and Michael Barlow, this time focusing on the inaccuracies in Dr Levitov's portrayal of the Cathars themselves, and his seemingly scant knowledge of the historical facts of the 'Great Heresy'. He hypothesises that the manuscript might have been brought to England around the year 1163, four years before the peaceful 'Cathar International' at St Felix, over forty years before the start of the Albigensian Crusade, and more than sixty years before the trials of the Inquisition. At such a time the *Endura* rite was unheard of and unneeded. Indeed, the Cathars of this period were known for their attempts to preserve life by ministering to the sick and the foundation of hospices. When the *Endura* rite did become necessary towards the end of the thirteenth century, it was used only as a way to hurry the inevitable end, thus ensuring the dying of their unsullied *Perfect* status, rather than a form of euthanasia to relieve pain as Dr Levitov's translations seem to suggest. His interpretation of the naked nymphs quietly cutting their veins as part of a suicide pact also fails to square with the known facts of the *Endura*, which was simply an abstinence from food, a final fast designed to bring about a quicker death, carried out alone without need of liturgy or ritual. Dr Levitov even mistakes the *melioramentum*, a Cathar prayer expressing hope for a death worthy of a *Perfect*, with a plea for 'someone, even close kin...to hasten the death of one dying in agony'.[17] As for Dr Levitov's most astonishing claim, that the devout Cathars represented the inheritors of a pagan cult of Isis, no other historical evidence can be found to back up this pronouncement, and in all probability it must be consigned to the realms of fantasy.

But why should the good Dr Levitov, a seemingly rational and well-educated man, be so seduced by such an unlikely and fantastical hypothesis? Undoubtedly there is the lure of the Voynich manuscript itself, which has seduced and deluded many others before. But there is also the one lasting legacy of the Cathars themselves; an aura of malleable mystery that has been reshaped by many over the last two hundred years. The Cathars have been interpreted variously as proto-feminists or medieval European Buddhists, and their legacy has been claimed at various times by the French Resistance of the Second World War II, hippies, New Age mystics and even, most worryingly, by the Fascists of the 1930s. In the final chapter of his recent book, *The Perfect Heresy*, historian Stephen O'Shea charts this reinvention and reconfiguring of what is fast becoming a Cathar mythology. Just as southwest England has King Arthur, inextricably linked to Tintagel and Glastonbury, so southern France has a burgeoning cult of the Cathar, centred around the evocative ruins of Montsegur.

Tellingly, one of the few books from which Dr Levitov quotes directly is *The Holy Blood and the Holy Grail*, by Michael Baigent, Richard Leigh and Henry Lincoln. This multimillion-selling publishing phenomenon of a book presents an *über*-conspiracy theory in which an all-too-mortal Jesus survives the crucifixion and flees Palestine with his wife, Mary Magdalene, to settle in southern France. There they founded, according to the book, a dynasty of Merovingian kings, whilst this secret – the Holy Grail – became known to both the Knights Templar and the Cathars, who were naturally persecuted by the Catholic authorities wishing to maintain the religious status quo. Add to this heady mixture a dash of secret societies and a whiff of buried treasure and one is presented with a delightfully far-fetched though certainly tantalising tale. Might it be possible that Dr Levitov was seduced more by this kind of fanciful myth-making that currently shrouds the Cathar story, rather than the harrowing and sobering historical truth of the 'Great Heresy'? Dr Levitov was dealing with two highly potent historical mysteries: the inscrutable Voynich manuscript and the mystically romantic Cathars. Perhaps, then, he can be forgiven for letting his imagination get the better of his rational investigations.

Before we attempt to draw together these various cryptographic threads, there is one other baffling linguistic feature of the Voynich manuscript that needs to be considered. Throughout the many years of study devoted to the manuscript, most scholars have assumed it to be the work of a single person, a conclusion based on the apparent homogeneity of style present in the Voynichese script. In the mid-1970s, however, this seemingly indisputable principle of Voynich lore was to be seriously questioned thanks to the work of Captain Prescott Currier.

After careful study and statistical analysis of the manuscript, Currier, another military cryptographer, eventually concluded that there were two distinct forms of handwriting present in the herbal section, which have subsequently been dubbed **Currier A** and **B**. Currier concluded that the first twenty-five folios appeared to have been written in hand **A**, with the following forty or so being a mixture of both **A** and **B**. Hand **A** appears to be better formed, more flowing and vertical than the rather lax and slanting script of hand **B**. Even more puzzlingly, the two hands are not only different in appearance, but also vary in their use of Voynichese characters when forming words; for example, ligatured letters appear far more frequently in hand **A** than in hand **B**. Brigadier Tiltman, in a lecture given in 1975, gave another startling example of Currier's analysis (quoted here from D'Imperio): 'In his account of suffixes following a number of common roots, the suffix 89 occurs eight times in twenty-five **A** pages, and five hundred and fifty-four times in twenty-five **B** pages...'[18] Researching further, Currier concluded that, amongst other features, the balneological section was written all in one hand and 'language', and that one section of the pharmaceutical and one clear folio in the recipe section are in other, different hands. According to his final reckoning, Currier went on to identify the presence of up to *twelve* different hands in the manuscript as a whole.

The appearance of differing 'hands' is still debated. Currier's supposed findings do not even, as they may at first appear to do, imply that a whole group of scribes worked on the manuscript. An individual's handwriting may be variable, according to changes in writing conditions (age, health), and the materials used (pens and inks). Even the apparently different vocabularies need not imply alternative languages or dialects, merely a change in the subject matter about which a lone scribe was writing. Currier's findings, if correct, do seem to back up the hypothesis that the Voynich manuscript was probably copied, as has already been suggested by the lack of corrections and the arrangement of the script around presumably pre-drawn illustrations. Are we then faced with a medieval monastic or scholastic community contributing their calligraphic talents in a strange handwriting exercise, using a fabricated alphabet to accompany a set of pre-arranged illustrations? Even if this is the case, we remain none the wiser as to why they should have undertaken such a unique and perplexing task.

So what conclusions can be drawn from these various claims of decipherment for the Voynich manuscript, and more importantly, are any of them likely to be correct? Although many studies have thrown up interesting results worthy of further analysis, none has been accepted as conclusively determining the actual cipher system used in the manuscript, or uncovering the true plain text hidden within its pages. Perhaps the best we can hope to achieve is to say with some certainty what encryption system was *not* used in the Voynich manuscript, and by eliminating the impossibilities, suggest new avenues of study for future cryptanalysts.

Let us begin by examining the possibility that the Voynich manuscript is a monoalphabetic substitution cipher, such as a Caesar shift, as was suggested by the lawyer James Feely. By discussing the arguments for and against the use of such an encryption system, we shall be better able to pronounce upon the validity of the claimed decipherment. In favour of a monoalphabetic cipher is the tentative dating of the manuscript by some experts to the era of Roger Bacon, or the centuries immediately following. If the Voynich manuscript is the product of the late Middle Ages, then a simple substitution cipher would be the only likely encryption method available to

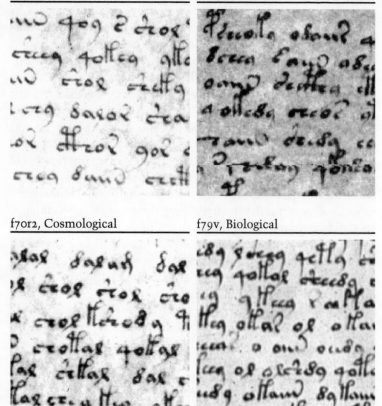

f2r, Herbal

f26r, Herbal

f70r2, Cosmological

f79v, Biological

our mysterious author. Furthermore, the Voynich manuscript is a long document, over two hundred pages, and to encipher such a quantity of text would realistically require an encryption process that could be carried out quickly and easily. Here again, our monoalphabetic cipher fits the bill. However, as we have already demonstrated, this form of cipher should be equally quick and easy to break using frequency analysis, especially given the huge amount of cipher text to work with. Over the last ninety years, most attempts at deciphering the manuscript via this route have failed miserably, and even in those cases where success has been claimed, such as with James Feely, the nonsensical quality of the plain text produced seems to argue against a correct decryption.

f86v5, Text-only/Cosmological   f188v, Pharmaceutical

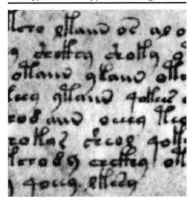   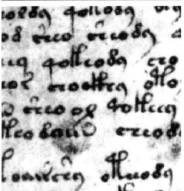

f116r, Recipes

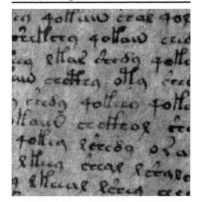

Different hands as identified by
Prescott Currier
(courtesy René Zandbergen)

But perhaps there are some mitigating circumstances for Feely's failure in what should have been a relatively straight-forward cryptanalytical task. We must remember he had access only to a small sample of cipher text with which to attempt his decryption; perhaps he got the relationship between the Voynich and plain-alphabet characters wrong. In other words, maybe the Latin alphabet letters he deduced to be the equivalents of Voynichese symbols were incorrect, thereby producing an incorrect decipherment. The fault might not lie in the cipher, but in the key. In fact, the Voynich manuscript presents any would-be solver with a number of unique problems that make the implementation of frequency analysis particularly difficult. For a start, there is the

recurrent difficulty of determining exactly how many characters there are in the Voynichese alphabet, a question that has
troubled many Voynich scholars over the years, and to which
no definitive answer has ever been produced. Even more prob-
lematic is the uncertainty of what language the original plain
text of the manuscript was written in, because it is precisely
this piece of information that makes frequency analysis possible. For example, given that the most frequently used letter in
English is **e**, as it is in French and German, the most frequently occurring symbol in a cipher text produced by a monoalphabetic cipher from one of these languages will most likely
be the equivalent for **e**. However, the most common letter in
Russian is **o**, so if our cipher text was from a Russian original,
the most common cipher symbol would represent **o**. In Serbo-
Croatian the most frequent letter would be **a**, and so on. It is
therefore vitally important for the cryptanalyst to know in
which language the plain text was written, because without
this knowledge, the use of frequency analysis to break the
cipher becomes extremely difficult. Most scholars of the
Voynich manuscript have assumed that because it looks like a
product of the late-medieval or early-modern era, the underlying plain-text language is most likely to be Latin. Yet frequency analyses of the Voynichese text based on this assumption
have all failed, as have those using Greek, English, German,
Italian and most other major European tongues as the plain-
text language. Perhaps a way forward for future research is to
carry out frequency analysis of less widely spoken languages,
in the hope of producing a match with Voynichese.

Any cryptanalyst basing a theory on the use of a monoalphabetic cipher in the manuscript would also need to
account for a number of odd phenomena that appear in the
Voynichese text. The average length of words in Voynichese
is around four or five characters, roughly the same as in
modern English. However, unlike English and most other
languages, there are almost no one- or two-letter words in the
Voynichese lexicon, or words over ten characters in length.
Also, there are no doubled letters, such as **oo**, **tt**, **ll**, **ee mm**,
etc., which are common in many languages. As a simple substitution cipher does not disrupt such letter patterns during
the encryption process, and if such a cipher were used in the
Voynich manuscript, the language of the plain text must have

been very strange indeed. This is further demonstrated by some unusual patterns of words that can be found in the manuscript. On most pages of the manuscript strings of the same word are repeated up to five times, or on other occasions, even longer strings of words with only the odd change to individual letters. This would be like writing the word **that** five times in succession in a phrase in modern English, or producing a sentence along the lines of **Brought bought bough, though tough, through trough**. It is almost impossible to conceive of a language where this would happen regularly, if at all. As Mary D'Imperio says, reporting the words of several Voynich researchers, 'the text just doesn't act like natural language'.

Perhaps then we could be dealing with a simple cipher with the addition of homophones or nulls, meaningless dummy characters inserted into the cipher text, which might disguise the natural patterns of the original language? In the example quoted earlier in the previous chapter, twenty-six numbers were used to represent the letters of the alphabet, with a further seventy-three numbers used as nulls that could be scattered throughout a cipher message to confuse a cryptanalyst. But this system requires a total of ninety-nine numbers to make up the cipher alphabet. When we compare this to the Voynichese alphabet, which D'Imperio estimates to contain between fifteen and twenty-five characters, we realise there are not nearly enough symbols to suggest a cipher system utilising nulls.

But what of the polyalphabetic ciphers, those Rolls-Royces of cryptology developed during the Renaissance, and which have been linked to the Voynich manuscript, though never in a fully coherent way, by Leonell Strong? Such ciphers, though going some way to explaining the manuscript's resistance to cryptanalytical attack, have been largely discounted by Voynich researchers; and Elizebeth Friedman went so far as to categorically rule out their use in the creation of the Voynichese script. To explain why polyalphabetic ciphers have been so flatly dismissed, it is necessary to understand the concept of 'entropy'. Originally a term used in physics, entropy has been borrowed by cryptologists: 'In both fields, entropy measures disorder, randomness, lack of structure.'[19] All languages have low entropy because they possess a clear and discernible structure imparted by the grammatical and syntactical rules that are the backbone of communication. But as we have seen with the example of frequency analysis given earlier in the chapter, it is just such linguistic structures that create the weak spots exploited by cryptanalysts to break ciphers. The problem with simple substitution ciphers is that these recognisable patterns of letter frequencies and combinations, present in the plain text, are transferred directly into the cipher text, where they can be identified by careful cryptanalysis. Polyalphabetic ciphers were specifically developed to overcome this weakness, by removing any such recognisable patterns; as demonstrated by Vigenère's cipher and the seemingly random string of letters it produces. Therefore polyalphabetic ciphers are designed to *increase* the level of entropy: in effect, to create disorder. But the Voynich manuscript has very low entropy. There is a vast amount of superficial structure on its pages, though the deeper meaning and significance of these patterns is not clear; and because a polyalphabetic cipher would have produced an altogether more jumbled and chaotic cipher text than is apparent in the pages of the manuscript, such a cipher system can be discounted.

A complex, multistage encryption process, such as the one described by Professor Newbold, seems highly unlikely due to the time-consuming effort involved in enciphering a document of the length of the Voynich manuscript. But what if there were a relatively short cipher message, encrypted using a system that is both easy to learn and quick to execute, but which is subsequently hidden within a longer sequence of meaningless gibberish? This is one of the possibilities presented by Robert Brumbaugh. Any of the cipher systems described above could have been used to encrypt the original plain-text message, but the resultant cipher text is then concealed, either by the use of a grille, or by a predetermined letter or word-counting system, within a vast sea of dummy text. If this were the true scenario, then with the grille lost for centuries, or the recognition pattern long forgotten, the chances of ever discovering the relevant text would be almost nil. And if the whole of the Voynich manuscript was created just to hide a relatively short cipher message, this raises the tantalising prospect that the original plain-text communication must have been of great import to merit such a huge steganographic effort.

11. Folio 16r

12. Folio 52r

13. Folio 106r, 'recipe' section

14. Jan Van Eyck, 'Eve',
Ghent altar wing

15. Lucas Cranach,
'The Fountain of Youth'

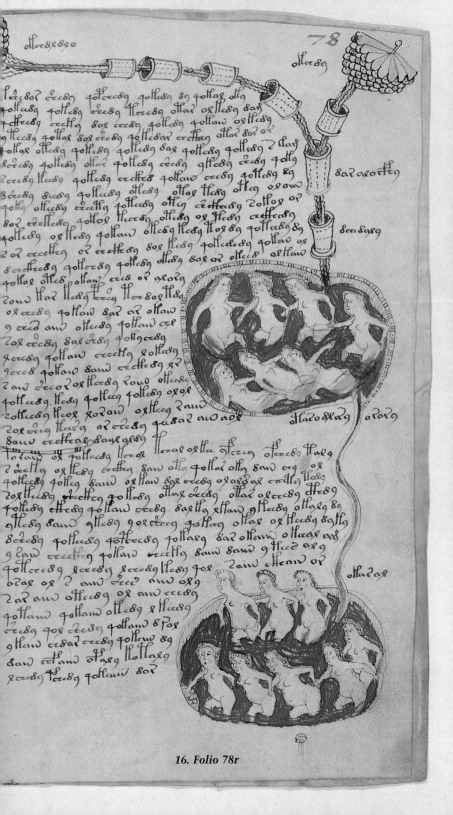

16. Folio 78r

17. Folio 79v

18. Folio 86v3

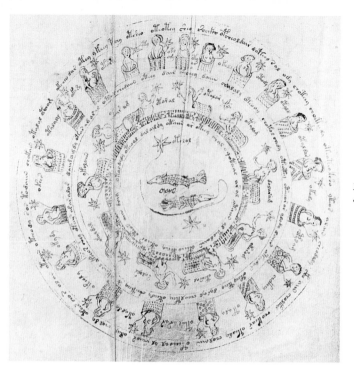

*19. Folio 70v2,
'Pisces'*

*20. Folio 73v,
'Sagittarian
archer'*

And finally, what can we make of the Friedman/Tiltman hypothesis, that the Voynich manuscript is written in a forgotten synthetic language? This theory must surely merit serious consideration, not least because of the impressive credentials of those who proposed it. An artificial writing system would certainly explain many of the structural phenomena observed in the Voynich text; though there does remain one persuasive argument against the theory. All the examples of artificial languages that have been quoted so far date from the middle of the seventeenth century; much later even than the latest possible date of creation for the Voynich manuscript. We know the manuscript existed by 1608, thanks to the faded signature of Jacobus de Tepenecz, and could well have been written some considerable time before this. The Voynich manuscript therefore falls outside the historical period when the development of such synthetic languages was *en vogue* ... though this does not rule out the intriguing possibility that the manuscript is actually the earliest surviving example of such an ambitious linguistic endeavour. However, with this exciting thought comes a sad corollary: if this really is the case, then there is little prospect that the code will ever be broken. Without an explanation of the fundamental principles of the language; either a description of the particular priori-type classification system, or a more prosaic codebook in which the plain-text equivalent of every code word is listed rather like a French/English dictionary, an understanding of the encoding system remains far off. Indeed, if the Friedman and Tiltman hypothesis is correct, and if no other example of Voynichese text ever comes to light, the chances of decoding the manuscript shift from the highly unlikely to the almost impossible.

If, as seems most likely, the text has yet to yield up its secrets, what other avenues of investigation remain? Perhaps it is in the enigmatic illustrations that the answer to the Voynich riddle lies?

→ 6 ←

A GARDEN OF UNEARTHLY
DELIGHTS

Gerry Kennedy once again takes up the story of his visit to
Yale.

The realisation of a fantasy is proverbially fraught; the
long-sought-after has a habit of failing to live up to the dream,
and, to make things worse, is subject to the fickle vagaries of a
first impression. In July 2001, having travelled up from the Big
Apple to Yale University to inspect the fabled Voynich manuscript, I was hoping to gain a clear and calm overview of its
delights that up until then had been supplied remotely by a
computer screen.

Initially, the sheer privilege of being granted an audience
with the volume was excitement enough; I had never before
sat reverentially in front of any book, let alone a medieval
tome. But somewhere at the back of my mind I possessed
images of such rarities, of exotic embellishments to first-line
letters or the stylised perspectives of scenes and figures that
unfolded as part of a recognisable story. Regardless of one's
acquaintance with ancient volumes, Mary D'Imperio was
right to state that the Voynich manuscript stands 'totally
apart' from other 'remotely comparable documents'.

Each page (or folio, as I learned to term them, recto facing,
verso on the other side) that librarian Ellen Cordes turned, as
we progressed through the various sections, revealed fresh
wonders for which I had no reference points of any kind. The
collection of plants seemed gaspingly surreal, the naked
nymphs, whether splashing in ponds or disported on star-
wheels, sensually whimsical, the medicine jars voluptuously
oriental. I struggled to find something of the everyday in it,
but felt, like others, that some coherent meaning would
emerge if only I looked long and hard enough.

The session lasted about forty-five minutes. This inadequacy was compounded by the aloofness of my bibliographic minder. I attempted to ask a few unprobing questions about how often the volume was shown and to whom, only to be met with complete silence. The 'look don't touch' treatment may have been understandable, but the 'seen and not heard' addendum was an unnecessary stricture, turning me from a would-be suitor into a Voynich voyeur. Not only did the book itself seem unreal but the whole context in which I viewed it. Most people, for example, on a visit to savour New York, city of gleaming skyscrapers, would be well advised to take in a bird's-eye panorama from the top of the Empire State – rather than merely ride its cavernous avenues in a taxi. It was like sightseeing New York on a video played within the taxi.

I exited the revolving doors of the Beinecke Library, carrying a $40 unsatisfactory photocopy of the whole Voynich, feeling as dizzy as if I had spent the last three-quarters of an hour trapped in its portal's clutches. I wasn't sure what I had seen except for some document of star-status, clearly so rare and precious that it required the attendant services of a strict bodyguard. Fortunately I had arranged an interview that followed shortly after with another starstruck admirer, whose open enthusiasm reminded me that I was not alone in my infatuation. Phillip Marshall, a postgraduate student in biology at Yale, had seen the manuscript, and as a biologist had naturally concentrated his scientific attention on the large section devoted to plants. We discussed some of the possible identifications he had made. Outside the Beinecke glass box I found it soothing to think that it might be possible to temper a possibly irrational personal attraction with some kind of rational analysis.

Marshall has spent a good deal of time trying to make sense of the illustrations, but like others has met with scant success. If it is extraordinary that the manuscript has resisted decipherment by the most pre-eminent cryptographers of the twentieth century, it is even more so that the copious drawings have not really provided a solid basis to our understanding of it. Codes and ciphers perhaps belong to a specialist realm of study; one would expect concrete images to be more amenable to interpretation. It may turn out that the Voynich script hides a large quantity of written gibberish, but the illustrations do not seem to represent the visual equivalent of mere scrawl or doodling. The strange fact, agreed by many commentators, is that there does appear to be some overall sense of intention behind them, a tentative thematic link.

The illustrations described in chapter 1 divide fairly readily into sections, suggesting a systematic purpose rather than a random rambling. Voynich analysts differ over the precise boundaries of these sections but in general concur that these fall into the herbal, astronomical, astrological/cosmological, balneological (or bathing), and a pharmacopoeia section, including a list of 'recipes'. We shall view the illustrations utilising these useful headings but perhaps more importantly try to put them in an overarching thematic context.

At a general level the Voynich manuscript's illustrations evince creative and positive life-generating natural forces, whether relating to the heavens or earth. There are no antagonistic images – no blood, dragons, lightning, monsters or mythical beasts that haunted the medieval imagination. There is none of the conflict or destructive tendencies that might be generated pictorially where human interaction and social institutions are concerned. For a medieval document it is surprising that there are almost no references to organised religion or the trappings of secular power, or more mundanely to everyday objects – tools, furniture, means of transport, and so on – that might point historically to a way of life. This creates a sense of otherworldliness and timelessness enhanced by zodiacal drawings of suns, stars, moons and 'cosmic' phenomena. Yet this in turn is brought down to earth by the apparent purity, youth and innocence of the naked bathing women undergoing perhaps some esoteric aquatic medical treatment associated with the benefit of the many depicted plants. Are we looking perhaps at some kind of magical herbal treatise that holds contentious secrets for the eyes of only a few?

Amongst all the wide-ranging estimates of what the Voynich manuscript represents, commentators tend to a consensus on one aspect of its content at least – that the illustrations show a high proportion of what seem to be herbal plants. If the volume's origin can be placed somewhere between the thirteenth and seventeenth centuries, the chief purpose of such a collection would most likely be for its medical use. Plants were, of course, described and illustrated for other reasons. Horticulture was well developed and its knowledge put to good use in the gardens of abbeys, infirmaries and the estates of the rich, as well as working farms. Pietro Crescenzi, for example, compiled his *Ruralia Comoda* circa 1306, considered the best medieval treatise on all aspects of farming including the cultivation of edible plants. The Voynich manuscript vegetation looks to be small in stature, mostly without fruits, suggesting either decorative or medicinal use. Many of the species portrayed have exotic flowers that might point towards ornamental purposes, but the definite inclusion of often very elaborate root structures indicates not just identification but some practical application.

Herbal medicine has a long history but on its own is unlikely to have coped adequately with the ravages of medieval ill health. As Carole Rawcliffe puts it, 'Epidemics and famines apart, medieval life was beset by constant threats to health arising from poor diet, low levels of hygiene, high rates of mortality, risks of childbirth and rejected pregnancies, accidents and injuries.'[1] Life could be, as Thomas Hobbes declared, 'solitary, nasty, brutish and short'; for even the rich.

Despite being without the modern awareness of bacterial infection, and possessing a woefully inadequate knowledge of the body (the function of the heart in blood-circulation, for example), medieval medical theorising achieved a remarkable degree of sophistication. Health was a matter of balance and harmony. The four elements of air, water, earth and fire reflected the macrocosm of the world with their inherent qualities of cold, moist, dry and hot respectively, influencing the microcosm of the body through four corresponding humours, seen as bodily fluids: blood, phlegm, black bile and yellow bile. Each humour partook of the four temperature and moisture properties; blood being hot and wet, for example. Predominance of one humour over another could be seen to affect even personality type – thus too much yellow bile (hot and dry) produced the fiery choleric person prone to anger; in turn open to influence by other corresponding aspects of the macrocosm – youth, summer, the west wind, Mars and the constellations Aries, Leo and Sagittarius. Despite its complete redundancy, aspects of the system have lingered on in our imagery; we speak of being sanguine or phlegmatic.

All these diagnosable factors were evident primarily in the body's symptoms and appearance, further discerned by scrutinising faeces, blood and urine. All of these were seen against the larger congruent forces of the wider world and the stars, creating a complex continuum of causality between the earthly and the universal. The celestial bodies had an over-arching effect on all happenings and conditions below, but not, as we have mentioned before, to the exclusion of the important Christian notion of free will. Thus leprosy was somehow associated with lust and pride, and at a collective level, as with Sodom and Gomorrah, the Black Death was regarded by many as a Divine Retribution for human way-wardness, or by others as the result of a malign conjunction between Jupiter and Saturn.

The physician would attend his patient with a panoply of diagnoses and hints from the mundane to the celestial. Any substance used to repair the body would play its part in bring-ing harmony through the virtues of its own nature. At one end of the scale he might employ the rare and exotic, such as gold or gemstones immersed in liquid, in the hope that their dura-bility and longevity might 'wear off' on his client, whilst at the other, for those who could not afford such luxury, the more evident qualities of herbs were used for their emetic, sedative or analgesic properties.

For the humble cottager unable to afford a physician, herbal lore sufficed. This form of medicine was a combination of practical observation and superstition handed down locally and orally and applied often by a village wise-woman. Herbal wisdom, however, had its own inconsistencies. Goodness and evil in plants could exist side by side; the elder, for example, gave benefit as an eye lotion yet was imbued with pagan malevolence supplemented by being the tree on which Christ was supposed to have been nailed.

Whether medicine was practised by the learned physician or the local herbalist-cum-savant, the importance of herbs was fundamental. The need for their recognition would be of greater importance to the professional using plants possibly brought in from much further afield than to the village practi-tioner. Hence herbal reference works as illustrated manu-scripts were highly valued possessions and circulated widely. Yet strangely enough, until the advent of the printed herbal in the fifteenth century there were only three major works that served as the basis for other renditions, two of which dated back to Roman times. The most important of these was the *Materia Medica* by the Greek physician Dioscorides, compiled about AD 60, but remarkably still of influence until the nineteenth century. The most famous copy of his work, the *Codex Vindobonensis*, made in the sixth century, resides in Vienna and consists of 400 full-page coloured drawings of herbs, people, animals and birds accompanied by lists of plant virtues and applications. The illustrations vary in quality, and Blunt and Raphael maintain they have been produced by more than one hand.[2] One of the best is that of the bramble, whose changing appearance can be traced through many copies. The texts were translated into Arabic, Persian and Hebrew. The other basic herbal, the *Herbarium*, is a derivative of Dioscorides with a Latin text by Apuleius Platonicus, compiled around AD 400 and copied widely until the fifteenth century with varying degrees of success, including an Anglo-Saxon version circa 1200.

Not until the early fourteenth century, based on the botanical school at Salerno in Italy, did a new basic work emerge to serve as a model for other productions. The *Tractatus de Herbis* uses texts from the other two herbals but the illustrations are more naturalistic as a result of using live local models rather than ghostly relics from a millennium before. Centuries of copying herbal drawings necessarily meant that, like Chinese whispers, exaggeration and distortion could render likenesses inadequately, depending on the skill of the copyist. Nevertheless they were clearly put to use by those who could afford them and had need for them: physicians, pharmacists, teachers and clergy, for their scientific use, or the well-to-do bibliophile for their aesthetic value. In the fifteenth century, with the advent of printing and the use of wood blocks, herbals became cheaper and more accessible, still based on Dioscorides, but including new botanical discoveries from America and the Far East

Minta Collins in her authoritative study *Medieval Herbals* suggests that herbal artists were faced with four challenges: how to depict all the parts of the plant proportionately, how to indicate its growth habit – climbing, trailing, etc., how to relate the illustration to the surrounding text and how to make the image represent the stages of growth.[3] With these criteria in mind she further suggests that three degrees of success result. 'Schemata' tend to have reduced parts to better represent the whole and lack three-dimensionality. A 'recognisable image' possesses a faithful rendering of a plant's structure and colour and indication of its growth habit, and may look rather like a 'pressed' plant demonstrating no great artistic expertise. A 'naturalistic' specimen, however, possesses three-dimensional qualities helped by shading and crossing or overlapping parts with realistic effects of fallen petals, broken stems, etc. Where does the Voynich manuscript as a herbal fit into all of this?

The essential problem is, of course that, unable to read the text, we do not know what any of the plants are supposed to be, other than, as we have suggested, assuming them to be herbs or 'plants with a purpose'. Traditional herbals at least possessed the starting point of a label. The artist's title gives sufficient information for identification even where the illustration is of rather a stylised nature. The example from Bodleian 130, 'hart's tongue', an Apuleius Platonicus derivative, looks fairly strange, but the nomenclature helps us easily to recognise the characteristic leaf. Without a label we are left looking for resemblances from a huge range of plants. Following Minta Collins' criteria, the Voynich manuscript illustrations would not perhaps be classed as 'schematic'; they seem to have a sense of proportion and are neither completely flat nor a mere outline. Further, they are unlikely to be considered 'naturalistic'. The middle category of 'recognisable image' seems to fit in terms of a degree of three-dimensionality and distinguishable structure. This would seem to indicate that the Voynich manuscript herbal illustrations are credible, despite their amateurish execution, suggesting a dating from post-Salerno fourteenth century.

Of the 126 full-page specimens viewed here by the authors (avowedly inexpert taxonomists), approximately one third could be classed as 'strange', having at least one feature of root, stem or flower that does not look authentic – folio 1v (plate 4), for example, in which the roots look like clawed feet. A further third have more than one feature tipping the exhibit towards what might be considered biologically unlikely, fantastic or even preposterous (plates 5, 6 and 7). The remaining third seem to exist in the realm of the possible – there have even been claims by some that particular specimens might actually merit the botanical accolade of 'recognisable image'.

Hart's tongue, Bodleian 130, folio 11v

The most interesting of these claims was made back in 1944. Hugh O'Neill, a Benedictine monk at the Catholic University of America, made in his words some 'none too certain' identifications of a number of plants, the most important probably being the 'sunflower' (f93r, plate 8). As the plant was not introduced into Europe until post-Columbus this would be a significant help in dating the Voynich manuscript. There is indeed a strong immediate sense of recognition, the thick straight stem and the large-seeded flower-centre. These, however, are features of the modern, cultivated sunflower, a factor to be remembered with any comparison between the two periods. The medieval 'wild' version would possess a smaller head, non-conical calyx, larger petals and a more divided stem. The leaves too are more characteristic of a European relative – the Jerusalem artichoke.

Another Voynich illustration that has tentatively been identified as a sunflower is f33v (plate 9) but here again there are problems. Jorge Stolfi has pointed out that the leaves, although attached to the stem appropriately, are very uncharacteristic, and the petals are the wrong shape and colour, not to mention the complete weirdness of the tubers resembling some kind of flotilla of naval mines. The sunflower of any epoch has 'ordinary' roots and although the Jerusalem artichoke does have tubers they are in no way similar.

'Viola', folio 9v

There have been other identifications hazarded, most notably by Dana Scott. He suggests twenty-one possibilities, but only five with some confidence. These include f9v, a form of viola, pansy or heartsease, which has been noted by others too, including Phillip Marshall. The heartsease's romantic association was used by Shakespeare in *A Midsummer Night's Dream*, when Oberon squeezes its juice into Titania's eyes, resulting in her love for Bottom when she awakes. More mundanely it seems to have been used as an emetic, purgative and to treat heart disease, epilepsy, asthma and bronchitis.

It is tantalising that so little can be positively identified from the manuscript. It is as if the drawings themselves were encrypted. There are simply none of the collateral clues to be found in a traditional herbal. In contrast, Egerton ms 747, f12 (plate 3) shows not only three easily recognisable plants – wood sorrel, a strawberry-tree and the culinary sorrel – but a woman collecting resin from a balsam tree from which balm of Gilead was obtained. The walled garden and her attire provide useful information regardless of the quality of the tree's depiction. Mythological figures, doctors, birds, animals are often found in herbals but very infrequently in the Voynich manuscript. The only exceptions connected with the full-page plants are a sweet little dragon on f25v and two snakes intertwined in the roots of f49r (plate 10). The latter drawing hints at cyclamen with its convoluted stalks and flowers, which was associated, along with herbs such as vervain and wormwood, with protection against snake bites. Neither the leaves nor the

'Dragon', folio 25v

corms (could they be potatoes?), however, quite fit. This possible identification is given more in a spirit of demonstrating a typical piece of Voynich detective work rather than with any certainty – there always seems to be one part of the jigsaw missing. Other tentative identifications have been made of a fern, f56r, and a myrtle, f4v. Two London-based herbalists, Sara Hamer and Richard Adams, who appeared in the television documentary, 'The Voynich Mystery', suggested that the weirdness of most of the plants may have been a deliberate exaggeration to serve as an aide memoire. They joined the consensus in identifying the viola of f9v and promoted a water lily for f2v plus a thyme-like leaf for f4r.[4]

Perhaps one of the strangest features of the drawings is shown by the twenty in which stems seem to have been grafted on to a peculiar root stock such as f16r (plate 11), and which is echoed in the hart's-tongue fern. Karen Reeds, an expert on medieval botany, who has described many of the plants in the Voynich manuscript as 'phantasmagorical', has also suggested that they remind one of those children's 'flip' books in which several sections such as the head, torso and legs of a person can be combined humorously, or in the case of the manuscript, the roots, stem and flowers, awkwardly. The 'grafting' adds considerably to the effect.

As early as Theophrastus of Eresos (387–287 BC), the different

159

methods of grafting were comprehensively discussed, most of which would still be relevant to a modern manual. Bacon expounds his own views on the subject, but typically focusing philosophically on the question of which plant soul would dominate in the coupling. Giovanni Battista Porta (1535–1615), a Neapolitan, Dee-like magus (whom we encountered in chapter 4 in relation to cryptography), was also interested in astrology, alchemy and optics. In his third book of *Natural Magick* he expounds a typical mixture of magic and scientific observation. He follows conventional wisdom in asserting the importance of humours and the 'circuit and motion of celestial bodies', but proposes wild assertions; for example, that asparagus grows from the horns of rams. He nevertheless expounds many sound practices of grafting, 'in plants the same that copulation is in living creatures'. This in general applies, correctly, only to woody shrubs and trees, but he does suggest that cucumber seeds can be directly implanted into bramble or fennel stalks. Perhaps the Voynich grafts are experiments of this kind? Experts consulted at the Royal Botanic Gardens at Kew in London felt that they were most unlikely to succeed.

A species of herbal that falls outside the conventional, but may be relevant to the Voynich manuscript, has been classed as 'alchemical'. According to Professor Sergei Toresella, an expert on Italian herbals, about seventy versions of these circulated in Northern Italy, possibly used by travelling practitioners, from the fourteenth to sixteenth centuries. Although they incorporate some influences from traditional works such as Apuleius, they feature rather surreal illustrations from a constant corpus of plants that, despite their fanciful names, such as herbia barbaria and herba capilaria, are recognisable. The surreal quality of the images is not unlike the Voynich manuscript but makes much more use of animal figures and plants with eyes, for example. In the alchemical herbals a root can look like a wolf or a fish and the mandrake becomes clearly anthropomorphised. Accompanying texts in Latin describe, sometimes fantastically, how the plants can aid the finding of treasure or the useful knack of becoming invisible. One of the three herbals of this school, ms 337, housed in the Wellcome Trust's London library, includes recipes relating to conception and pregnancy (subjects to which we shall return later in this chapter). Another, ms 334, bought from Wilfrid

Voynich himself in 1912, contains an image of a female man-drake with a dog attached to its feet performing the function of excavator, whilst a human kneeling nearby puts his hands to his ears to blot out the screams of the poor plant as it is wrenched from the ground. Interestingly, this is the kind of unharmonious image that does not accompany the mandrake-like roots that appear in the Voynich manuscript.

Toresella questions to what degree this group of herbals deserves the adjective 'alchemical'; few of the plants have sig-nificant alchemical connections, although a regular example, lunaria (honesty or money-plant), has some significance as an apparent aid in transmuting base metal into gold. D'Imperio suggests that an illustration of the plant can be found in Ashmole's *Theatrum Chemicum Britanicum* which has a Voynich-like look to it. We remain unconvinced; but is she right, however, to assert, contrary to Toresella, that the Voynich manuscript 'could well be, at least in part, an alchemical treatise'?[5]

Bacon, like many another, drew the distinction between practical and theoretical alchemy; the former being a search for the secrets of gold-transmutation and an elixir of life, the latter for the 'nature of things'. The more well-known mer-cenary aspect, however, belies the unity of alchemy and its appeal to the questing of Bacon, Dee and others to attain knowledge of and communion with matter from the lowest (microcosm) to the highest (macrocosm) of the celestial and divine world, echoed in its famous dictum, 'as above so below'. This was to be achieved by the adept via the intuited

Lunaria, Ashmole 1652

understanding of complex but practical processes that would not only purify the individual but benefit mankind as a whole. The hermetic tradition of alchemy recognised the four elements, astrology, the importance of numbers and the Galenic humours, but attempted to link its notion of the three basic substances, sulphur, salt and mercury, to correspondences with spirit, body and soul, and to the Christian trinity of Father, Son and Holy Ghost. Its use of abstruse symbolism made alchemical knowledge rather elite, but some of its practical processes were more accessible, for example, in the use of herbs as medical treatments. Tinctures and essences were made in ritual ways with special emphasis placed on the purity of the producer as well as the product. Astrology played a vital role, as the Swiss philosopher and alchemist Paracelsus (1493–1541) noted, 'The physician should know how to bring about a conjunction between the astral Mars and the grown Mars (the herbal preparation), as a remedy cannot act without the heavens it must be directed by them.' This interconnectedness is not merely instrumental but part of the wider physical and spiritual cosmos, to be interpreted holistically. Some commentators have suggested that the Voynich manuscript might contain alchemical/mystical references to be seen in this way. The root stock of f52r (plate 12), for example, has a certain resonance with John Dee's monad. The herbs, as we have already noticed, seem to divide clumsily into three – roots, stem and flowers. The Voynich Wellcome herbal, ms 334, regularly features small flower heads neatly divided into three, not unlike a fleur de lys. Might this be a reflection of triadic numerology? It might be worthwhile counting flowers, roots and leaves to find clues, as well as other repeated images such as stars. Do the few animal images or the strange shapes of the 'plumbing' in the bathing section (which we shall encounter shortly), have deeper meanings associated with the alchemical quest to preserve and prolong life? This is open to a limited scrutiny, however. One leading expert in the world of alchemy, Adam McLean, thinks that there are no such connections with alchemical symbolism or imagery in the manuscript.

One possibility worth exploring to explain the weirdness of the plants is that their geographical origin might, like the putative sunflower, extend further than Europe and hence explain their exotic appearance. As Carole Rawcliffe points out, the dissemination of Arabic additions to the classical Greek work of the physician Galen and Dioscorides widened the pharmacopoeia used to supply the rich and ill, who tended to put more faith in rare rather than common wayside herbs. An account for the Infirmarer at Westminster Abbey of 1351 lists, for example, the purchase of gum Arabic, tragacanth, sandalwood, rhubarb, musk, pepper and senna. Other more magical substances like seed pearls, ambergris, elephant's tusks, and so on, part of Bacon's physic, continued to be imported.

The search for an elixir of life was a medical El Dorado. One recipe included theriac, an expensive distillation taken with wine, made with over sixty herbs and substances including viper's flesh. It was a like-curing-like remedy used for bites from snakes, dogs and scorpions, but the drug was also generally promoted as a health-giving scourge of phlegmatic and melancholic humours – and was probably of no medical value whatsoever. The original formula dated back to Ancient Greece and required a period of years before it allegedly became efficacious. The manufacture of theriac was closely regulated against poor ingredients and counterfeiting until its use gradually died out by the eighteenth century, although the word lived on in corrupted English as 'treacle', becoming affixed to that equally non-health-giving syrup of today. The relevance of this slight digression (to which we shall return) consists in mooting the possibility that the strange ingredients of roots and herbs, unidentified in the Voynich manuscript, might be part of a secret or guarded process, since fallen into disrepute, for making a life-promoting elixir with constituents garnered from far-flung places, their origin and use masked by the strange accompanying language.

Despite our suggestion at the beginning of this chapter that the Voynich manuscript seems to echo harmony and life-generation, given the potency of herbs and their centrality to medieval conditions, it is also worth considering that their properties might equally be life-denying, perhaps another solid reason for the employment of secret writing to combat the prohibitions of the Catholic Church.

John Riddle, in his book *Contraception and Abortion from the Ancient World to the Renaissance*,[6] notes that neither practice was unequivocally condemned in ancient or medieval times by the laws of civil authorities or dogma of the main faiths. Up until as recently as 1869, Rome had asserted that until the foetus was forty days old it did not possess a soul and therefore could not be the victim of murder. The Church realistically recognised that the health and poverty of the mother could be a factor in turning a blind eye to abortion. Contraception was more complicated given the view that the only proper function of sex was procreation rather than pleasure. Nevertheless, Albertus Magnus (1193–1280), theologian, scientist, and contemporary of Bacon, although condemning birth control, lists herbs helpful in practising it. Macer Aemilius (1035–1123), Bishop of Rennes, gives information in his tenth-century herbal about penny-royal as a contraceptive. Dioscorides, and all the herbals derived from him, mentions in the prescriptive text herbs of similar use such as rue, juniper and wild-carrot seeds. In Chaucer's *The Parson's Tale* we read of a woman who 'drygnge venemouse herbes thurgh which she may not conceive'.

Indifferent to canon law or scholarly treatise, ordinary women facing the daily grind of poverty, ill health and too many mouths to feed produced their own birth-avoiding formulae under the guidance of wise-women and midwives. Some of these may have been mere magic – 'spit three times into an open frog's mouth' – but mostly derived from a practical empirical observation that Bacon would have endorsed. Where abortion is concerned, as Riddle points out, there can be no placebo effect in operation: either the substance works or not (although which preparation of several had an effect is more difficult to say). A 'rustic' pharmacy shelf would probably stock, in addition to those already mentioned, extracts from wormwood, birthwort, artemisia, cyclamen, asafoetida, valerian and others, some of which have been recently tested – rue, for example, being found very abortifacient.

Folkloric knowledge, passed on by generations in local communities, tended to be rather static, but the triumvirate of physician, apothecary and surgeon gradually became more professionalised through registration of practitioners, preferably holding a university degree. The competition between the two worlds, it has been suggested by Riddle in his book, *Eve's Herbs*, led ultimately to the suppression of the former in the witch crazes that obsessed the fifteenth to seventeenth centuries, replacing their knowledge with a less down-to-earth, professional quackery.[7] Wary of priestly opprobrium and jealous of a monopoly of hard-earned trade secrets, might the manuscript's author have encoded them? Could the Voynich manuscript possibly be a treatise directed towards abortion and contraception by yet another secretive physician or herbalist using, once again, exotic and hence expensive plants from distant shores including the New World? Or perhaps there are no useful secrets at all to hide in the first place, the herbal drawings being perhaps a poor approximation of his pharmacopoeia, 'recognisable images' only? Might he simply have carried it with him as an estate-to-estate sales-man out to impress clients with sham products? Such tricksters of the trade were not unknown.

Leonard Thurneisser was rather similar to Edward Kelley – his rascality did not prevent the patronage of the rich and powerful including the Holy Roman Emperor Ferdinand II and Queen Elizabeth of England. Born in Basel in 1530, even as a seventeen-year-old he was faking gold by gilding lead. Fleeing to Strasbourg to continue his metallurgical acumen, he sold amulets, potions and gemstones as medicines to the wealthy and gullible. Intending to write a ten-volume compendium on medicine, he completed one herbal volume consisting only of umbelliferous plants, impossible to recognise, and linked to specious astrological texts regarding harvesting and preparing, aided by obfuscating charts.

The apothecary was less liable to suffer suspicion of poor practice. He had the trappings of expensive premises and Latin-inscribed jars to convey authority. This perhaps moves us on to another part of the Voynich manuscript, the pages near its end that seem to indicate plants being used as part of a pharma-copoeia (f100r, plate 1), and which is followed by what has been assumed to be a connecting 'recipe' section – folios 103–16, twenty-three pages of close script only, with small marginal star 'bullets' indicating between ten and nineteen recipe para-graphs per folio (f106r, plate 13). The drawings consist of rows of what appear to be miniature plants and roots, often labelled in Voynichese. In general they are more like Collins' schemata and cartoon-like, suggesting once again an aide memoire, although few of the 230 or so specimens seem to couple with the full-page drawings of herbs. The combination of both sections, it should be noted, adds up to a grand total of something like 350 botanical species in the manuscript, hardly any of which can be positively identified – a feat of invention or catalogue of unrecognisable flora that is quite remarkable.

One illustration, however, has become the focus of much attention. On f1oor (plate 1) sits the pepper or capsicum identified by Brumbaugh that served as a starting point for his decryption, and if correctly identified, like the sunflower, it dates the manuscript post-Columbus. It is not a very compelling match, however; the shape of the fruits could just as easily be leaves and they are in fact coloured green not red, although they could just be unripe. There are other pimento-like shapes of fruit on leaves on folio 88r and several other pages.

At the end of each row are stationed what appear to be medicinal or apothecaries' jars, sometimes labelled. Earthenware storage vessels for herbs, seeds and berries date back to antiquity, having been found in Greece and Rome. As with many modern artefacts, it was an Arab influence that refined a common need, in this case with the introduction of a tin glaze to make fired clay impermeable. The term for such ware is majolica, possibly because it was introduced by way of Majorca. This was a practical but exotic development allowing for much better storage and decoration, made even more necessary as the pharmacist's stock consisted not just of dry products, but included syrups, distillations and ointments. The demand for glazed jars inspired and helped create whole industries of pottery-making in centres across Europe. It became particularly sophisticated in Italy during the fourteenth century. Latin labels could be fired into the design, and elaborate, delicate artwork with stylised foliage, accompanied by classical or religious themes, became part of a display designed to impress customers.

The shapes of the pots depended on what they were intended to contain and seem to conform to regular patterns. The simplest was the *albarello*, a tall, thin vessel waisted to make handling easier and holding herbs or spices sealed with parchment or wax. Small jars would contain ointments; infusions and oils would be held in urn- or globular-shaped idria, usually with two handles at the top. Syrups would be decocted from chevrettes, urn-shaped with one handle plus a spout for pouring.

The reader might be forgiven for thinking that this is more information on medicine jars than is necessary but the relevance consists in placing what appear to be jars of a similar purpose in the Voynich manuscript. Some of the jars, regularly cylindrical in shape and relatively unadorned, appear to be in three sections (alchemically relevant again?), a lid, vessel and a base. There is little indication of scale in relation to the plants – are they as small as pepper pots or tall as letter boxes? The majority, however, appear to be multilayered, Arabian Nights concoctions on the larger scale of samovars or stoves, but all are elaborately crafted and decorated. They do not appear to be remotely functional for any tradesperson; a shelf full of them on their precarious feet would crash to the floor as the chemist's door slammed in the wind.

Yet there might be a link back to the potter's art and the apothecary jar. The showpieces of an apothecary's emporium, the so-called *vases de monstres*, were highly decorated idria of much greater height than normal. Their status was due to what they held inside, the so-called 'sovereign remedies', of which theriac was one. Another would be *confectio alkermes*, as non-beneficial as its monarchical peer. Nicholas Culpeper, the seventeenth-century herbalist, lists a recipe including apples, rose-water, silk, cherms, sugar, ambergris, cinnamon, wood of aloes, pearls, leaf-gold and musk. The last three ingredients, owing to their cost, would probably have been deemed the most effective. The 'cherms' were tiny berries found on East Mediterranean oaks producing a rich red dye, but were later discovered to be a cochineal-type of insect after the invention of the microscope. Culpeper had no doubts about the concoction's worth. 'Questionless this is a great cordial having its value as strengthener of the heart', and, 'resister of pestilences and poisons'.[8]

Very often these princely jars had two handles for ease of manipulation, but not always, as their prime use was betokening imperial majesty. The drawing demonstrates the rich fluting and double narrowing of the shape which bears some resemblance to jars on f102v2. With characteristic verve and unfettered imagination, might not the author of the Voynich manuscript be taking a cue from such vessels? If this is the case it carries an interesting implication – the development of the potter's art to such giddy heights, as the accompanying

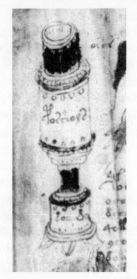

Theriac vase de monstre   *'Apothecary jar', folio 102v2*

SEC.XV   SEC.XVI   SEC.XVII   SEC.XVIII

Development of idria

drawing shows, was not known until the seventeenth and eighteenth centuries.

The apothecary jars (if that is what they are), given their unusual appearance, do at least seem to indicate a connecting sense of purpose with the array of equally unusual herbs that they may have contained. This nexus, however, becomes looser, but not completely sundered, when we consider the bath or balneological pages, folios 75r to 84v, nineteen in all.

The prominent spectacle of bevies of naked women seated or splashing about in green pools of liquid greatly enhances the surreal quality of the manuscript. It has an immense allure; without the nymphs, one suspects, the manuscript would not be quite as entrancing as it is; they seem so very

168

human in a volume often veering towards the other-worldly. How might these pages extend our medical theme?

Contrary to popular belief, bathing was not unknown in the Middle Ages. Whilst sewers may have run openly in crowded towns for want of civic plumbing, personal hygiene was not overlooked but celebrated according to one's wealth. The rich would have sloshed and steeped in large wooden tubs filled with hot water perfumed by herbs such as rosemary, sage and lavender. These would often have perches for sitting and a canopy over the top for privacy. Keeping water hot was costly and laborious, requiring firewood and servants to do the boiling and pouring. For the less well-off, urban public baths were available, and for the peasantry, washing in a basin or the laundry-water might suffice. Whilst the Church tended to decry bathing as a luxurious indolence, doctors and the civilised recognised the benefit of sweating to help balance the humours, and cleanliness to create a positive healthy environment.

Three of the manuscript pictures show the chorus lines of women in some form of large container, one like a large sardine-can, another seeming to be built of barrel-like staves, (f81r), and a third appearing to be brick- or stone-built with a colonnade of arches (f78v). Medieval public baths consisted of a number of tubs, rather than a Roman-style swimming pool, so unless the ladies are part of some potentate's harem, it is difficult to explain the size of the pools apart from the

Bath, folio 81r

possibility that they are wallowing in communal therapeutic baths.

This might perhaps account for the colour of the liquid in the baths; the green colouring is certainly not being employed for the artist's lack of pigment – blue is used too – and it may suggest a sulphurous content. Hydrotherapy as a treatment for skin disease, scabies, gout and rheumatism, for example, grew in popularity until the sixteenth century when syphilis was suspected to be waterborne. A number of books were written about mineral waters and their uses. One well circulated and copied was the thirteenth-century *Balneis Puteolanis* by Peter of Eboli, which describes the healing properties of thermal baths in Sicily. The set of brightly coloured miniatures depicts large receptacles, sometimes surrounded by pillars crowded with naked members of the same sex, often pointing to or holding a hand over their afflicted part. C. M. Kauffmann, author of a study of the baths, suggests that the packed pools were rather unusual, and that bathing scenes of this kind were not really found until the fifteenth century.[9] Some of the pictures are clearly outdoors, as is suggested in the Voynich, but the Eboli illustrations tell us rather more with a wealth of identifying features – vases, a veritable wardrobe of clothing and Christian iconography. As with the manuscript's herbal section, there are few collateral clues with which to build any useful theory as to what is represented. We are left with but one immutable fact: that they include almost entirely women.

Perhaps the bathing section supplements the suggestion of the herbal abortifacients already discussed. Are the women taking the herbally treated waters in order to abort unwanted offspring, reminiscent of the old gin-and-a-hot-bath? Do their pronounced stomachs suggest that they are pregnant? The crudeness of the drawings makes it difficult to tell but, in general, pregnancy was seen as a source of shame and not to be celebrated. It is possible to find examples of slimness in medieval art as well as the more matronly look; de Eboli's women, better depicted, have discernible stomachs. Perhaps the stockiness of the ladies in the manuscript suggests a podgy peasant diet or the comfortable bloat of well-fed women of substance, rather than incipient motherhood. Unlike the Greeks and Romans, nudity in life and art was

Balneum sulphatara, folio 4, 'Balneis Puteolanis', Peter of Eboli

frowned upon by the Christian Church. Its very founding belief asserts that the covering of the body was a punishment for mankind's loss of innocence as a result of Eve's folly. It was difficult to deny the nakedness of Jesus at birth, however, or at his demise on the Cross (although with discreetly posed loincloth), or the nakedness of martyred saints like St Sebastian. In the predominantly illiterate Middle Ages, art in stained glass or painting, viewed in a church setting, was the provider of important images to the masses. As Madeline Caviness points out, 'the thirteenth-century painter (and his patron or audience) had to depend on a "real" event to give licence to his depiction of the nude female body as desirable object'.[10] The potentially erotic could not be avoided but was sanctified by its moral purpose. Mary, otherwise heavily draped, could be shown breastfeeding Jesus or, in the Vision of St Bernard by Alonso Cano, even shooting a stream of her milk into the saint's mouth.

Far more ambiguous was the portrayal of woman as Eve. As the Renaissance freed some artistic constraints she was often shown as a tall slim beauty, probably arousing the very opposite of the reproach that her mythical role intended. In Jan van Eyck's Ghent altar piece of 1432 (plate 14), her charms are displayed with a fairly opulent belly. This same body-shape is well evident in a non-biblical scene, directly relevant to our theme, in Lucas Cranach's 'The Fountain of Youth' (1546, plate 15). In the painting elderly women enter the bath on the left disconsolately droopy, but thanks to the water's elixir of youth, exit right firm and confident. The whole scene is reminiscent of the manuscript bathers, except that they, unlike their rejuvenated sisters, show no signs of preening and enjoyment, looking as down-hearted as the 'before' of Cranach's painting rather than the 'after'. Maybe this suggests not their collective anxiety over pregnancy but their earnest desire to attain it and overcome sterility. The treatment of 'female disorders', especially in salt/bromide baths, was high on the list of hoped-for ameliorations. The overall impression is that, at least regarding body-shapes, the women's figures express the artist's penchant for paunches, and they are not pregnant. Whatever the function of the baths the sheer number of shamelessly unadorned women is unusual. As to the other clues revealed alongside their nakedness, such as hairstyle, we shall save comment until we consider the astrological section of the manuscript.

All the vague clues from the nature of the baths and their inhabitants tend, however, to be adumbrated once again by the surreal apparatus that links and seems to hold the women in bondage once removed from the baths. The overall impression is that some process of organic healing or transformation is taking place, designed for and executed by women specifically. The potent source of the essence or elixir emanates from a strange 'fruiting-body' like a custard apple with an underside cluster of sometimes dotted seeds like a giant blackberry. Some tentative suggestions for what this vegetative form may be have included giant pineapple weed or pineapple itself, or the pomegranate. Does the stylised artemisia head from the Apuleius Platonicus herbal look familiar here? The doctrine of signatures provides an interesting theoretical basis for other contenders.

This latecomer to the pantheon of medieval thought has been attributed to Jakob Bohme (1575–1624), a German shoe-maker. Like Giovanni Battista Porta, whom we have already

Artemisia head, Bodleian Ashmole 1462, folio 17r

encountered, Bohme believed that plants exhibited their God-
given purpose by signs or hints given by their appearance.
Hence the walnut, looking not unlike a brain, might have cur-
ative powers connected to it. By the same token, plants characterised by overlapping seeds should be connected to the
body's layers, and relevant therefore to skin conditions. A
woodcut from Porta's *Phytonomica* shows an array of plants
including the pine cone, the thistle and bulblets clustered
together, sharing a broadly similar feature reminiscent of the
Voynich manuscript. The Mediterranean asphodel plant regularly included in medieval herbals is often shown in this way

Asphodel, Bodleian Ashmole 1462, folio 23r

173

and has noteworthy characteristics. Growing prolifically on barren sandy soils to a regal height of a metre, it came to have a magical reputation by association; its 'sign' of habitat suggesting a powerful force bringing growth from sterility that must be, therefore, of some benefit. By further analogy, planting it near burial grounds would help nourish the dead. It was once used to combat menstrual complications. If our theme of rejuvenation is appropriate and the author of the manuscript was acquainted with the doctrine, this may help limit our search not only historically but to plants in which appearance and function are associated with youth and fertility.

In other pages of the manuscript this curious form becomes less coherent. Wherever the form is fairly evident, a liquid emanates from it. On folio 75r nymphs cascade and dance in it, on folio 78r (plate 16) it is 'filtered' by what look like elongated washing-machine drums, on folio 79v (plate 17) they are replaced by short lengths of tubing sometimes opened out to form receptacles, like pulpits, in which the women lie or dip their toes. After a protracted four floors of 'treatment' (which begins with the 'asphodel' pouring forth past a lady in a pulpit, holding unusual evidence of token Christianity in the shape of a small cross), the liquid pours into an elongated pool, also showing rare animal signs – four creatures, including a lizard, gathered to 'enjoy' its properties. A similar cluster motif occurs on other folios, although less coherently (see page 175), taking the form of a nest in which the women stand, or a 'beehive' from which 'spores' or indeed 'bees' fly out – to no obvious purpose. The tubes take all manner of configurations, sometimes stretching in long arcs between the operatives/patients, or twisting and turning in short lengths like intestines, their ends reamed open, into which the women often place a hand – testing or receiving treatment.

Commentators have agreed with Professor Newbold that there is something perhaps gynaecological about all this, hinting at fallopian tubes and ovaries. This may be so, but the overall impression, however, is of something outlandish and dream-born. Folio 83v takes this one stage further. To describe it reveals its remoteness from anything else one could imagine. Two naked inmates of the establishment are each dwarfed by gross round bladders from which the clusters are excreted in lengths, like home-knit scarves, terminating

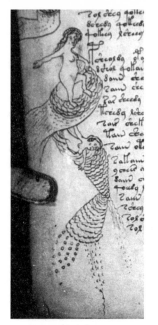

Detail, folio 76v

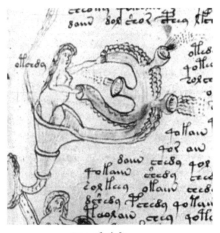

Detail, folio 77r

Detail, folio 83v

by spouting caviar-like roe. This image is somehow more sinister than most others and of a similar order of grotesque fabulousness as that found in Hieronymus Bosch's 'Garden of Earthly Delights'.

Making an equal claim to top the bizarre league table is folio 86v3 (plate 18). Newbold's 'nucleated ova' are here again in profusion, accompanied by humans and birds. In the top left corner a nymph appears from behind the fruiting-body, here looking like a beautifully arranged greengrocer's pyramid of apples piled on a barrow adorned in curtain-drapes, one of which is spurting a column of 'spores'. Opposite it, a bird, apparently bathing itself, is trapped in a gush of spores as if the whole fruit display had exploded at once, leaving the scaly calex intact. At the bottom left and right, two of Newbold's '*membrum virilia*' stand erect ('so schematised as to avoid giving offence'), the one on the left like a Gaudiesque, rocketing jellyfish spouting spores and carrying all aloft, including a waving passenger. Its opposite partner has a sitting duck in control or a foolishly unwitting phallonaut having made a poor choice in nesting site. Any hint of facetiousness in these descriptions seems entirely apposite. What is one to make of all this? If one focuses on the women bathing together we remain perhaps on the right side of the possible, but if we add to the picture the vegetation and the 'plumbing', the illustrations become entirely singular, eccentric and incredible within the original meaning of the term. Despite endless searching through herbals and artwork, no one seems to have offered any reference to any aspect of European culture that makes overall sense of these pages.

With this in mind, at first sight it is an immense relief to come across a coherent section of the Voynich manuscript with some recognisable iconography. What identifies the astrological pages, folios 70–73 (several of the folios have multiple-page foldouts), is the presence of a conventional zodiacal star sign in the middle, medallion like, of two outer bands of script serving as terra firma for collections of mostly naked women in containers of various kinds. There are twelve of these pages, one for each sign of the zodiac – but, naturally, with the Voynich manuscript nothing is ever straightforward.

Folio 74 is missing, presumably representing January and February (Aquarius and Capricorn). April (Aries) and May (Taurus) have been drawn twice, making up the conventional twelve. To add further confusion the order of binding does not follow the months of the year. As if to help us out, someone, probably at a later date, has written in the months in non-Voynich script – 'marc' and 'may' and 'abril' being quite clear (and in French it has been claimed), but although the others make appropriate hints they are largely illegible. The astrological figures themselves are an indistinct mishmash atypical of medieval iconography: Leo, for example, looks more like a leopard than lion and Cancer more lobster than crab. The Gemini twins shown as man and woman may point to a late-medieval dating, but the crossbow of the Sagittarian archer is unhelpful in this respect.

Perhaps the chief feature of the pages is the array of women, sometimes clothed, but mostly naked, who radiate from the centre star sign of each page and who, on the pages where they are entirely deshabille, look not unlike an aerial view of Busby Berkeley's swimming babes, only more risqué. Apart from the Pisces page, f7ov2 (plate 19), where some of the troop are emerging from washing-machine drums, the dressed women appear to be standing in their own bins to retain some vestige of modesty. The one unifying feature is that each nymph is associated with her own six- or nine-pointed star floating just above her right shoulder, to which she hangs or which she regards floating, tethered to the container or the circle on which she stands. The roughly drawn stars would convey a car-nival-like atmosphere if the naked ladies, as in the bath section, were not each wearing an expression of open-mouthed dismay.

What clues can be gleaned from this section? The nymphs' appearances per page have some regularity: seven pages have exactly thirty, four have fifteen, but Pisces is at odds with twenty-nine. Interestingly the four less-crowded pages are the duplicated Aries and Taurus. From these one obtains the impression that the two expositions of each sign are different enough in style to have been executed by two different hands. This is further emphasised by the maverick Pisces, which is the only page combining the larger number of nymphs, placing them all in tubs or strangely emerging horizontally from their drums. Equally recalcitrantly, the inner ring of women face anticlockwise. Several of the deviant group even cheekily seem to be holding their own star possessively like a balloon tied to a string. The whole page artistically exhibits greater penmanship and much finer attention to detail, despite the crowded assembly on the page. The decorative embellishment to the tubs is much more imaginative than elsewhere and the women are daintier. Have three hands been at work in this section?

The other potentially useful clues lie in the cultural collat-eral of these pages – clothing, hairstyles and headware. Folio

Detail, folio 71r *Detail, folio 71r* *Detail, folio 71r*

Detail, folio 72r2

71r appears, however, to have allowed three male interlopers into the entourage, two of whom from their headgear in particular make passable imitations of Canadian mounted police, whilst their fellow officer, nippleless, sports only the hat. Three more possible males have inveigled their way on to f72r2, less dashingly than their mates wearing belted tunics and boots. In amongst them, emphasising their likely maleness, is a long-haired woman in a full gown. Brumbaugh has asserted that the Sagittarian archer (f73v, plate 20) is definitely sporting a Florentine hat. Overall the dating-evidence from clothing styles is rather limited. On Taurus (f71v, plate 21), for example, half of the women are clothed, but only their top halves are evident above the tubs, showing a variety of fashions but not revealing their otherwise helpfully dateable footwear. A consensus of commentators suggests, however, the latter half of the fifteenth century.

Crown, folio 72v3

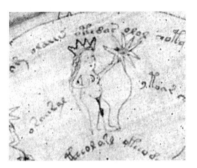

Crown, folio 72r3

The headwear exhibited seems to cover a variety of styles; very definite, however, on f72v3: a determined-looking lady carries an imposing crown, her authority seeming to drive her naked subjects further round the dial. Altogether less convincing on f72r3, another nude nymph wears a less impressive crown that looks as if it had been added in later. Hairstyles are more evident amongst the women when naked and appear in general to be curly, shoulder length, occasionally waist length, but never covering any part of the body. Apart from eccentric Pisces, the five hundred women drawn seem to be invariably blonde. This may seem strange seeing that one consensus locates the manuscript in late-fifteenth-century Northern Italy, where light hair was not the rule. Fashion, however, did place an emphasis on bleaching the hair with chemicals like alum, sulphur and soda. Records show that wealthy Venetian women would sit in special turrets on their rooftops wearing broad-brimmed hats without crowns to encourage bleaching by sunlight. There seems little evidence of coiffures connected to the rich, no braiding or elaboration, such as the style with two 'mounds' on either side of the head, the tight beehive or netted hair. The overall impression of women's hairstyles both in the bathing and astrological sections of the manuscript is of healthy-headed but unstylish peasants. Their bubbly curls are somewhat reminiscent of the 'dumb-blonde' character played by Barbara Windsor in the British *Carry On* movies, whose body-shape is also fairly apposite.

The dominance of the herbal section in the Voynich manuscript and the possible evidence of apothecary jars, both linked to an underlying medical context of the bathing women, should neatly connect with the astrological section to confirm the manuscript as an instrumental guide to some, albeit esoteric, medical practice. As we noted in chapter 2, astrology was inextricably bound up with the medieval world view as a factual schema for interpreting God's world. Medicinal plants possessing certain qualities derived from their relation to the planets, and picked if possible at the most propitious astrological time to make use of their full potency, would be administered to patients, bearing in mind their own astrological characteristics. But the zodiacal pages seem to loosen, not consolidate, the link, heading away towards a sketchy and unrecognisable schema of the heavens, ever nearer that latent undertow of the fanciful. The final two linked sections of the manuscript accelerate this tendency at warp-speed.

Although stylistically similar, one group of eight pages has been designated as 'astronomical' owing to the presence of star configurations of various kinds within concentric circles, similar to the astrological folios; a further dozen or so have been given the designation of 'cosmological'. Newbold's Andromeda, f68v3 (plate 22) is classed as the latter but does have some stars within its spiral. The other predominant characteristic of the astronomical folios, perhaps akin to an almanac, is the presence of a variety of suns and moons, usually with faces, mostly looking anxiously out of the page. On f67r1 (plate 23) the sun wears a headband, and is surrounded by an elaborate twelve-pointed starwheel of a vaguely floral design, but the shading makes it look oddly like a set of rotorblades for a windmill. Folio 67r2 (plate 23) does not contain

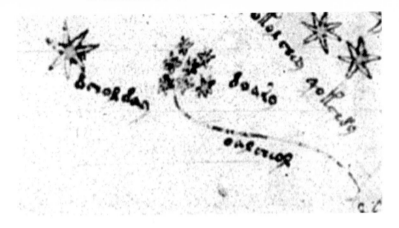

'Pleiades', folio 68r3

clusters of stars but is included in this classification because of the twelve moons resembling portholes and arranged within segments.

The drawings are executed in typical Voynich amateur style, the diminutive stars inconsistently possessing six or seven points, and are arranged in some folios in clusters within segments of a wheel or scattered generally. More specifically, the suggestion has often been made that a labelled group of seven stars clustered tightly within one of the segments of f68r3 might represent the Pleiades with Aldebaran, also labelled, nearby. This specific information has, however, not provided a crib to decryption, nor has the presence of labels to each of the twenty-four and twenty-nine stars of the folios 68r2 and 68r1.

'Tycho Brahe', folio 67v1

Robert Teague, however, has conducted some research with the aid of a computer-generated 'star-searching' programme, and posted details on the Voynich mailing list (January 2003). He maintains that the cluster in f68r3 is in fact the Pleiades but the lone star is not Aldebaran. Teague, also, makes a connection in f67v1 with the heaven-breaking Tycho Brahe (1546–1601), Imperial Mathematician to Rudolf II's court from 1599. In the central sun he identifies the face of Brahe with beard and full moustache, and whilst this is debatable, there is no doubt of Brahe's relevance to the times, particularly in his discovery of a supernova in November 1572. Could the Voynich sun image, much more pronounced than others, with seventeen flames emanating from it, represent a celebration of his find? Brahe's refusal to abandon the notion that the earth was the centre of the universe, in favour of the societally undermining heliocentric Copernican revolution, despite what he saw with his own eyes, is also perennially relevant to much inquiry (including that of the Voynich manuscript) – we often believe what we want to see.

The cosmological section, that is, those without stars, comprises a further dozen or so eccentric folios. In the plates depicted in this volume (f67r2 and f69r) one common feature can be shown. Both have a central star of six or seven points that more resemble 'starfish' than stars. Folio 69r (plate 24) shares with f69v a curious array of pipes joined together in a circle, forty-five in the former, twenty-eight in the latter. They seem to echo the plumbing found in the 'balneological' section.

Interestingly, three of the other cosmological folios feature human beings. The strangest is perhaps folio 86r2 (page 183). Placed around a flaming sun is what looks like an aerial view of a castle round tower with six parapets divided into four by elongated plumes or spouts extending beyond the customary outer circle. D'Imperio suggests that there may be some sort of system behind the diagrams in general, that 'may relate to contrasted hours of night and day, times or events governed by different classes of stars, with effects of the sun and moon on the humours, elements, seasons, ages of man, winds, directions, etc.', all of which relate to the number four.[11] Certainly, stationed on each of the fortifications are four male figures, two of whom seem to be youths, and an old man bent double supported by a stick and struggling with a large chain. This

Folio 86r2

fourfold division occurs in f57v (plate 25) also, consisting of five circular bands of script in the middle of which are four people of indeterminate sex, two of whom, one holding an egg or stone, appear to be looking down the central circle as if it were a well. The fourfold theme is also present in one of the

 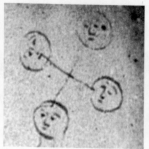 

Details, folio 67v2

crankiest folios, 67v2, in which almost everything occurs in fours – small suns partially extinguished by the 'asphodel' motif from the balneological section, and cartoon moons in strange configurations. The ubiquity of four in the natural world, particularly, may point us in certain directions, although in general it is difficult to connect any of the other numbers contained within the folios to medieval cosmology; counting stars and segments and numbers of rings produces a list of 3, 7, 8, 9, 12, 17, 24, 29, 39, whose significance is not readily apparent.

D'Imperio's suggestion of numerical clues contained within the Voynich manuscript exemplifies the unforgiving search for a rational basis to the document, one we have pursued within the framework of a medico/herbal treatise. As we have seen, the herbal, pharmacopoeia and aspects of the bath section might substantiate the quest for an interconnected order and purpose. The bizarre plumbing of the last-named pages and the other sections, however, seem to be just too idiosyncratic to sustain an overall hypothesis. If the reader is somewhat disappointed and wearied by this conclusion there is a yet more weird and wonderful wackiness to encounter in the manuscript. If the apothecary jars perhaps represent one end of a continuum of earthbound, everyday tangibility, the cosmological folios 85/86, the 'rosettes', represent the other. Here we wander off into a complete world of fantasy; even the foliation astounds, consisting of a large foldout sheet like a map of spheres beyond the clouds. Its special quality adumbrates the rational model explanation we have been trying to follow so far, but we shall attempt to describe and examine it in the next chapter with the aid of rational and scientific tools.

→ 7 ←

PRIVILEGED CONSCIOUSNESS

So where now do we find ourselves in the twisting, turning maze that is the story of the Voynich manuscript? Historical research has produced many names and uncovered fascinating characters whose lives have been connected with the manuscript, but none has been shown categorically to be the author. Decades of cryptanalysis have delivered no decrypted material that has been universally accepted as genuine plain text, and the underlying message beneath the Voynichese script remains hidden. The hundreds of illustrations at first yield vague similarities with other medieval works, but on closer inspection these congruences seem to vanish, and we are left no closer to an understanding. In which direction, then, should our investigation progress?

Rather than searching for other historical artifacts which demonstrate a close linguistic or graphical resemblance to the manuscript (herbals, alchemical documents or cryptographic treatises), might we not look for something that appears to possess the same apparent intensity of creative purpose and endeavour? Is it possible, by studying the manuscript in whole or part, to detect what creative impulse or intent was in the mind of its long-forgotten author? Could there be other writings or images in existence which, whilst not sharing an exact likeness or even probable date with the Voynich manuscript, might nonetheless possess a similar 'other-worldliness', and thereby present us with a clue as to the motivations behind its creation? Such a line of inquiry was first suggested by a strange coincidence on the return journey from Yale University after visiting the Voynich manuscript itself. Gerry Kennedy once again takes up the story.

Still bewildered from the dizzying experience of my first encounter with the manuscript at the Beinecke Library, I did not relish the prospect of an immediate return to the bustle of New York, and so with some relief accepted an invitation from a friend to attend the annual Tanglewood Festival of Music, staged amongst the beautiful wooded hills and glistening lakes of west Massachusetts. To further delay my return to the metropolis, I also decided to visit the Hancock Shaker Village nearby.

Now a museum dedicated to the memory of this cloistered nineteenth-century religious sect, the settlement still retains the feeling of order and purpose that once dominated the lives of its inhabitants. The dignified agricultural buildings combine with the utility of the barrack-like living areas; where men and women, separated from each other, conducted their daily routines in an atmosphere of frugality and asceticism. In a high summer setting of plenty, it was easy to imagine how a life of discipline and subservience to God would nevertheless feel full and rewarding. In the depths of a New England winter, however, the cold and poor diet would need the compensations of comradeship and inner faith. Such fraternal warmth and spiritual intensity were ignited and maintained in the hysterical 'shaking' dance that also provided the community with their enduring nickname of 'The Shakers'. Individual religious expression within the sect manifested itself in 'gift' drawings, the first sight of which immediately suggested an echo of the Voynich manuscript: highly stylised plants and birds were drawn and painted in elaborate, jumbled, yet still dignified settings with what can only be described as a quiet fervour or calm passion. Some less representational drawings took off into circular realms of hatching and shading, looking not unlike restrained versions of the 'rosette' pages of the Voynich manuscript. What did strike me, however, were several drawings employing not only gift images, but also containing gift 'tongues', written in a flowing yet totally original script. Whilst not as developed or detailed as those of the Voynich manuscript, these images conveyed a sense of drive and intensely personal meaning that seemed very familiar. Returning to London, laden with books on Shaker art, I had unwittingly opened a new chapter in my relationship with the manuscript.

Founded by James and Jane Wardley, The United Society of Believers, or the Shakers, originated in England in the eighteenth century. The Shaker movement split from The Religious Society of Friends – better known as 'Quakers'. The Shakers pursued a goal of a personal expression of their Christianity and relationship with God, combined with a desire for a simple existence away from the outside world; similar in many ways to the Anabaptist Mennonites of North America, more commonly known as Old Order Amish. In their early days, the Society of Believers, or simply 'Believers' as they referred to themselves, built their community around the central tenets of celibacy and the Catholic doctrine of the confession of sin. However, the direction of the society, both spiritually and physically, was to change with the arrival of Ann Lee in 1772. A textile worker from Manchester, and also a charismatic visionary prone to receiving prophetic messages from heaven, Ann Lee quickly rose to prominence within the society, where she became known as Mother Ann.

After an accusation of blasphemy and an interview with four Anglican clergymen to determine her guilt or otherwise, Mother Ann received the most important of all her visions. In it, she was divinely directed to lead the community to America. Despite the four clergymen finding in favour of Mother Ann, there must have been a growing sense within the community that it would only be a matter of time before the religious authorities in England clamped down on their 'enthusiastic' and physical methods of worship; which had already gained them the epithet 'the Shaking Quakers'. Led by Mother Ann, a total of nine Shakers arrived in New York City on 6 August 1774. In the New World the Shakers began to flourish.

By the early nineteenth century the ecstatic form of Shaker worship had changed dramatically. The Shaker communities, now ranging from Maine to Kentucky, had formalised their religious and social structures. This regulation entailed the communal ownership of property, the dissipation of normal familial ties and a more pronounced withdrawal from the world at large, alongside a gradual disappearance of the visionary religious experiences. As these new social rules took hold, a worrying trend made itself manifest, as the younger generations began to drift away from the community to seek lives for themselves in the outside world. To counteract this, the elders concluded it was necessary to rekindle the mystical intimacies that had characterised the early years of the society, and so began a period in Shaker history known as Mother Ann's Work. In the 1830s the community began to receive 'gifts', messages from Mother Ann, saints, and other biblical and historical figures. These messages were relayed via 'instruments', what we today might call mediums, who were usually, though not exclusively, young women, often of a low social status. During a trance-like state, often accompanied by dancing, shaking and babbling in unknown languages, the gifts would be imparted, and later recorded in the form of songs or drawings.

Today, approximately two hundred of these Shaker gift drawings survive, and it was the sight of a number of these in the Hancock Shaker Village that suggested a possible link between visionary experiences and the Voynich manuscript.

The more 'straightforward' gift drawings, adorned with recognisable images of trees and flowers, and obvious religious symbols such as crosses and doves, bear similarities to secular nineteenth- and twentieth-century needlework samplers. However, alongside these are a smaller number of far stranger drawings, sometimes referred to as sacred sheets. On the sheets, weird, unintelligible writing, supposedly an angelic or heavenly language, traces swirling patterns across the page. The sheets possess such titles as 'A sacred sheet sent from Holy Mother Wisdom by her Holy Angel...For Brother Giles Avery', or 'A sacred sheet sent from Holy Mother Wisdom by her Angel of Many Signs'.

The period of Mother Ann's Work lasted just over a decade, and by the late 1840s the deliverance of 'gifts' via 'instruments' had all but died out. The whole episode of visionary revelations has been seen by the more sceptically minded as an attempt by women in the Shaker community to regain at least a little of the former status and power which they had lost after the introduction of the strict social rules following the death of Mother Ann in 1784. To a modern, secular inquirer, it is indeed difficult to accept that these 'gifts' were really divinely imparted messages; but one must concede that to those who created them, the sacred sheets were produced in the truest sense of the phrase 'good faith'. What the physiological basis for these ecstatic visions might have been is now impossible to determine. We can only be certain that the Shaker 'instruments' who painted their gift drawings genuinely believed they were conduits of holy wisdom.

A comparison between the images and scripts used in the sacred sheets and those found in the Voynich manuscript produces only a few, superficial similarities in design, which themselves tend to disappear on closer inspection. The Shakers' angelic languages possess none of the apparent linguistic structure of the Voynichese script, but the swirling patterns of the sacred sheets do bear a resemblance to the more abstract images in the Voynich manuscript (plate 26). However, what does strike an observer of both Voynichese and the Shakers' angelic script is the obsessive, driven quality that seems to underpin their creation. Although the 'languages' themselves may be entirely different, a similar impetus or compunction seems to be present in both. It is not so much *what* was written, or even *how*, but *why* it was written that may be important. Perhaps it is into the twilight realms of visionary mysticism or mental illness that we must venture in order to gain an understanding of the Voynich manuscript?

Today, art produced by people marginalised from society in general, by an author/illustrator obeying some creative instinct outside that which would be considered rational or 'normal', is known as 'Outsider Art'.

> The specific term Outsider Art was first coined in 1972 by the British writer Roger Cardinal, in his eponymous book, as an English-language equivalent for the French term 'Art Brut', originally formulated by the painter Jean Dubuffet (1901–1985) in the mid-1940s. The artist outsiders are, by definition, fundamentally different to their audience, often thought of as being dysfunctional in respect of the parameters for normality. Psychiatric patients, self-taught visionaries and mediums are the groups at the heart of early definitions of Outsider Art.[1]

Comparisons of what different societies, separated from each other by physical distance and many centuries, consider to be normal or rational behaviour are fraught with danger. Whether the term 'Outsider Art' can strictly be applied to visionary creations of the Middle Ages is open to debate.

However, the term is useful, as it describes what is produced by those existing in some way beyond the normal experiential constraints of the given society, and so will be used in this way in the following pages.

Jean Dubuffet became interested in the art of the insane after reading Hans Prinzhorn's seminal book *Bildernei der Geiteskranken* (*Artistry of the Mentally Ill*), published in 1922. Prinzhorn, a doctor from Heidelberg in Germany, aimed to examine and analyse the art produced by the clinically insane for diagnostic purposes, years before the concept of art therapy had been developed. He was not the first to attempt this – others such as the psychiatrist Karl Jaspers and the philosopher Luwig Klages had suggested just such an approach – but Prinzhorn took up the challenge with such dedication that he amassed a collection of around five hundred works by some four hundred and fifty individuals from mental institutions in German-speaking countries. The collection, according to Prinzhorn, was made up almost entirely of works created by people with no formal artistic training and who were clinically insane. Armed with this mass of material, Prinzhorn began to search for 'the roots of the creative instinct'.[2] He estimated that roughly three quarters of the works were produced by schizophrenics, the remainder being the creations of epileptics, imbeciles, psychopaths, manic-depressives and paralytics. At pains to avoid any evaluation of the artistic or aesthetic worth of the works, Prinzhorn concentrated his analysis on the psychological processes that shaped them.

Prinzhorn refrained from referring to the works as 'art', preferring the word *Gestaltung*, which can be translated as 'shaping' or 'configuration'. He did, however, identify certain expressive impulses which he believed led to the production of such configurations: the urge to play, the urge to decorate, the urge to imitate, and the need for self-expression. These were linked with the more aesthetic drives to impose pictorial order, symmetry or form on the creation, accompanied by a need for a personally symbolic content. Moreover, the spontaneous production of drawings by the insane was seen as 'a means of reasserting order on a chaotically changed world',[3] in a sense, creating an artistic environment in which they regained just the sort of control and understanding that they

had lost in their day-to-day lives. In the worst stage of schizophrenic illness, these creative urges became manifest in
nothing more than obsessive scribbling, which Prinzhorn saw
as 'nearest to the zero point on the scale of composition'.[4]
However, at the other end of Prinzhorn's scale were 'a large
number of creators who produce highly individual, alternative
world systems that are often extremely sophisticated'.[5]

Such Outsider 'world creators' cited by Rhodes include the
Americans Henry J. Darger and Achilles Rizzoli.

The world of Achilles Rizzoli has been bequeathed in the form
of grandiose architectural schemes whose realisation lies in a
fantastic elsewhere. A trained technical draughtsman, he
worked full time for more than three decades for the San
Francisco architect Otto Deichmann. Rizzoli's central project
was a city that he called YTTE (Yield to Total Elation) whose
inhabitants included figures associated with his life – his
mother, work colleagues and local children – who were themselves immortalised in the large-scale architectural elevations
he referred to as 'Symbolizations'. His mother, at the foot of
whose bed he slept until her death in 1937, was invariably
depicted as a cathedral, drawn on birthday cards that he sent to
her at his own address for twenty years after she died. He held
his first Achilles Tectonic Exhibit (ATE) in his own sitting-
room in 1935, although only some of the neighbourhood children came to see it. Yet, together with his workaday life, these
small contacts constituted the full extent of his relationships
outside that with his mother.[6]

Darger's mother died when he was four and his father aban-
doned him four years later. This loss informed his prodigious,
though entirely secret, artistic output. At the age of twelve
Darger was committed to the Lincoln Asylum for Feeble-
minded Children, in Illinois, from which he eventually
escaped, spending the rest of his life in menial jobs, mostly in
Chicago hospitals. In his spare time, however, he created huge
quantities of drawings and writing. He produced a five-
thousand-page autobiographical work which consisted largely
of an account of a tornado he witnessed as a child, and detailed
comparisons between weather reports and actual climatic
conditions. His most astonishing creation was a vast fantasy

titled *The Realms of the Unreal*, in which, over the course of fifteen volumes consisting of over fifteen thousand typed pages, Darger related 'The Story of the Vivian Girls in What is Known as the Realms of the Unreal or the Glandelinian War Storm or the Glandico-Abbiennian Wars, as Caused by the Child Slave Rebellion'. Accompanying the text were hundreds of illustrations, often graphically violent, filled with figures traced or cut from magazines, comics and even children's colouring books. The work, created solely for his own use and never intended to be viewed by others, was discovered by his landlord shortly before Darger's death in 1972.

What strikes the viewer of these disparate works is not the similarities in the artistic styles and representations of Darger and Rizzoli (of which there are very few), but their shared attempts to bring personal order to their 'chaotically challenged world' through the creation of alternative realities. It has been argued that the Voynich manuscript is unlikely to be the product of mental illness because of the size of the volume and the amount of material it contains. Yet when compared to the work of the Outsider artists mentioned above, does it not seem possible that, purely in terms of quantity, the Voynich manuscript could be the product of just such a mental dysfunction? Might it be the product of some medieval scholar or scribe, who, suffering from an unbalanced state of mind, attempts to recreate a sense of order in their now strange and forbidding environment by creating a work of 'natural science' that represents their altered perception of the worlds around them?

Mediumistic art – that is, art produced by spirit mediums – could be considered the most extreme form of Outsider Art in that the physical creators believe themselves to have no intentional influence on the works produced; they are merely the conduits for the true artists, the spirits that control them. Such a practice is known as automatism. English spiritualist artist Madge Gill began to create after losing a son in the Spanish flu pandemic of 1918, later followed by the traumatic birth of a stillborn daughter. It was during attempts to contact her dead children that she encountered a spiritual force she called 'Myrninerest' who subsequently guided her creative activities. Anna Zemánkova (1908–1986) and contemporary French mediumistic artist Marie-Jeanne Gil both began

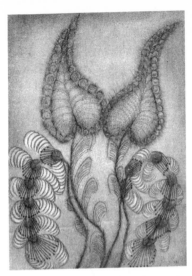

Example of Anna Zemánkova's 'fantastic plants'

receiving other-worldly guidance after suffering illness; Gil experiencing a vision of the Virgin Mary during her recovery from polio at the age of seven, and Zemánkova after a severe bout of depression. Both women are led by their spirits to represent: 'The sense of an organic cosmos, replete with a life force that is in a constant state of formation.'[7] Zemánkova has produced images of plants not unlike illustrations in the Voynich manuscript (though executed with considerably more artistry), whilst Gil sees 'celestial presences' in natural phenomena, leading to such works as *Cosmic Roses*, comprising kaleidoscopic arrangements of flashes and swirls. What precise, physiological conditions lead to these mediumistic experiences, and hence to the creation of artworks, is uncertain. There is, however, another mystical visionary whose art may hold the clue to their psychical origin, and which may have a direct bearing on our interpretation of the Voynich manuscript.

The older medical and religious literature contains innumerable references to 'visions', 'trances', 'transports', etc., but the nature of many of these must now remain enigmatic to us. Many different processes may have similar manifestations and some of the more complex phenomena described may be hysteric, psychotic, oneiric,* or hypnagogic† in origin, no less than epileptic, apoplectic, toxic or migrainous in nature.

A single notable exception may be mentioned – the 'visions' of Hildegard (1098–1179) – which were indisputably migrainous in nature.[8]

(*specifically, 'belonging to dreams' and † 'drowsiness preceding sleep')

The divine visions of St Hildegard of Bingen led directly to the creation of three of the most remarkable works of religious writing of the Middle Ages. Within these volumes we have not only visionary medieval work with which to compare the Voynich manuscript, but also, according to Dr Sacks, quoted above, evidence of the pathology or cause of such mystical revelations. Furthermore, a resultant understanding of the psychological and physiological roots of Hildegard's inspired creativity may cast some light on to the more abstract and inexplicable drawings in the Voynich manuscript.

Hildegard was born in 1098 in the town of Bemersheim, which is situated twenty kilometres southwest of the modern German city of Mainz. The tenth child of aristocratic parents, Hildegard was placed by her family in the Benedictine monastery of Disibodenburg in the Rhine valley, sometime in her seventh year. By the standards of the day, the monastery – named after the Celtic saint Disibodus – was well endowed and comfortable, and housed both monks and nuns within its walls. She became Abbess in 1136 by the unanimous acclaim of her peers. Some years later Hildegard was divinely instructed to lead the nuns to a separate, and comparatively spartan new home in Rupertsberg, in 1148. She seems to have been a determined woman, with a strong and independent personality, and, thanks to an upbringing within the confines of Disibodenburg, was relatively well educated for a woman of the twelfth century. Once settled at Rupertsberg, the nuns became noted for their manuscript illuminations, and Hildegard, in addition to her religious and administrative duties as head of the convent, continued to pursue her own intellectual interests. She composed many hymns, and wrote a play, *Ordo Virtutum*, which was performed by the nuns (this, combined with a relaxed attitude to the 'dress code' of her flock, further demonstrates her open and forward-looking disposition to convent life). She also wrote copious correspondence and even produced a 'medico-scientific' work which today survives only in fragmentary form. As if all this were not enough, Hildegard supposedly created a secret language during the 1150s, known as the *lingua ignota* or 'unknown language', and a secret alphabet, the *literae ignota*, with which to write her encoded hymns or *carmina*. The exact purpose of this language is still debated. Mary D'Imperio suggests that the '*ignota lingua*', as she refers to it, was spoken or sung by Hildegard 'while under the sway of her mystic visions', and the record we have of it today was 'preserved in a sort of glossary written down by her contemporaries'.[9] However, it has also been suggested that Hildegard deliberately created the language so that the nuns in her convent could communicate with each other without strangers understanding them,[10] whilst a recent biographer, Sabina Flanagan, argues that the *lingua ignota* may have been nothing more than an 'intellectual diversion on a level with crossword puzzles'.[11]

But above and beyond all her other achievements, St Hildegard is remembered and revered today for her three great visionary religious works: *Scivias*, *Liber vitae meritorum* and *Liber divinorum operum*. By her own admission, Hildegard had been experiencing visions since infancy, normally in the form of 'a light of awesome brightness',[12] but it was not until the year 1141 that she experienced the mystical revelations that led to the writing of her books. She was apparently inspired by a particularly powerful vision in which, in her own words from the *Scivias*, 'the heavens opened and a blinding light of exceptional brilliance flowed through my entire brain'. This light created an instant, deeper appreciation of the works of Christian literature, combined with a divine instruction to make her revelations known to others. Overwhelmed, not only by the import of the vision itself, but also by the responsibility of communicating this divine understanding, Hildegard became ill; and only after confessing to others the task appointed to her did she recover. However, it was to take her a further ten years to complete the task of transcribing her visions, the result of which was her first major work, *Scivias*, a contraction of the Latin *Sci vias Domini*; 'Know the Ways of the Lord'. Almost from the outset, Hildegard's visions were accepted by the religious establishment as a genuine divine gift, and at the Synod of Trier in 1147, after inspecting the still unfinished *Scivias*, Pope Euginius III instructed Hildegard to record all further visions she might receive. It is clear that her peers 'thought of her as a prophet, empowered to know and make known the *secreta Dei*, whether past, present or future. Hildegard, too, assiduously promoted herself in this role, both in her writings and in her daily dealings with others.'[13] Between 1158 and 1163, Hildegard produced her second great theological opus, the *Liber vitae meritorum* or *The Book of Life's Merits*, which detailed the vices and virtues present in human nature. The writing of this book seems to have coincided with another bout of illness that affected Hildegard from 1158 to 1161. The third work, *Liber divinorum operum* (*Book of Divine Works*), was produced intermittently between 1163 and 1174, and built upon certain themes first encountered in *Scivias*, which are expanded to form a commentary on the opening of St John's Gospel. All three books contain illustrations which show in detail the religious iconography that filled the visions of St Hildegard.

Whatever the modern, secular explanation for St Hildegard's mystical experiences (which we will come to in a moment), there are no such overtly religious images in the Voynich manuscript. Indeed, the lack of any such identifiable Christian imagery in the manuscript has led some to dismiss out of hand the possibility that a form of mystical or visionary experience may have played a part in its creation. However, by examining the current scientific thinking regarding the visions of Hildegard, it may be possible to explain the physiological foundations of her experiences, and, divested of their religious interpretations, see if the same or similar experiential factors could have affected the creator of the Voynich manuscript.

The idea that Hildegard may have been a sufferer of migraines was first put forward in the 1950s by Charles Singer, and has been taken up and expanded by renowned neurologist and writer Dr Oliver Sacks, and by Hildegard's biographer Sabina Flanagan, who presents the implication of the theory thus:

...since Charles Singer first made the suggestion, it has become something of a medical, although not hagiographical, orthodoxy to claim Hildegard among other distinguished sufferers from migraine…Two questions now arise. The first is whether Hildegard's descriptions of her visions accord with accounts of migrainous phenomena. If they do, the second question is whether the visions are then reducible to this physiological cause.[14]

What is a migraine? It is not, as is so often the misapprehension of non-sufferers, simply a bad headache. In fact, although this is one of the physical manifestations that *can* be associated with a migraine attack, a sufferer may experience some or all of the other migrainous phenomena without developing a headache. The common migraine develops in a sequence of four stages, beginning with an emotional 'excitation', comprising feelings of anger, irritability, or perhaps even happiness. The early stage then gives way to the attack proper, or 'prostration' as Sacks describes it, in which the patient suffers the full-blown physical manifestations of the migraine: nausea, drowsiness, faintness, weakness, and occasionally the agonising vascular headache which is so often associated with an attack. Recovery may occur abruptly (known as *crisis*), or gradually (*lysis*), either over time or during sleep, with some sufferers experiencing a *rebound* stage, in which they have feelings of euphoria and renewed energy.

The classical migraine sufferer will experience some or all of the phenomena present in the common attack, with the addition of two further symptoms during the early prodomal stage: *paraesthesiae* and *migraine hallucinations*. Paraesthesiae is a tingling sensation which may begin in the extremities such as the toes, fingertips or nose, and which may then spread or travel around the body. More common, though arguably more extraordinary and disturbing, are the *scotomata* or *migraine aura* that can invade and disrupt the field of vision. These migrainous hallucinations generally (though not always) take the form of 'blob-like' shapes or geometric patterns. Dr Sacks distinguishes three types or *levels* of migrainous hallucinosis. 'The first is, colloquially, "seeing stars" (phosphenes); the second is the classical expanding spectra or scotoma, with its edge of fortifications; the third – less described, but no less common – consists of rapidly-changing, intricate geometrical patterns. There is a certain tendency for these three levels to occur in this order, the sequence being launched with phosphenes.'[15]

From autobiographical snippets, Hildegard's biographers have attempted to piece together the link between sickness and the mystical experiences that occurred throughout her life. Frances Beer suggests that it was the mystical experiences which invariably came first, and the illness was an unfortunate corollary induced by the strain of the visionary event: 'The very effort involved in keeping visions of such great intensity bottled up would almost inevitably result in headaches and other psychosomatic symptoms.'[16] However, Sabina Flanagan sees in Hildegard's life the patterns of a life-long migraine sufferer.

> Hildegard's description of her health as a child exhibits several features typical of migraine sufferers. They include the early onset of the condition and the picture of her generally 'delicate' constitution. We might surmise that in childhood Hildegard suffered from isolated migraine auras (that is, manifestations not followed by an attack proper) and common migraines or possibly migraine equivalents which she did not connect specifically with her visions. As she reached middle age, however, there was some change in the pattern of her illness, or in her perception of it, which she describes in several different contexts. The simplest possibility is that the earlier mixture of isolated migraine auras and common migraines coalesced to give Hildegard her first experience of a classical migraine. Such shifts in the overall pattern of the disease throughout a sufferer's life are well attested.[17]

Hildegard was always at pains to stress that her visions were *not* dreams. She was always fully awake during her mystical revelations, a fact that rules out hypnogogic or hypnopompic experiences (the dreamlike states at the onset and end of sleep, in which the brain can confuse dreaming with actual events). But what of the visions themselves?

Singer reached his conclusion after examining illustrations in *Scivias*, in which he identified 'scintillating scotomata' or 'phosphenes' of a first-level migraine aura, and indeed a number of the illuminations do seem very likely candidates for artistic representations of migrainous hallucinosis. The most often quoted is the 'Extinguished Stars' (plate 28) or 'The Fall of the Angels' as Hildegard named it. In the illumination, bright stars tumble from the firmament, only to darken and go out in a turbulent, boiling ocean.

> I saw a great star most splendid and beautiful, and with it an exceeding multitude of falling stars which with the star followed southwards... And suddenly they were all annihilated, being turned into coals... and cast into the abyss so that I could see them no more.[18]

Not all of the illuminations, however, can be so readily explained as the 'shooting stars' of the first-level migraine, which transforms into the 'abyss' of the scotoma of the second level. Some have naturalistic and representational qualities, showing detailed images of figures and structures. But when these less explicable illuminations are examined in conjunction with the text that accompanies them, a migrainous interpretation still seems the most likely answer. Flanagan takes for her example the first vision of the third book of *Scivias*, which is illustrated not only by the 'Extinguished Stars' but also by a miniature which depicts:

> ... a bearded male figure, dressed in a blue gown, green mantle, and red and gold cope, sitting on a golden throne with his feet on a red and gold cloud above a set of concentric circles of varying shades of blue It is only with a willing suspension of disbelief that the figure on the throne can be assimilated to a play of scotomata. Yet when we turn to the written description of the vision we find:

> > and then I saw... a round kingly throne on which sat a certain living light of wondrous glory, of such brilliance that I could in no way apprehend him clearly... and from that light seated on the throne there extended a great circle of colour like the dawn. (Scivias, 3, 1)[19]

It is little wonder that the devout Abbess, whose whole adult life had been spent in the environment of the convent, should deduce a religious meaning for her hallucinations. Indeed, it would be all the more improbable if she could have produced any *other* interpretation.

> Invested with this sense of ecstasy, burning with profound theophorous and philosophical significance, Hildegard's visions were instrumental in directing her towards a life of holiness and mysticism. They provide a unique example of the manner in which a physiological event, banal, hateful or meaningless to the vast majority of people, can become, in a privileged consciousness, the substrate of a supreme ecstatic inspiration.[20]

Might it just be possible that some similar form of physiological event could have worked its creative magic on the 'privileged consciousness' of the Voynich illustrator? A visionary explanation of the manuscript has often been discounted because of the lack of identifiable religious imagery of the kind found in the works of Hildegard. However, Singer, Sacks and Flanagan have suggested that Hildegard experienced migrainous hallucinosis, which *she* interpreted as mystical visions, and to which she 'added' a level of Christian iconography. So rather than flatly dismissing such a visionary explanation of the Voynich manuscript, should we, perhaps, be searching its pages for evidence of hallucinosis? Are there any illustrations within its pages that bear the hallmarks of hallucination? It is just possible there are; in one of the least studied and baffling sections of the Voynich manuscript: the 'rosettes'.

Folios 85 and 86 (plates 27, 29 and 30) of the Voynich manuscript stand alone, even in the intriguing world of the Voynich manuscript, through their almost indescribable weirdness; unfolding to reveal abstract 'medallions' that defy logical explanation. Here is an edited version of the description given by Mary D'Imperio (the italics have been added to highlight certain aspects of the illustrations which, as we shall see, may represent identifiable hallucinatory phenomena):

> This elaborate array of circular medallions covers several segments of a large, multiply-folded page. It has received little or no study or mention by students; this may be partly because

its complexity and bizarre character boggles the mind already overburdened by the 'queerness' to the modern eye of so much else in the manuscript...

There are nine *elaborate circular designs*, in three rows of three each. The central design in the middle row is larger than the others, and contains six pharmaceutical 'jars' arranged in an *oval pattern with stars in the centre*...One medallion shows a structure like *a castle and other buildings around its periphery; the castle has a high, crenelated wall and a tall central tower*...In the other two corners [of the folio] are *sun faces surrounded by wavy rays*. Some of the medallions have *petal-like arrangements of rays filled with stars*...Many medallions are provided with curious structures like bundles of *pipes or gun barrels clustered around the periphery of their circular outlines* (plate 27).[21]

Compare the above description of the Voynich rosettes with Hildegard's third vision from book one of the *Scivias*, a startling and apparently migrainous vision known as 'The Universe in the Shape of an Egg' or simply 'The Cosmic Egg' (plate 31). It consists of concentric oval rings; the outermost of which is a band of petal-like flames, immediately inside which is an area of turbulence containing, as Hildegard describes it, 'dark fire'. Within this is a region of incandescent stars which fill almost the whole of the oval apart from a central globe, which itself contains a white mountain. Hildegard interpreted this revelation as showing the purifying and consoling power of God, surrounding the redemptive rock of faith that cannot be tainted by the powers of evil. To a modern viewer it seems to be one of the most obvious candidates for a direct representation of migraine aura, and also bears a striking similarity with the rosettes of the Voynich manuscript. Could both 'The Cosmic Egg' and the Voynich manuscript be composed of visual phenomena which are today recognised medically as elements of classical migraine hallucinosis?

Take also this quote from Hubert Airy in 1870, quoted by Oliver Sacks, of his personal experience of a migraine aura: 'When it was at its height it seemed like a fortified town with bastions all around it, these bastions being coloured most gorgeously...All the interior of the fortification, so to speak, was boiling and rolling around in a most wonderful manner as if it was some thick liquid all alive.'[22] Could Airy's 'fortified town with bastions' be the same as D'Imperio's description of 'a structure like a castle and other buildings around its periphery' with a 'high, crenelated wall'? Might the 'boiling and rolling' interior of Airy's castle be the same as the 'wavy rays' of the Voynich medallions?

Perhaps, then, we can suggest a possible link between the disorientating auras of a migraine attack and the rosettes of the Voynich manuscript, which have so far eluded any logical interpretation. But this is only one small part of the manuscript. Does some form of hallucinosis offer an explanation for any of the other illustrations? Certainly there could be many candidates for the first-level aura of dancing phosphenes or shooting stars in the Voynich manuscript. The astronomical section is awash with stellar objects; the circular diagrams filled with tiny stars could, with only a slight stretch of the imagination, be an attempt to represent the 'dance of brilliant stars, sparks, flashes and simple geometric forms across the visual field'.[23] As the aura progressed to the second level of scintillating scotomata with its characteristic fortification outline, might it not approach something resembling Newbold's spiral nebula, with its central 'blob-like' area filled with tiny stars enclosed within a crenellated border? Sacks also relates a case in which the sufferer visualised the progression of phosphenes as a procession of small white animals. Could our little 'naked nymphs', frolicking in their green baths with architectural and corrugated edges, be another attempt to express in diagrammatic form a hallucinatory episode? Finally, what of the third-level migraine auras, consisting of rapidly changing patterns and networks of geometrical shapes? Surely there is no evidence of this in the Voynich manuscript? We will conclude this section with a further quote from Dr Sacks, and leave the reader to decide if this is reminisicent of any Voynich illustrations:

> Sometimes these networks have a circular or crystalline appearance, and may grow visibly, sometimes with sudden jerks, like frost on a windowpane or *primitive plants*. Sometimes there are radically symmetrical forms like *flowers* or *pinecones*, continually unfolding in a constant revelation of themselves [authors' italics].[24]

If mental illness (such as schizophrenic episodes) or migrainous hallucinosis might present themselves as possible stimuli
for the creation of at least some of the Voynich manuscript,
might there be other 'psychical' phenomena which could have
a bearing on our investigation? Oliver Sacks relates a number
of case studies of 'incontinent reminiscence', in which long-
lost memories return, unbidden, to the waking and fully conscious mind. Such reminiscence and experiential hallucinosis
are usually the product of thrombosis (stroke) or infarction in
the temporal lobes – 'those parts of the brain associated with
the central representation of sounds and music, and with the
evocation of complex experiences and scenes'.[25] Could our
medieval illustrator have been influenced by this altogether
more debilitating form of hallucination brought about by a
seizure, after which, perhaps, they were recreating in the
Voynich manuscript an impressionistic representation of
earlier documents they might have seen or even worked upon,
images of which now flooded back into their present consciousness in an unwanted torrent? Or what of autistic
'savants', of which the popular media have made so much in
recent years? Sufferers of severe autism are barely capable of
'normal' social function, yet are endowed with prodigious
artistic and representational skills, with which they can recreate detailed and highly accurate drawings of complex subject
matter after only a single, brief viewing of the original. Might
the illustrator of the Voynich manuscript fall into this category; an unfortunate soul reproducing a replica of some once-
seen document, perhaps a standard medieval herbal, of which
they had no real comprehension, only a compunction to
reproduce in minute detail, thereby creating a form of script
and set of illustrations that bear a superficial similarity to
what they observed, but none of the meaning?

So perhaps we begin to see other, less rational explanations for
the mind-bending drawings in the manuscript. But what of the
Voynichese 'language' and text? Are there any examples of linguistic outpourings that could be the basis of the unreadable
script? There are a few, and one in particular, a mystical religious phenomenon that continues to this day, is observable
and open to scrutiny. It is glossolalia, more commonly known
as 'speaking in tongues', and is defined as the paranormal

ability to speak in another, usually unknown or mystical language. Some biblical scholars detect the presence of this phenomenon in the pronouncements of Old Testament prophets, but in its recognised form, glossolalia is firmly rooted in the Christian era. The first manifestation of speaking in tongues is recorded in the Book of Acts, when, on the Day of Pentecost, ten days after Jesus' ascension to heaven, the disciples were filled with the power of the Holy Spirit and found themselves able to speak to all those around them in their own languages; languages, moreover, of which the disciples had no previous knowledge. This is, technically, xenolalia – the ability to speak in a recognisable foreign language hitherto unknown to the speaker – and was a miraculous gift, 'charisma', bestowed upon the disciples to communicate the Christian message. However, as that message spread, this gift transformed into glossolalia, or the uttering of an unknown language, supposedly that of God and the angels; so that in the New Testament book of First Corinthians we find Paul advising this fledgling Christian flock on the use and importance of this 'gift'.

Glossolalia, as a usual practice within the wider Christian Church, diminished after the early centuries and became the tool of visionaries and mystics, used for prophecy rather than everyday worship. David Christie-Murray, in his exhaustive study of the subject, *Voices from the Gods*, outlines a number of reasons for this decline. Certainly such charismatic and vocal behaviour was not always in the best interest of the Christian community in those early years, drawing attention to the practitioners at times when persecution was a regular and very real occurrence. But there was also an influence from within the Church; a change in emphasis in the expression of Christian faith away from the charismatic in favour of the 'ethical'. Christie-Murray suggests such shifts happen in many religions, marking a departure from the 'gnosis' or self-knowing form of spiritual experience found in young faiths, towards more sober, ordered and hierarchical forms of worship. Another influence may have been the desire to distance the Christian faith from pagan religions in which prophetic babblings and trance-induced chantings were also common, coupled with a suspicion that speaking in tongues was just as likely to be the work of evil spirits or demonic possession as it was to be a divine gift.

With the Reformation, and its emphasis on a personal relationship with God, bypassing the formal structures of
Catholic doctrines and priestly intermediaries, glossolalia
began to occur once more. It was common among the
Protestant Huguenots, who carried this gift with them when
they fled France, and may have been responsible for its appearance in the non-conformist sects in England. It was known in
Cromwell's time, and was subsequently taken to America by
the Shakers, only to decline again after the period known as
'Mother Ann's Work'. Yet by 1900, this seemingly irrepress-
ible phenomenon had surfaced again in the rural southern
states of America, in a number of new churches calling themselves Pentecostals in commemoration of the original miraculous ability of the Apostles on the Day of Pentecost. By the
1960s, speaking in tongues was occurring in some Protestant
and even Catholic congregations, and it has been encouraged
further by the rise of the TV evangelists in the US. Glossolalia
today is a divisive issue within the worldwide Christian community; those who profess a charismatic style of worship
deem it a vital element of their faith, demonstrating that they
are 'spirit-filled' and truly possessed by the power of the Holy
Ghost, while conservative churches are inclined to be more
sceptical.

Yet apart from the sacred sheets of the Shaker communities,
and possibly the received *carmina* of St Hildegard, glossolalia
is an oral expression of religious fervour which rarely achieves
a concrete, written manifestation. Indeed, in the state of
heightened transcendental, often trance-like religious experience that usually accompanies glossolalia, it would seem difficult to write *anything* down. However, as has been discussed
earlier in this book, many Voynich scholars believe the lack of
corrections or errors suggest the manuscript may well have
been copied, possibly even by a team of scribes. Could the
manuscript therefore be the work of some isolated religious
community, such as was described in the analysis of Captain
Currier's 'multiple handwriting theory' in chapter 5, with a
dedicated brethren faithfully transcribing the glossolalic utter-
ances of their charismatic leader? Could the Voynichese script
be an attempt to set down the divinely inspired pronouncements in a language specifically designed for this purpose,
in the style of Dee and Kelley's Enochian? As D'Imperio

states 'The possibility cannot be ruled out that a made-up language of this type underlies the Voynich script, devised by an exceptional individual under the power of religious inspiration.'[26]

There is another related glossolalic phenomenon, however, that requires neither a team of copyists nor an agreed synthetic language to record its ethereal wisdom. As the Shaker communities of North America were dying out in the 1850s, a new interest in all things mystical was gripping America and Europe. This was the birth of Spiritualism; the attempt to communicate with the souls of the dead or the realm of the spirits through seances and mediums. As well as vocal pronouncements from the afterlife and strange rappings on Victorian parlour tables, the spirits found other ways of passing on their wisdom, such as Ouija boards, automatic writing (in which a pencil grasped by a medium is guided across a sheet of paper by spirits), and xenolalia or glossolalia. In one of the most famous and well-recorded cases of such communication, the medium received not only the power of speech in other languages, but also the ability to write.

Hélène Smith was the pseudonym of Catherine Elise Müller, a French-speaking Swiss woman from Geneva. Born in 1861 to a Hungarian merchant father and a 'mediumistic' mother, by the age of thirty-one Hélène had begun to receive spirit messages via typtology or table tapping. With the aid of a spirit guide named Leopold, her mediumistic powers increased, as did her fame, until in January 1894 Hélène announced herself to be the reincarnation of Marie Antoinette. This marked the beginning of a ten-year period in which Hélène was to produce four 'romantic cycles' of seances: the Royal Cycle, stemming from her experiences as the former French Queen; the Oriental Cycle, in which Hélène became Simandini, the daughter of a fourteenth-century Arab sheik; the Religious Cycle, during which she painted religious tableaux after experiencing a vision of Christ; and most extraordinarily, the Martian Cycle. This began in October 1894 when Hélène was visited by the spirit Alexis Mirbel, the dead son of a woman attending the seance. Having departed this world, Alexis must have been somewhat surprised to find himself on the planet Mars, whence, in 1896, he began to communicate to Hélène in Martian. During the

Hélène Smith's 'Martian' script

Oriental Cycle, while possessed by Simandini, Hélène had spoken a few words of Hindustani, but her Martian revelations were altogether more impressive. Over a period of eighteen months the Martian language developed a distinct vocabulary and linguistic patterns, until finally Hélène received a complete Martian alphabet with which she would eventually write forty messages from Alexis – now living under the Martian name of Esenale. Luckily for posterity, these Cycles were observed and recorded in objective detail by Thomas Flournoy, Professor of Psychology at the University of Geneva. In 1899 he published *From India to the Planet Mars*, in which he found convincing psychological explanations for Hélène's supposedly paranormal experiences.

Thanks to the amount of time he was able to spend with the medium herself, and his careful observations of the seances, Flournoy was eventually able to provide a rational explanation for almost all the strange phenomena that Hélène produced. In the case of the Princess Simandini, Flournoy began his investigation by attempting to ascertain whether such a person had ever existed. Not surprisingly, he was unable to find any real historical counterpart for Simandini, or for her supposed husband Sivrouka. Yet how was he to explain the xenolalic episodes in which Hélène recounted detailed information about her previous existence?

> Then one day Flournoy came across a six-volume history of ancient India written by De Marles. Lo and behold it contained all of the information found in Hélène's oriental fantasies. Although De Marles was considered to be a very unreliable historian, it was clear this was the source of Hélène's information.[27]

To investigate the xenolalia, Flournoy submitted examples of Simandini's language to oriental experts who confirmed it was a hotchpotch of Sanskrit and invented words. What little actual Sanskrit there was could, according to Flournoy, have been picked up subconsciously even from the quickest and most cursory look at a Sanskrit grammar. Further evidence in support of this thesis was the poor quality of Hélène's pronunciation, which suggested she had read the words in a book and never heard them spoken.

Moving on to the Martian language, Flournoy also observed the development and subsequent use of the Martian language over a period of years, and concluded it was the product of a gradual, incremental autosuggestive process in which Hélène was more or less able to induce the visions necessary for the creation of glossolalic episodes. Of the language itself:

> Flournoy was able to analyse the syntax and trace much of the vocabulary to its origins. Martian was simply French with sounds and letters changed, each French word being replaced by another. For example, the Martian for 'Quand reviendra-t-il?' was 'Keri berimir-m-hed?'[28]

When confronted with this, Hélène began to produce other extraterrestrial languages – Ultramartian, Uranian and Lunar – along with outlandish and lurid descriptions of the various planets visited. Again these languages arrived first as auditory hallucinations, only to develop over time until Hélène could produce them via automatic writing, and once again Flournoy was able to demonstrate their basis in simplistic twists on Hélène's native French. 'Ultramartian was a more puerile language than Martian and Uranian even more of an eeny-meeny-miny-mo type.'[29] As Flournoy continued to produce rational explanations for Hélène's visions and spirit possessions, there could be only one inevitable outcome. In the summer of 1901, it was made clear to Professor Flournoy that he was no longer welcome at the seances of Hélène Smith.

In his book on the subject, Christie-Murray produces a long list of the supposed causes of speaking in tongues that have been put forward over the years. These include neurosis, auto-suggestion, self-hypnosis, hysteria, catalepsy, schizophrenia, disease or derangement of the nervous system and even mob rule or mass hysteria. Freudian psychologists see it as an out-pouring of the repressed inner child, whilst to Jungians it is an expression of the collective unconscious. Whatever the root cause may be, and this could be different for every individual who has ever experienced it, what concerns us in connection with the Voynich manuscript is not *what* compulsion leads to the creation of entirely new and unknown languages, but *how* these languages are created.

The baffling phenomenon of xenolalia is a product of what Flournoy termed 'cryptomnesia' (meaning literally 'hidden memory'), and is the power of the mind to recall things of which there is no conscious memory. The ability of the sub-conscious to unknowingly store experiential data, which might then be retrieved unbidden and at unexpected times, has been linked to other anomalies of the memory such as hypnotic regression to past lives, and 'false memory syndrome', in which people believe they have uncovered memories of childhood abuse repressed by their conscious mind, but which are in fact their own confabulation. Hélène Smith's fragmentary and admittedly limited ability to speak Hindustani came from a brief and long-forgotten glance at a phrase book.

Glossolalia seems a better candidate for the kind of processes that might have been involved in the creation of the Voynich manuscript. Throughout the years he spent assessing Hélène Smith, Flournoy never doubted her motivation, observing that for her, the visitations seemed genuine. Flournoy suggested that the creation of the languages was actually the product of 'secondary personalities' which were accessed during the self-induced trance-like state of the seances. The ability to devise such languages, though an act of linguistic skill in its own right, was outweighed by Hélène's abilities to summon them up and speak them during the seances. 'Flournoy was impressed not with her creations but with her extraordinary feats of memory.'[30]

So we have seen that it is eminently possible for an individual, either through some form of altered mental state, often perceived as a religious or spiritual intercession, or through an almost wilful release of subconscious memories and suggestions, to create spoken and written forms that bear many of the hallmarks of true languages. Once again, we have no way of knowing if a variant glossolalia was instrumental in the creation of the Voynichese script, but it now, perhaps, seems an option that must be given some serious consideration. It might also go some way to explaining the odd, repetitive nature of the Voynichese language, which could be seen as the creation of the same psychological processes which give rise to magical chanting or mystical incantations. But what if the Voynich illustrations and language were not the product of an involuntarily changed perception, rather a deliberate and conscious attempt to create a meaningless babble? Our image of the anonymous creator of the manuscript shifts, as we shall see in the next chapter, from that of a merely misguided or delusional individual to something altogether darker and corrupt.

→ 8 ←

SHAMS OLD AND NEW

For all those mediums who truly believe in their spiritual gifts, there must be others for whom the mystical messages are just an act of controlled imagination, a conscious creation or improvisational performance to capitalise on the gullibility of unquestioning believers. The world is full of unscrupulous individuals always on the lookout for their next credulous victim, and it would be wrong to assume this is a recent phenomenon. In light of this we must force ourselves to accept the possibility that the Voynich manuscript might be the product of a deliberate attempt to dupe or hoodwink. Could the fact that so many years of study have produced so few results be evidence of duplicitous hands at work? In other words, could the Voynich manuscript be a hoax?

Others, as we shall see shortly, have toyed with this idea, but Michael Barlow in his article in *Cryptologia* has pointed out that, despite a sense of coherence in the Voynich manuscript, no experts from the fields of botany, astronomy, astrology, pharmacy, cryptography, or art and book historians can adduce anything other than nonsense in it from their perspective.[1] Barlow's line of thought is clear: some agency or other has conspired to create a manuscript that deliberately conveys a tantalising sense of meaningfulness and integrity without allowing any evidence of its actual origins or the relevance of its component sections to become clear; the sort of artifact that would become celebrated, attracting and teasing a wide group of interested parties motivated to unlock its secrets for the pure pleasure of cerebral stimulation plus an ensuing fame, not to mention the financial value that would accrue to it. Put bluntly, he believed the Voynich manuscript to be a forgery or a hoax, the difference between the two concepts depending on the cynical monetary motive of the former or the whimsical 'joke' value of the latter.

Barlow was not the first to make this suggestion. D'Imperio writes, 'I could accept a finding that the manuscript was a hoax or a forgery', unlike other doubters of its falsity who maintain that 'it just doesn't look like a hoax'.[2] But as Robert Brumbaugh, son of the cryptographer Robert S. Brumbaugh, adroitly pointed out in a recent TV interview, 'a good hoax isn't supposed to look like a hoax'.[3] D'Imperio quotes John Tiltman, who 'expresses his considered confidence in its authenticity', noting that it is not 'the ravings or doodlings of a lunatic, nor do I believe it is just a hoax – it is too elaborate and consistent for either'.[4]

The extraordinary elaboration of the manuscript in style and length is indeed impressive, involving a great deal of concentrated work; so much so that even as far back as 1639, George Baresch reasoned that the creative effort would only be worth it if there were something of genuine importance to say. It is, of course, just as easy to maintain that the effort and elaboration are precisely intended to make it appear of importance. The trick for a hoaxster is to provide material for those who want to believe in its significance, who, whatever their objective detachment, harbour a faith that clouds their judgement.

Hitler's 'forged diaries', for example, attest not only to the extraordinary effort and gamble in producing sixty-two volumes, but the inventiveness in establishing the scam; in this case the notion that they were flown from Berlin just before his suicide and recovered from the crashed plane by farmers. Those who were taken in by this magnificent ploy were duped by the potentially huge publishing returns to be gained by providing the public with subject matter of gripping importance.

A more contemporary example of an expert forger is that of Mark Hofmann, whose speciality was to trade on the gullibility of the Mormon Church. The Church was founded on the spurious 'Book of Mormon' supposedly based on the golden plates etched in hieroglyphics dug up by Joseph Smith in New York state in the 1820s. Smith claimed that an angel named 'Moroni' had guided him to the plates (which later inexplicably vanished), but nevertheless, with the aid of a 'show-stone', enabled him to translate them and reveal the history of a pre-Columbian people descended from ancient Israelites, visited and instructed by Jesus.

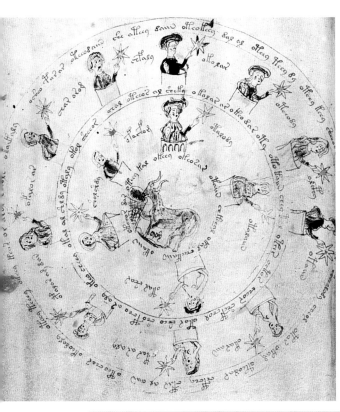

21. Folio 71v, 'Taurus'

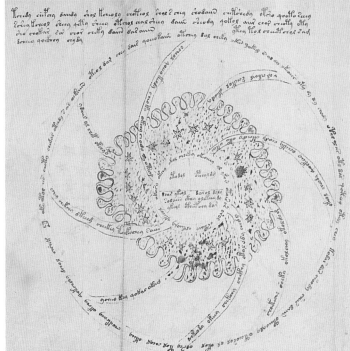

22. Folio 68v3, Newbold's 'Great Nebula of Andromeda'

23. Folios 67r1 and 67r2

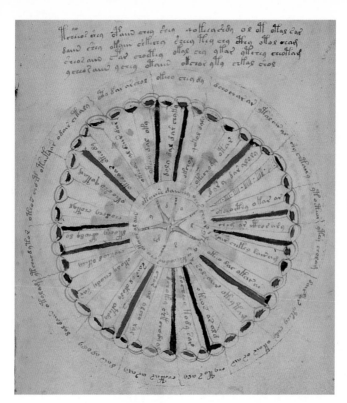

24. Folio 69r

25. Folio 57v

26. *Shaker sacred sheet*

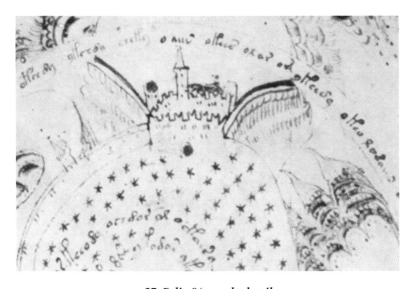

27. *Folio 86, castle detail*

ϚEϚ
hom
ſump
abaſ
hom
vuſ q
ñſuɩ
nanc
nari homo ppr̃ ũſgreſſione leg
di. cũ deberem ẽ uɩſta ⱥ ſũ inuɩ
ñ qd̃ di creatura ſũ ɩpſí gr̃a. qu
me eɩ̃a ſaluabɩt. uɩdi adorient
ⱥ ecce ɩlluc conſpexɩ uelut lapide
unɩſ rorũ integrũ inĩſe laɩru
nɩſ atꝗ; alrɩrudinɩſ. habenr̃ ꝼer
colore. ⱥ ſup ɩpſum candɩd̃a nul
ac ſup ea poſɩrũ regalem rronum
rundũ. inquo ſedebar quid̃a uɩ
lucɩduſ mɩrabilɩſ gl̃e. ranreꝗ; clar
rɩſ ur nullaren̂ eũ pſpɩcue poſſe
ɩcuerɩ. habenſ q̃ɩ in pecrore ſuo
mũ nɩgrũ ⱥ luruleirũ. ranrꝗ la
rudɩnɩſ ur alɩcuɩ magnɩ homun
pecruſ ẽ. cɩrcũd̃arũ lapɩdɩb; pcɩo
arꝗ; margarɩrɩſ. Ʇr de ɩpſo lucɩd
ſedenre ɩrrono prendebar magn
cɩrculuſ aureɩ colorɩſ ur aurora. c
amplɩrudɩne nullõ cõphendeɩ
porɩu. guanſ ab orienre ad ſepren
nẽ ⱥ ad occɩdenre arꝗ; ad merɩdɩe

28. Hildegard of Bingen, 'Extinguished Stars'

29. Folio 86v4

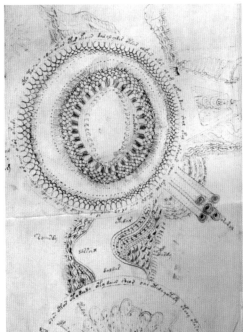

30. Folios 85/86, rosette with pipes

31. *Hildegard of Bingen, 'The Cosmic Egg'*

The yawning credibility gap in all this allowed Hofmann, using his profession as historical book dealer, to embroider the story with fake religious documents that *undermined* the faith, and were consequently bought up by the Church itself in order to conceal their alleged truths. So adept was he in discovering lost 'treasures' that he was nicknamed by other dealers 'the Mormon Indiana Jones'. One of his major secular literary coups, as recounted by Simon Worrall in *The Poet and the Murderer*, was to fabricate a poem by Emily Dickinson, using his own paper and specially aged inks, which was bought by a New England library via Sotheby's for nearly $25,000. Hofmann had written on the back of the poem, 'Aunt Emily', cleverly adding a touch of naivety to augment the fact that her life was surrounded by myth and conjecture.[5]

A far more heinous recent forgery, exposed in 2000, centred on the mummified body of a Persian princess that came to be housed in the National Museum of Pakistan, valued at $11 million. This most elaborate of frauds fooled many authorities who accepted the embalming, the gold mask, the cuneiform writing on the coffin and stone sarcophagus that had been uncovered in Pakistan as a result of an earthquake. Detailed examination later revealed that there were errors in the writing in particular. The grisly truth emerged that a woman had probably been murdered to bring about the hoax. Curator Asma Ibrahim expressed a common sentiment when confronted with the reality of a forgery. 'I didn't want to admit that "she" was a fake. Maybe I was emotionally attached to her.' What is perhaps less common in a case of forgery is the number of conspirators that must have been involved in the scam, making it more at risk of discovery, but clearly where there is a huge pay-off this is seen as acceptable.

These few examples of hoax or forgeries are the merest tip of a huge volume of solid, well-executed and elaborate schemes upon which many an expert's credentials have foundered and sunk. When an artifact like the Voynich manuscript survives and defeats nearly a century of intense scrutiny by professionals from many fields, it is not churlish or untrusting to look for devious goings-on.

As we have seen in chapter 5, Brumbaugh, after his partial decryption using his 'numerological box cipher', suggested that the dubious quality of the text he had uncovered might indicate the presence of a less-than-honourable motive behind the creation of the Voynich manuscript. Accepting that there might be another level of encryption yet to be discovered (though apparently never questioning the veracity of his own supposed cipher system), Brumbaugh began to suspect that much of the text was dummy, 'filler' material, and had no discernible meaning whatsoever. Such dummy text was designed to 'pad out' the book between the occasional piece of easily decipherable script, which itself was placed in the manuscript with the express purpose of keeping a would-be solver intrigued by the possibility that a full decryption was almost within their grasp.

According to Brumbaugh, just such a 'false' clue, designed to mislead a hopeful cryptanalyst, was to be found on the last page of the Voynich manuscript; the same page, no less, that Newbold thought contained the vital key sequence. After careful examination, Brumbaugh read the opening of the first line of the 'key' thus: MICHI CON OLADA BA (compared to Newbold's: MICHITON OLADABAS). Ignoring the opening letters, Brumbaugh suggested that the CON...BA was a simple anagram, the rearrangement of which produced BACON. Next, using a standard Caesar shift cipher, OLADA becomes RODGD, giving us RODGD BACON, or 'Roger Bacon'. Brumbaugh was not returning to the fallacies supported by Newbold and Feely, but was convinced that this easily decipherable clue was created to suggest a *false* attribution to Bacon. Brumbaugh's conclusion was that the manuscript was a deliberate fabrication, designed to convince a potential buyer of its importance and value thanks to its thirteenth-century origin.

But who, then, was the real author? From his analysis of the manuscript as a whole, Brumbaugh had concluded it was a product of the sixteenth century, with the various sections either copied from earlier originals or freshly written. And if one is searching for a candidate for a confidence trickster and hoaxer in the sixteenth century, one need not look much further than Edward Kelley, scryer and confederate of John Dee. Searching for corroborative evidence to support his theory, it was Brumbaugh who first suggested the connection between the 630 gold ducats mentioned in Dee's diary of

1586, and the 600 ducats supposedly paid for the manuscript by Emperor Rudolf as mentioned in the Marcus Marci letter. Brumbaugh's theory was now falling into place. At the centre are Dee and Kelley, travelling around Europe in the hope of convincing rich and credulous noblemen of their alchemical and spiritual abilities. Knowing of Rudolf's fascination with all things esoteric, they arrive in Prague in possession of a precious volume, supposedly the work of Bacon, and written entirely in cipher. It was, of course, completely their own creation, with just enough decipherable material to convince Emperor Rudolf and his experts that not only was this the work of Roger Bacon, but that it would also be possible to decrypt the remainder of the manuscript. Having swallowed their story, hook, line and sinker, the Emperor buys the manuscript from Dee and Kelley for a sum of around 600 ducats.

The possibility that the Voynich manuscript could be a historical forgery had first been mooted in 1951 by Brigadier Tiltman (though, as we have seen, he later rejected this theory as being 'rather improbable'), but Brumbaugh was the first to produce 'evidence' to support his theory. There are, however, a number of problems with Brumbaugh's argument. Although he never made a categorical accusation against Dee and Kelley, in Brumbaugh's theory they still remain the most likely candidates for a sixteenth-century fabrication. Yet from what we know of John Dee, was he really con-artist material? Intelligent though he certainly was, and equipped with enough cunning and self-serving acumen to survive the religious and political slings and arrows of late Tudor fortunes, he was also possessed of a naivety and credulity that made him such easy prey for the likes of Kelley. Let us not forget that Dee, scientist, mathematician and spy, also believed in angelic commands divined in a crystal ball; commands, no less, that forced him to burn his books and allow another man to sleep with his wife. Dee seems more like the gullible punter than the deliberate trickster. Furthermore, one inevitably feels a slight uneasiness with the quality of Brumbaugh's original decipherment of the Voynich manuscript. Brigadier Tiltman, considering Brumbaugh's numerological box cipher system and his resultant decryptions, commented: 'All this is so ambiguous that it can only be justified by the production of a great deal of confirmatory evidence, but he supplies hardly any evidence at all and I remain quite unconvinced.'[6] However appealing his theory may be, it is built upon the shaky foundations of a vague and finally unlikely decipherment; and for this reason we must treat the Brumbaugh hypothesis with some caution.

A variant on the Dee and Kelley hoax theory has been developed recently by Voynich scholar Tim Mervyn, whose uncle, Peter Long, was a senior figure in British Signal Intelligence with an interest in the Voynich manuscript stretching back over many years. Long's position at GCHQ in Cheltenham, England, brought him into contact with his American Intelligence counterparts, such as Mary D'Imperio and Prescott Currier, who shared his passion for the mysterious manuscript. After Long's death in 1999, Tim Mervyn gained access to his uncle's archive of Voynich-related material and transatlantic correspondence, thus beginning his own fascination with the subject. Mervyn has produced a highly detailed and exhaustively researched theory in an, as yet, unpublished manuscript, which he kindly made available to the authors of this book. Mervyn refers to his theory as **K:D:P**, taken from the initials of the three main characters in his dramatis personae: Kelley, Dee and Pucci. What follows is a brief summation of the labyrinthine trail of clues he uncovered.

Mervyn also rejects the connection Brumbaugh made between the 630 ducats mentioned in Dee's diary and the 600 reportedly paid by Rudolf for the manuscript. As noted in chapter 3, Dee and Kelley had already left Prague and were living in Trebon at the time Dee made the diary entry. Mervyn reiterates how unlikely it would have been to expect an Emperor to *pay* for a precious manuscript. He suggests it would have been more usual to present a volume as a gift in the hope of future patronage and favour; as indeed Dee did, presenting Rudolf with a copy of the Monas Hieroglyphica during their brief meeting in September 1584. The greatest departure from Brumbaugh's hypothesis, however, comes with the role of Dee himself, whom Mervyn sees as an innocent dupe at the mercy of a conniving Kelley.

In February 1589, when he and Kelley finally parted company in Trebon, Dee recorded in his diary: 'I delivered to Mr Kelley the powder, the books, the glass, and the bone...' These unnamed books, suggests Mervyn, provided the raw materials from which Kelley would create the Voynich manuscript, and included the works of angelic writing such as the *Book of Enoch* and the *48 Great Calls* that Dee and Kelley had produced during their 'actions' between 1583 and 1584. Furthermore, according to Mervyn, Kelley also had in his possession at the time of his departure a quantity of vellum containing illustrations by Dee. These drawings, which now make up the botanical and balneological sections of the Voynich manuscript, were originally intended by Dee to be part of a humorous tribute to the then Holy Roman Emperor Maximilian II, father of Rudolf. Dee had been treated with great kindness by Maximilian when he visited him in the year 1563, and proposed to present him with a compendium of topics that he thought would amuse the Emperor, such as a fantastical herbal and the 'mildly erotic' naked nymphs. The work, however, was never completed, and Maximilian died in 1575. Dee held on to the unfinished set of illustrations, perhaps hoping one day to present them to Rudolf, until in 1589, so Mervyn's theory goes, they were taken by Kelley. It is also possible that some of the biological section could have been devised as a separate tribute to their previous patron, Count Albrecht Laski.

The erstwhile crystal-ball gazer or 'scryer' was now the brightest star in the alchemical firmament. As Dee made his slow progress back to England, Kelley found wealth and favour at the court of Emperor Rudolf, and saw no reason to leave Bohemia. It was just before this sudden and somewhat surprising ascendancy that Kelley, according to Mervyn, created the Voynich manuscript. In this endeavour Kelley was aided by that other self-serving and dubious character, Francesco Pucci: emissary of the Papal Nuncio, probable spy and double agent, and the only other witness to the famous book-burning incident.

This multiplicity of scribes (Dee, Kelley and Pucci would have been involved in the creation of the manuscript at different times) could explain the **A** and **B** hands observed by Captain Currier. Mervyn agrees with Currier, identifying at least three handwriting styles. But whereas Brigadier Tiltman, a contemporary of Currier, saw the work of more than one scribe as evidence that the manuscript could not be a forgery, Mervyn interprets this fact in totally the opposite way.

Mervyn also claims some success in deciphering the manuscript, believing the language to be the product of a simple
substitution cipher, in which letters of the Latin alphabet are
translated into the fabricated angelic script we know today as
Voynichese. Mervyn deduced his Latin/Voynichese equivalents by a careful analysis of the frequencies of the Latin characters in the *48 Great Calls*. Decrypted material from the first
folio (recto) of the Voynich manuscript, representing Currier
hand **A**, is the work of Dee himself, part of his attempt to
create a mystical book as instructed by the spirit Ave on 26
June 1584, which was to become part of the *48 Great Calls*.
The decrypted plain text reads not unlike the sort of
glossolalic material discussed in the previous chapter, and
contains, according to Mervyn, garbled references to classical
mythology. Here is a sample of the decipherment:

leus gvia cciom rom gia cod rod rod com red
go rod goles cga cra lom roleus go crox
aro bria roceis gio zgod lalal pa leipa
abo god gi colgia hieda leteis leis valt
lrem gpeus oceum ria mra zobod podt ldocbe
goc rom ria leis via
obod leius

Within these few lines Mervyn selects *gia*, *bria roceis* and *ria*
as being suggestive of names from Greek legend. *Gia* could be
'Gaia' or 'Ge', the Earth goddess, whilst *ria* recalls 'Rhea', the
Titaness and daughter of Gaia. The words *bria roceis*, if run
together, are not unlike 'Briareos', one of the monstrous
creatures known as 'Hecatoncheires'.

What we appear to have is a sixteenth-century example of
'stream of consciousness' writing. Although acting under different constraints, John Dee is writing a work that comes
closest in literary terms to James Joyce's *Finnegans Wake*!
Instructed to 'think' of names of God and angels, Dee is only
able to come up with the names of the early Greek divinities.
(Mervyn, p. 484)

By 1589, when Kelley and Pucci were putting together the
final version of the Voynich manuscript, they added extra

pages to produce a volume worthy of a prospective patron. This resulted in new illustrated material (identified by Mervyn as the less polished drawings of the astrological section), and the unillustrated latter parts of the manuscript. Decryptions of this Currier **B** text show, in Mervyn's opinion, a distinctly different character to Dee's writings from the first folio: lacking the classical references but now with traces of a natural Gaelic tongue. In a sample from folio 83, Mervyn produces the decryption:

> *teus ruca gua nocila gila odla*
> *todrila rua nola citi odla*
> *tocula nocula noca teims*
> *birila nobrila ocula dla*

In this extract, Mervyn identifies the second line as being close to the modern Irish '*Ta drioghladh rua nola citl*' ('red-brown oil is distilling from a kettle'), which is redolent not only of Gaelic origins, but also has the whiff of alchemy about it.

> Although Kelley was not *speaking* in tongues, but writing down the material, I suspect he went through phases where inspiration was at a minimum. In these periods he would repeat short sections of highly repetitive monosyllabic material. (Perhaps he was mentally speaking in tongues.) I suspect that this explains those sections in the manuscript that intrigued Currier and other statisticians. (Mervyn, p. 490)

What did Kelley do with his fabulous creation? Mervyn believes it was most probably presented to Emperor Rudolf, either in April or May 1589, upon Kelley's triumphant return to Prague. Although a massive creative undertaking (even if the task was made easier by the use of Dee's illustrations and Pucci's scribing), the fabrication of the Voynich manuscript would have been a sensible investment of time and energy for Kelley. His burgeoning reputation may have been based on his skills as an alchemist, but Kelley must have been only too aware of the pressing need to find other ways of impressing his patrons. Knowing, as we do in our modern scientific age, of the impossibility of alchemy, one must assume that

Kelley's ability to transmute base metal into gold had more to do with prestidigitation than the philosopher's stone. Not only was there the danger of his acts of legerdemain being discovered. The continual need to purchase the gold, which would later miraculously appear during the alchemical 'experiments', must have become prohibitively expensive for Kelley. Far better, surely, to cobble together some seemingly arcane but essentially meaningless tome with which to impress a credulous emperor, than watch your ill-gotten gains returning to Rudolf's coffers in the form of 'transmuted' alchemical gold. And what of Kelley himself? Mirroring the history of his extraordinary creation, his fortunes were to fluctuate over the following years in a roller-coaster ride from wealth and success to imprisonment; before he eventually disappeared from the pages of history into legend and myth.

Anyone wishing to examine Mervyn's theory in more detail will sadly have to wait until his manuscript is published in full. Until such time as his research and decipherments are made available to a wider audience, the authors of this book will refrain from passing comment on the hypothesis, save to say that it adds one more fascinating and tantalising lead in the story of the Voynich manuscript.

So we have two different yet related hoax theories, both centring on the colourful, amoral charlatan Edward Kelley. But let us now return to Barlow's hoax theory, which puts forward another, even more surprising candidate for author of the manuscript. An author who, though born centuries after Kelley, shares with him a life of adventure, espionage, danger and dark secrets.

Although Barlow was not alone in suggesting the possibility that the Voynich manuscript was a hoax, or more accurately a forgery intended to raise money, he was probably, however, the first to seriously suggest a new contender for fraud – Wilfrid Voynich himself. If we shoulder the mantle of wary museum-buyer of exhibits, or head of fraud squad operations, the timeworn *modus operandi* in such cases is to investigate 'motive, ability and opportunity'.

It is inescapably true that Voynich wrestled with financial problems over much of the forty-year period from his arrival as a refugee in London in 1890 to his death in the US in 1930.

The establishment of his antiquarian book empire from the turn of the century until the First World War may well have been a golden interlude. He was certainly penniless in 1896, and although living graciously in the US (if his hotel letter-heads are anything to go by), he was badly in debt as demonstrated by correspondence to his friends, the Levetus family back in England (where he stayed at the London Savoy). Why did he decamp to New York in 1914 when so successful in Europe? Perhaps he feared an influx of refugees calling upon his services, or his revolutionary past catching up with him. Evidence on the other hand suggests that his continuing political links may have actually benefited him. According to Carol Spero, who collected material for a biography of his wife Ethel, Voynich was helped in securing his stay in the US by the influence of Ignace Paderewski, the famous pianist and later Premier of Poland, who had moved to the US in April 1915 to rally support for the Polish cause. Voynich must have performed some important services over the years to justify this patronage but, beyond his aid to refugees in London, we cannot be sure what they were. It may have been this same connection that came to the Voynichs' aid when they were finally threatened with expulsion from the US in 1927 as illegal immigrants (it seems that they had both been travelling back and forwards between continents on visitors' passports to avoid this). Voynich wrote, 'I have used very powerful backing and visited twice Washington.'

In chapter 1 it was also suggested that fear of the war was the probable reason for his emigration to New York, but it seems that the outbreak of European hostilities may have had precisely the opposite effect on Voynich's business interests. During the war Voynich returned to Europe on several occasions and, as again reported by Spero in an interview with Ethel's adopted daughter, Winifred Gaye, he continued to travel in France and Italy, picking up rare and valuable books from people desperate to obtain funds in troubled times. All this suggests that it was ambition rather than fear of European collapse that motivated him. As for many another, the war was a business opportunity not a constraint. Or maybe in 1914 Wilfrid was already in fear of one of his financial 'smashes', as he put it. We simply do not know for sure, so much of his life is shrouded in secrecy. We do know, however, that if realised, the asking price of $160,000 (nearly two and a half million at today's prices) for the manuscript he unearthed in Italy in 1912 would once and for all have made him rich.

Let us move on from 'motive' to our next watchword – 'ability'. Barlow too had clearly read enough good crime novels; he writes, 'one would have to know much more about Voynich as a man to know what he was capable of...'[7] In chapter 1 we glimpsed his character through the somewhat hero-worshipping eyes of Millicent Sowerby, who worked for him in London from 1912 to 1914. Voynich does indeed merit her accolades; his revolutionary credentials in the struggle for Polish freedom seem impeccable – Warsaw, Siberia and his work with the Society of Friends of Russian Freedom in London from 1890 to 1895 under the direction of Stepniak.

Voynich's involvement with its sister organisation, the Russian Free Press Fund, reveals other aspects of his character. Formed in 1891, it was mainly composed of exiles, although Ethel was included as an honorary member. It published and distributed a flysheet and raised money through sales of its own publications and revolutionary works at its Hammersmith bookshop. Voynich was its business manager. According to Donald Senese he was 'capable and energetic', but 'insufferably brash and rude'.[8] This may have been due to him being younger than his colleagues and a Pole amongst Russians, but he also clearly regarded himself highly in matters of both ideology and business. As a result, he established a breakaway organisation, 'The League of Book Carriers' in late 1894, which foundered, however, due to lack of money. This did not seem to stop either of the Voynichs being involved in Russian affairs; they were still smuggling books there in 1895, but were very poor, and Wilfrid was suffering bad health. However Stepniak's death in December of that year did put an end to Ethel's activities, but not her husband's.

Also in 1895, Sidney Reilly, a Russian-born fortune-seeker, mercenary and later infamous spy, arrived in London. Andrew Cook, in his book *On His Majesty's Secret Service: Sidney Reilly Codename ST1*, maintains that Reilly was subsequently recruited by Special Branch to infiltrate the Society of Friends of Russian Freedom.[9] He was to become entangled in the lives of both Wilfrid and Ethel.

Reilly's association with SFRF appears to have been successful, because according to another biographer, Bruce Lockhart, in his book *Ace of Spies*, he wooed and won Ethel for some months in 1895, when the pair went to Italy.[10] Although in later life she denied the liaison (and it does seem out of character), she did spend May to September there, according to her letters working on her famous novel *The Gadfly*. The relevance of this diverting but fascinating episode being that Reilly claimed later as a result of their 'affair' to have been the model for the novel's epic revolutionary hero. If the story had been true, the resulting irony would have been magnificent; British agent Reilly was later involved in plots to undermine Soviet Russia where *The Gadfly*'s hero, fired with anticlerical revolutionary fervour, became idolised in opera and film. According to Cook, however, the story is quite definitely a pompous fiction of Sidney Reilly.

But more relevant to our story is Cook's assertion that Reilly must have got to know Wilfrid too, and that with abilities and interests in common – both were chemists, booklovers and shared the same accountant – there may have been a collusion to 'create "new" medieval manuscripts to order'.[11] Whether this fascinating suggestion holds water or not, somehow or other Voynich, penniless in 1896, mysteriously acquired enough money to establish his first antiquarian bookshop at 1 Soho Square in 1898, from where he issued the first of his catalogues. Cook states that the Okhrana (the Russian Secret Police) believed that Voynich was raising and laundering revolutionary funds. Taratuta reports as well that his political colleagues accused him of being 'greedy and envious' and of 'improper use of monies designed for revolutionary work'.[12] Could this have been a financial source? Cook's further evidence from the files reveals that in 1903 both Voynich and Reilly were still under surveillance by Okhrana agents. Could this imply a continuing suspect collusion between them? One other unsavoury possibility arises from his political activities. According to Senese, two of his fellow Fund conspirators, Chaikovskii and Volkhovskii, were engaged in the profitable business of gun-running. Probably only further research into British Special Branch and Okhrana files will reveal the truth about the funding of Voynich's book world. For some time at least he must have been leading a

double-life as an underground activist, Mack-the-Knife figure
– and an emerging respectable antiquarian book dealer.

Whatever the source of his finance Voynich did indeed
become known for his ability to unearth rare editions, some of
which he had been supplying to the British Museum in the
late 1890s. His collection listed in his 1902 catalogue as
'unknown and lost books' was garnered from his trips abroad
as early as 1895. That particular collection now resides in the
British Library Italian section, consisting of 158 sixteenth-
and seventeenth-century Italian books including 14 incunabula, 'discovered in different monastic libraries'. The curator,
Stephen Parkin, has commented on their remarkably interesting, eclectic nature, such as phrasebooks, herbals, devotionals
and schoolbooks, all unique and catalogued in great detail.
There can be no doubt at all about Voynich's rapidly gained
and sophisticated knowledge as a purveyor of fine books; he
knew where and what to look for. Yet, dual character that he
was, there is also something enduringly of the second-hand
car salesman about him. Behind the sale of that same collection to an institutional pinnacle of British society, he revealed
his underhand ways.

Voynich had his knuckles soundly rapped by the Director
of the British Museum for using his endorsement, without
permission, to drum up finances from the Duke of
Northumberland and a Rothschild amongst others. The collection was in fact purchased in 1906 but not until after the
'indignant' Director complained to Voynich about his 'most
improper' way of conducting affairs.

Voynich was not ashamed of the more dubious aspects of
his trade and generously full of encouragement for others to
jump on the bandwagon. Giuseppe Orioli writing in 1937 in
Adventures of a Bookseller relates how Voynich had told him
to 'stick to one subject at a time, buy the best and rarest books
on that single subject and don't let them go till you have
formed a big collection'.[13] Voynich described how he was
making a collection on cholera hoping that some day some
American would 'buy it for 300 times more than I gave for it.
That's what I call doing business.'[14] Shrewd enough, but less
standard practice was also unabashedly revealed to Orioli
about a trip Voynich made to Italy.

I once went to a convent and the monks showed me their library. It was a mine of early printed books, codexes and illuminated manuscripts. I nearly fainted ... but I managed to keep my head all the same, and told the monks they could have a most interesting collection of modern theological works to replace that dusty rubbish. I succeeded in persuading the Father Superior and in a month the whole library was in my hands, and I sent them a cartload of modern trash in exchange.[15]

With such a frank and compelling testimony in mind, Orioli did in fact start up, as Sowerby states, with his partner Davis in 1910. As far as can be ascertained Orioli arrived in England from Italy around 1908, so Voynich's story probably dates from before that. Orioli obviously had a poor memory; as Sowerby points out, he was wrong to describe Voynich as 'a Polish Jew, a bent kind of creature and getting on for sixty'.[16] Sowerby, forever girlishly loyal, counters that as well as being a Catholic, Voynich had a 'great Norwegian god-like appearance', and could only have been in his forties at the time. Orioli's recollection is odd too; monks do not live in convents or have Father Superiors, but, one wonders, irresistibly, could the happy hunting-ground referred to be the Jesuit College of Mondragone?

Even when Voynich's character can be seen in a more redeemable light there is an undertow of deviousness. An article in *The Times* on 11 May 1916 reported that he had returned a book in his possession to Lincoln Cathedral after it was established in a London court that it was stolen property. His financial loss included half the costs of the case, leading the cathedral authorities to speak of his 'sense of public spirit and generosity'. Yet behind the magnanimity Wilfrid could have avoided any loss if he had agreed to independent pre-trial arbitration. Not until identification was made in court did he accede. As *The Times* reported it, Voynich simply said, after looking at the volume in dispute, 'It's your book' – in other words: 'It's a fair cop.'

Wilfrid evidently had his fans, not just Millicent Sowerby. Even allowing for the fact that obituaries do not tend to dwell on the scurrilous aspects of the deceased, he seems to have been warmly regarded by acquaintances. James Westfall

Thompson, for example, Professor of History at the University of Berkeley, wrote of 'his genial humour, his kindliness', and stressed his scholarship and knowledge of languages. One curious detail, repeated by one of Voynich's employees, Herbert Garland, maintained that Wilfrid escaped from Siberia after the third attempt and joined a caravan in Mongolia bound for Peking, not arriving there until a year later. As we have noted in chapter 1, Ethel's version firmly states that his journey took only five months and probably involved westward trains rather than southbound camels. Wilfrid, without doubt, was an embroiderer of stories based, if not in fact, on a colourful life that made a certain deception inevitable.

Voynich could be described as a lovable rogue, living a flawed but admired life which sometimes took him to the edge of the law. Despite his international success as a book dealer he had problems establishing himself in the US, writing in 1921, 'private collectors are shy of me and my name', suggesting that his seven-year stay had not been all roses. In that same year the Bacon manuscript was launched on the world and Voynich's probity would be put to the test. He seemed initially to have passed, although in another letter that year he is mortified by an attack from an English journalist, Frank Vizetelly, suggesting that the Voynich manuscript is a forgery and that Voynich is a victim of a hoax.

This brings us back to the matter in hand. Voynich's double-life had been maintained both as respectable connoisseur of ancient books and disreputable dealer. But this does not, of course, make him ipso facto a forger. Barlow, despite having sown the seed of suspicion regarding the manuscript, lets him off the hook by suggesting that the hoax was being played on Newbold by Voynich to see if he was up to cracking the cipher. This is naive. If Wilfrid Voynich did create the manuscript, it was – as has already been suggested – for one reason only: money. Voynich also had the ability, the knowledge of literary styles and history.

Intriguing recent research by Rafal Prinke adds to the picture. Involvement in repressed political affairs automatically makes one some sort of criminal at odds with authority, and some skills are identical whatever their purpose. With this in mind, it is of interest that E. Taratuta, biographer of both Ethel Voynich and Stepniak, maintained that Voynich was forging passports as part of his activities with Proletariat, the Polish Revolutionary party. Prinke not only confirms this but augments our knowledge; police who raided some of his collaborators found letters written by him using ciphers and chemical 'sympathetic' inks. These are, in a sense, tools of the trade for an agitator, but it is impossible not to bear them in mind either in his connection with Reilly or in his later, more respectable book-dealing career.

A number of factors pose serious questions about the authenticity of the Voynich manuscript in general. Most importantly, how was it possible for such a unique and beguiling document to disappear from view for two hundred and fifty years after the Rudolf/Prague period, and possibly for two hundred years preceding it? Apart from its brief appearance then, there are no records of the manuscript whatsoever until 1912. At this point some accompanying facts sit uncomfortably on Wilfrid's uneven shoulders. He disguised its provenance from the outset, maintaining that he had found the manuscript amongst others belonging to the Dukes of Parma, Ferrara and Modena. His excuse for not revealing the identity of Mondragone, claiming he wanted to go back later, rings very hollow; he alone wanted to control the story of the manuscript. This is precisely what he managed to do for a decade and a half, masterminding the Roger Bacon attribution through the Marci letter.

Does it not appear also somewhat strange, as related in chapter 3, that he should have been the one responsible for the photocopying accident and the application of chemicals which revealed the de Tepenecz signature? It was a very lucky break indeed. Voynich must have known the history of de Tepenecz; the dates of his entitlement in 1608 to his death in 1622 neatly tie him into Rudolf's court. However, Rafal Prinke, tireless sleuth, has found interesting evidence offsetting the idea that Voynich might have added and erased the signature. In a manuscript owned by Jiri Berthold Pontanus, poet and rector of St Vitus' Cathedral in Prague, the signature of de Tepenecz appears in the same place as in the Voynich manuscript on folio 1, and 'has the same form', indicating that the latter appearance must be genuine. Prinke admits that prior to this, 'I was not quite sure what to think about [the] erased signature.' This evidence although significant does not quite remove the finger of suspicion from Voynich; after all, if he had set out to add the signature to help provenance he would hardly have added it without evidence from some other source, which given the extent of his research he must have possessed.

The most compelling evidence establishing the authentic origins of the Voynich manuscript remains the three letters to Kircher, bound within the volumes of the Carteggio Kircheriano, that turned up at Mondragone. The most important of these is a letter from George Baresch of 1639, as mentioned in chapter 3. In it he writes to Kircher for help in deciphering a manuscript which has 'pictures of herbs, of which the number in the Codex is enormous, of various images, of stars and of other things which appear like chemical secrets. I conjecture that it is all of a medical nature.' Such a description, plus the key mention of it being enciphered, seems to fit the Voynich manuscript well – although not exactly. Why have the naked women and the baths, probably the most striking and controversial aspect of it, not been mentioned? Was he just too shy to mention them?

The first of the other two letters in the correspondence, dated 1640, is from Marci to Kircher, sending some transcriptions of a manuscript by Baresch, but unfortunately they have not been found. The last letter is from G. A. Kinner to Kircher, in 1667, asking whether he had managed to transcribe the manuscript Marci had sent to him. Both of these letters may be referring to the Voynich manuscript, but unlike the 1639 letter neither can be viewed as sufficiently conclusive of its existence. Yet...

Supposing Wilfrid Voynich had, opportunely, come across the Baresch letter (he may never even have seen the other letters) in the volumes of Kircher's indexed correspondence at Mondragone at any time before 1912, and used the Baresch description as a crib upon which to build the manuscript. He took his time, probably employing other hands, using his chemical and forging expertise and the stocks of blank vellum that Sowerby maintains he sold in London for a shilling a leaf. He could be confident that there was no conflicting evidence of its existence by consulting the catalogues of Kircher's possessions, and set about designing a uniquely intriguing manuscript using his unrivalled expertise in 'rare and unknown' books. Let us recall, for example, his acquaintance with the off-beat alchemical look of the Wellcome manuscript mentioned in chapter 6, and bear in mind the singularity of the sexy nymphs (who Peter Collingridge, a specialist in rare books at Christie's of London, suggests have a distinctly nineteenth-century look). To this confection he attached the forged Marci letter of 1665/6 that he so nonchalantly noticed 'some time later' after coming across the manuscript. He then simply announced to the world the discovery of the manuscript and its circumstances, none of which could be checked by anyone else. He does, however, get an accomplice to ask about other Marci letters and makes more inquiries for himself about Baresch, happy that if his identity is unearthed it will eventually reinforce his whole story. Voynich writes emphatically in his 1921 lecture, 'research into the Bohemian State Archives will lead to discovery of the "intimate friend"'.

And the indecipherable script? Who better equipped than Voynich himself to fashion a melange of tongues, almost glossolalic but structured, and assign an alphabet? According to Sowerby again, 'He spoke eighteen languages in all, so he told us, equally badly...his English, [which] seemed on the whole a more or less literal translation from the construction of sentences in his native Polish.'[17]

The idea that the Voynich manuscript is a hoax or forgery, from whatever period, is certainly an attractive one. Its uniqueness inevitably commands attention, yet, without stylistic parallels, does not allow any simple verification or dismissal – a desirable quality for a fraud. The manuscript exhibits a fine balance between credibility and mystery that has kept so many people spellbound for just short of a century. Although it failed in the end to make Wilfrid Voynich rich, enigmas are also highly bankable – the very raison d'être for a forgery

Bearing all this in mind, one might well ask why the Voynich manuscript or the Marci letter have not undergone tests to establish their age. This would help lay to rest the question of authenticity and provide a historical base-line for further research. It is surprising that this is not part of institutional policy towards the manuscript, especially when the Voynich manuscript is a cause célèbre, almost too célèbre, as

Jim Reeds revealed back in 1994, when Robert Babcock, Head of Research at the Beinecke Library, 'implored' Reeds to decipher it, so 'Yale would stop being bothered by silly visitors'.

No museum or gallery likes to have a cuckoo in its nest. Just one impostor tends to discredit the judgement and calibre of the whole establishment, and Yale has already been bothered by another controversial case that has doubtless made them wary of the limelight. In 1965 they bought the Vinland Map without any clear record of ownership or provenance at a price of one million dollars. It showed in the Atlantic a large island named Vinland lying where Newfoundland should be. Dating from the mid-sixteenth century it appeared to demonstrate that Viking sailors had discovered North America, leading to a loud public outcry from Columbus-supporting Italian-Americans. In 1972 the latter, unlike Yale, were relieved to hear that a scrutiny of the ink showed the presence of a twentieth-century chemical, suggesting that the Map must be a fake. Yale did not enjoy the egg on its face. Controversy continued, however, and was abetted in 1987 by a new analysis opting for authenticity. More recent tests in 1995 using radio-carbon technology have dated a sliver of parchment to AD 1434, but to date the jury is still out.

In this context it is hardly surprising that the Beinecke Library would be nervous about the Voynich manuscript. Even if it did allow examination, however, available technology would not generate conclusive proof. Radio-carbon dating, depending on the period being investigated, can entail a wide margin of error, but in any case dating the base material such as vellum would not discount the possibility of the re-use of old supplies or the manufacture of new stock. This proved to be the case in the unmasking of the '1328' Gospel lectionary (a book containing the lessons read in church throughout the year), held by the Bancroft Library at Berkeley University, California. An x-ray-generating cyclotron showed that the parchment was a paper coated with white lead and tinted yellow, fabricated in the late nineteenth or early twentieth century, and apparently, according to Anthony Bliss, the detective at Berkeley, not uncommon as part of a cottage industry in Italy at that time. If this turned out to be true also of the Voynich manuscript, the finger of suspicion would point in only one direction.

Dating the inks tends to be more conclusive as it may reveal modern chemical composition, but even here, due to contamination and deterioration, there is room for uncertainty. Unless, of course, the vellum itself turned out to be modern. At which point the 'balance of probability' would certainly swing in favour of a hoax. Although, if the Vinland Map is anything to go by, or even more so the Turin Shroud – still revered as the real thing by the faithful despite conclusive tests to the contrary – this might be just a starting point for further disputation.

LETTING THE CAT
OUT OF THE BAG

The digressions, the false decryptions, the diverse theories and unprovable speculations of the preceding chapters have led us away from the Voynich manuscript itself, and its long and tortuous journey through history and around the world. The last time our narrative touched those faded vellum pages, the manuscript was still in the possession of Wilfrid Voynich, as he presented his and Professor Newbold's findings to the College of Physicians in Philadelphia. As this book draws to a close, we must complete the manuscript's story, firstly telling how it came to reside in the stacks of the Beinecke Library, and then stitching together the patchwork of contemporary thinking on all things Voynich: the current theories, its influence and resonance on the wider world, and perhaps even a hazarded guess as to its actual meaning.

No doubt buoyed up by the favourable publicity following the presentation in Philadelphia in 1921, Voynich soon announced an asking price for the manuscript of $160,000, a huge sum for that time. Despite, or perhaps because of the astonishing claims made for the importance of the document, no collector seemed willing to pay such an amount. His wife Ethel, upon the cessation of her revolutionary activities in the 1890s, had returned to her artistic endeavours, though her political beliefs were to inform her most famous novel, *The Gadfly*, published to much acclaim in 1897. Her enduring desire, however, was to compose music, and to this end, around the year 1910, she immersed herself in the activities of the Royal College of Music. Ethel finally joined Wilfrid in the US in the early 1920s, but lived a separate life from him in up-state New York (although they continued to meet regularly), and pursued her musical career. In early 1927 Wilfrid wrote that ELV, as she was known, had finished a large-scale cantata entitled 'Babylon'. There seem to have been a few performances of her works, but she never gained the recognition she so clearly sought. She continued to write, producing another four novels, but none achieved the success of *The Gadfly*.

In the autumn of 1926 William Romaine Newbold died, with his bogus transcription of the manuscript still far from complete, and around this time Voynich too seems to have lost faith in his 'ugly duckling'. His correspondence in the following years loses the wild optimism regarding the possible financial rewards it might bring, and he concentrates on the sale of other rare books in his collection. Things in general had not been going well for him. The Florence office had been closed in 1922, and his letters reveal that he was permanently tottering on the edge of another financial crisis, yet by all accounts he lived well, or perhaps beyond his means, staying, for example, in the Commodore Hotel on 42nd Street in New York.

In 1929 Voynich visited England once again, and whilst there contracted pneumonia. His health continued to deteriorate after his return to the US, and on 19 March 1930, with his wife Ethel at his bedside, he died. In accordance with his will, the Voynich manuscript passed into the joint possession of his wife and his secretary, Anne Nill, with the proviso that it might be 'sold for $100,000 to any public institution, but that no private collector should ever be allowed to buy it for any sum'. An immediate problem facing the executors of the will was to determine exactly how much the Voynich manuscript was worth. With the text still unread, and with Newbold's theories coming under increasing criticism from other academics, the manuscript seemed as opaque as it had done when it was discovered eighteen years earlier; how could a value be placed on a document no one could understand? This seemingly impossible task fell to an official appraiser, Eugene Homer, who, in November 1931, valued the manuscript at a mere $19,400, a fraction of Voynich's asking price.

As various experts and inspired amateurs continued to wrestle unsuccessfully with the problem of decryption, the manuscript spent the next thirty years in the New York Guarantee Trust safe deposit vault, until the death of Ethel Voynich in 1960, when it passed into the sole ownership of

Anne Nill. It was at this point that the mystery of where exactly Voynich had found the manuscript was solved. The only clue up to this time, apart from his vague mention of a 'castle in Southern Europe', had come from Professor Newbold, who recalled that at their meeting in 1915 Voynich mentioned that the mysterious castle was in Austria. However, at last, with the death of Ethel, the truth finally emerged. In a letter to Anne Nill, only to be opened posthumously, Ethel revealed that the manuscript had been part of a collection held in the Villa Mondragone, the former Jesuit college in Frascati, Italy. The Jesuits, in desperate need to raise funds for restoration of the villa, were forced to sell off part of their collection of rare manuscripts, and so it was that in 1912 Wilfred Voynich had found himself rummaging through the chest that contained what became the famous volume. It was only now, prompted by Ethel's fear that it would never be known, that Anne Nill disclosed the real story.

On 12 July 1961 the Voynich manuscript was purchased by the New York book dealer Hans Kraus for $24,500. He immediately attached a price tag of $100,000, which he later increased to match Voynich's valuation of $160,000; but just like Voynich before him, Kraus was unable to interest any buyers. In 1969 he donated the manuscript to Yale University, where it remains in the Beinecke Rare Book and Manuscript Library under the following catalogue entry:

MS 408
Central Europe [?], s. XV^^ex-XVI [?]
Cipher Manuscript
Scientific or magical text in an unidentified language, in cipher, apparently based on Roman minuscule characters; the text is believed by some scholars to be the work of Roger Bacon since the themes of the illustrations seem to represent topics known to have interested Bacon.

The single most influential tool for any would-be Voynich researcher in recent years has been the development of the world-wide web, and the subsequent emergence of a global group of manuscript aficionados, united via the internet in puzzled solidarity. This predominantly male group of scholars, sorely afflicted with the Voynich itch, have been scratching

BASIC EVA CHARACTERS

	EVA	Capitalised EVA		EVA	Capitalised EVA
'	?		m	ʃ	
a	a	ɑ	n	ɔ	
b	∂		o	o	σ
c	⌐		p	⅌	⅌
d	8		q	4	
e	c	c	r	?	
f	⅌	⅌	s	ƨ	ƨ
g	ƈ		t	⅏	⅏
h	⊂	⊂	u	∂	
i	\	⊤	v	∧	
j	8		x	⊼	
k	⅙	⅙	y	9	9
l	૪		z	ɾP	

Basic European Voynich Alphabet (courtesy of René Zandbergen)

235

their heads together since a mailing list was started up by Jim Gillogly and Jim Reeds in 1991. Subscribers' backgrounds include, amongst others, cryptographers, linguists, botanists, astronomers, paleographers, medievalists, historians and astrologers. In December 2002 it became managed by the Majordomo programme @voynich.net, which in fine democratic spirit allows anyone to make their own rash contributions to the Voynich body of knowledge.

The postings are polite, friendly and often jocular, but mostly erudite, covering all aspects from broad theoretical concerns to detailed observation of minutiae. Here is a selection of subjects discussed during July 2003 (if you subscribe you can expect up to thirty e-mails a day): missing pages, unvowelled Nabatean, word spaces, the Indian connection, folios 85 and 86, medieval numbers, hexadecimals, bifolios and smudges, old English plant names and 'bleed-through'.

A lasting and significant result of co-operation has been the production of a basic, accepted, machine-readable set of Latin characters standing for Voynich script symbols. Various attempts had been made before, but the European Voynich Alphabet (EVA) devised by René Zandbergen has been adopted. Using the 'Voynich EVA Hand 1 font' created by Gabriel Landini, the beginning of folio 1r is presented below, followed by the transcription into EVA.

The basic Voynich alphabet, made up of twenty-six letters transposed into our own alphabet, did not, of course, adequately represent the very large number of weird characters

```
fachys.ykal.ar.ataiin.shol.shory.cthres.ykor.sholdy
sory.chtar.or.y.kair.chtaiin.shar.are.cthar.cthar.dan
syaiir.sheky.or.ykaiin.shod.cthoary.cthes.daraiin.sa
o'oiin.okeey.oteor.roloty.cth*ar.daiin.otaiin.or.okan
sair.y.chear.cthaiin.cphar.cfhaiin - ydaraishy
```

Voynich EVA Hand 1 Font and folio 1r (courtesy of G. Landini)

and squiggles that dot the volume. To cope with these a set of some two hundred numerical codes have been devised, plus indications where letters are connected together or capitalised. (The 'splat' symbol in the Voynich passage opposite denotes an unreadable character.)

In July 2003 it was suggested that, amidst the plethora of imaginings and investigative meanderings linked to the manuscript, subscribers to the Voynich mailing list might like to put on view their current hunches about its provenance. Respondents posted a potted version of their own explanation of the manuscript, and a selection of these guesses are reproduced here with the permission of the original authors. They give a good overall impression of the latest ideas and the general direction in which current Voynich research is heading.

Gordon Rugg, computer scientist, Keele University, UK
When? 1551–1586
Where? Possibly England
Who? Probably Kell(e)y, possibly with the active help of Dee
Language? Probably meaningless gibberish, though a code is also possible, in which case English or Latin.
Contents? If code, then either a contentful hoax (i.e., a meaningful plain text, rather than gibberish, but a plain text whose role was purely as a source of 'padding', like the alphabetic strings in the Beale ciphers) or something which Kelley claimed that the angels had told him.
Decipherable/hoax? Probably recoverable, as opposed to decipherable – I think it would be possible to reconstruct the precise methods and materials used, though I'm far from certain about this. Procedure? Probably used a (now lost) north Italian and a (now lost) west mid-German manuscript as templates for the illustrations, to ensure fashions, etc. would be consistent with a late c15th alchemical herbal; perhaps supplied by Puccius. Used characters from a variety of scripts and shorthands, which make it harder for decoders (since we can't be sure which characters are random variants of each other and which are different) and also has the advantage of concealing the originator's own handwriting. Botanical section originally prepared in parallel by originator and accomplice; when they realised the divergence between the two sets of output (A and B), then they changed procedure, with one drafting and the other doing the fair copy. (Since the above was

written, Rugg has suggested that an Elizabethan espionage device called a Cardan grille could have been used to create the Voynichese language which is essentially gibberish.)

Petr Kazil, IT security auditor, Rotterdam
When: Between 1500 and 1600
Where: Europe, probably in the area between Rome, Avignon, Munich and Prague
Who: An unknown and unknowable author
What: A personal fascination/craziness or a fake document meant to impress credulous clients. Most probably there is no translation since both text and pictures are gibberish, but it is quite possible to make a good 'profile' of the author by: studying the conscious/unconscious pointers that he has left for us (just like in criminal profiling), searching for historical parallels for this kind of publication, doing more research into related historical areas like crypto, herbals, etc. That's why I just keep on reading related books and don't try to attack the VMS directly. I don't have the feeling the solution will come from there. I've given up on decryption. But I believe in studying the pages in minute detail, looking for possible clues and pointers. Then there is the slight chance that another page in Voynichese will be found in some remote library and we may be able to pinpoint the author more precisely. The horrible thought is that such a page may have been discovered already but not recognised as such.

Peter Riis
Riis agrees with Petr Kazil but adds:
My fairly uninformed opinion would be along the same lines. I would lean more towards the VMS being the production of a schizophrenic rather than it being part of a scheme to deceive – the intricacy of the VMS seems to go far beyond what would be necessary just to fool a buyer. That kind of mad intricacy, though, is sometimes seen in artifacts produced by schizophrenics. The bizarrerie of the balneological illustrations and even a certain menacing something in the botanical drawings leads me to think that all was not well mentally with the artist – but obviously that's a totally subjective impression. It does seem to me, though, that direct cryptological attack would be one of the less promising lines of inquiry. But then again, what do I know? Maybe tomorrow somebody will provide us with a complete, valid solution through pure crypto!

René Zandbergen, satellite navigation expert, European Space Agency

When? I trust the experts so believe 1450–1499 (if I didn't, I could believe that it was older rather than younger)

Where? Italy, Spain or the southern part of greater Germany (includes Bohemia)

Who? Someone who knows his (contemporary) science but has some different ideas. A fringe scientist. Language? No idea. I'm quite open. I could imagine an invented language where new words are made up and added to the vocabulary on the fly. I have a hunch that some number system could be behind it. Nothing as complicated as Newbold or Strong suggested.

Contents? I'm assuming that the text fits the pictures, but accept that there is a small chance that this is not true. Decipherable/hoax? I expect that the text has a meaning. I could very well imagine that the technique used by the composer of the MS to convert this meaning to its written form may have made this meaning irrecoverable, by accident. To clarify this last point: there used to be this 'magic' trick, I forget how it went, where a test person had to imagine a number. He would then be asked to make various calculations based on this number, and at the end the interrogator would predict that the outcome of the calculations was 1089. The point was that due to the selected set of operations, this was the outcome regardless of what was the original number. It was lost in the operation. I don't imagine anything as intricate in the VMS. I could well imagine someone 'transcribing' Arabic (or Sanskrit, or whatever) without having the first clue about what the original script is supposed to mean.

Matthew Platts

When? 1450–1500

Where? Northern Italy

Who? An unknown subculture

What? An encyclopedic work on a system of herbal medicine, derived somewhat from western European folk and esoteric thought, but with many original, shamanistic elements. Written in some Romance dialect, in a verbose word game-like cipher. My own belief is that it was written by a single natural philosopher, whose work in biology (i.e., dissections) was considered taboo at the time, and so had to be done in secret. Hence the figurative representations of bodily functions, with the naked nymphs and the pipes...I believe that it has some deliberate redundancy (like the 'King Tut' game) and that the glyphs are either alphabetical or phonetical – there are too few for a pictographic language...I don't think there is any special significance to the gallows characters. More so, that requiring it to be folded wouldn't make sense, partly because the ink would crack when the vellum was folded, or there would be otherwise a sure indication of folding by the original authors...who would, I am sure, have decoded it at one point or another...

Of the other replies posted, the majority agree on a creation date somewhere between the mid-fifteenth century to 1600, and give England as the clear favourite for country of origin, with Germany and Italy also-rans. John Stojko advanced a theory and partial decryption, developed some time before, that the manuscript was written in vowel-less Ukrainian. Other theories find themselves resting in the long grass just outside the ball-park, sometimes lobbed there deliberately. One such hitter is Jacques Guy, a linguist living in Australia, who developed the 'Chinese hypothesis':

I never was serious about it, it's just another I floated over the years to bring a bit of levity to our group. Perhaps it was when we were discussing a possible northern Italian origin for the VMS. Here it is: Marco Polo brought back with him two fellows from Southern China who, once settled in Venice, set about recording their medical knowledge. They devised an alphabet for the purpose of writing their language (a dialect of Southern China – perhaps Hakka, perhaps Holo, perhaps... there are hundreds of them!). There are clearly anatomic diagrams (the 'plumbing' and the bathing 'nymphs' who are clearly – sic! – embodiments of life principles); there are herbal recipes, (the pharmaceutical section); there is a lengthy herbal; and as for the astronomical/astrological diagrams, they are there just to make clear when the herbs should be collected. My 'Chinese hypothesis' was not based on any statistical observations. However, I had remarked time and again that statistical properties of the VMS were easily explained if it was written in a language with extensive sandhi [modification of the sound of a word caused by the context in which it is uttered] and/or with complex morphologies and holophrastic tendencies (such as many American Indian languages). The Chinese I know has some degree of tone sandhi, but that is about all. I never, repeat, never *ever* took it seriously, and did not even look into it.

In a similar vein he continues.

> Here is another hypothesis for your amusement. The Erzsebet Bathory hypothesis. Of course you know of the 'Bloody Countess'. The VMS is the notes of her alchemist who concocted an elixir of eternal youth and thought of rounding up and goring peasant girls for his mistress to bathe in their blood. The 'plumbing' of the anatomical section is real plumbing, the plumbing built in her castle for her gruesome bathtubs. The VMS is written in the alchemist's language, a language once spoken in darkest Bohemia, unrelated to any other (just like Basque, Pictish, Sumerian, Elamite, Etruscan...) and now long extinct. Fancy if a DNA analysis of the vellum turned up evidence that it was made from sheep of a flock documented as belonging to the Bloody Countess...

Jacques Guy's whimsical hypothesising has, in fact, led to some serious research by fellow Voynich enthusiast Jorge Stolfi. According to Stolfi's theory, the manuscript was written in Chinese (or another East Asian language), using a phonetic alphabet created by a Christian missionary as an aid to learning the language, or by a Chinese to help communicate with the missionary. There were indeed a number of contacts between the East and West before the sixteenth century, and a means to facilitate communication would have been important. The theory also posits that the manuscript conveyed a knowledge of herbs, medicine and cosmology that would have been of interest in Europe, but, proving unsuccessful, it became a curiosity, eventually bought by John Dee who passed it on to Rudolf II. Peculiarities of the Voynich script seem to connect it with some oriental languages: repeated words are frequent since most common words consist of a small range of single syllables intoned differently to convey meaning and connected together to make compounds; there are no inflected words (e.g. verbs) that have one root and take different endings to convey gender, plurality, etc.; and there is no punctuation. To date the theory rests undisturbed in the sward.

Another modern theory has been postulated by Beatrice Gwynn from Dublin, who once worked at Bletchley Park, home of the British cipher breakers of the Second World War, although Beatrice herself was not part of the decryption section. As a keen amateur cryptologist, however, she had been fascinated by the Voynich manuscript, and remembering that Leonardo da Vinci had used mirror-writing to hide his secrets, tried the same procedure on the balneological pages. Her verdict is that this is indeed the correct method of decipherment, and furthermore the language is Middle High German. With the aid of the 'michiton' key on the last page of the manuscript, she has managed to decrypt enough evidence to reveal that the Voynich manuscript is a sixteenth-century hygiene manual. The reader can check this out with a mirror of a suitable size and a quiet room. Beatrice is not alone, however, in linking Leonardo with the manuscript. Edith Sherwood, a Texas-based organic chemist, has gone several stages further.

Her attention has dwelt on folio 70vɪ, one of the Aries pages. She suggests that the tubs in which the nymphs are standing are birthing vessels, often used in medieval times to aid delivery. The figure on the inner ring of the page at '10 o'clock' is slightly unusual in that she stands clear enough of the tub to reveal an unashamed pudenda and seems to sport less of a belly than her sisters; the evidence of a nativity being seen in the 'baby' held in her right arm and celebrated by the striped string holding aloft a star. The folio, she suggests, is a calendrical representation of a birth, the exact date of which can be assumed from the number of 15 nymphs representing day 15 of April (Aries the ram), the 10 o'clock position, plus the year 1452 discerned in the decorative detail on the side of the tub. This, it turns out, is Leonardo da Vinci's birthdate; commemorated by him in the childish volume that we have come to know better as the Voynich. As for the mirror-writing, she does not claim to have penetrated far into reverse fifteenth-century Tuscan, but notes that the Voynich pages with nymphs holding stars are mostly facing clockwise, counter to the direction that the night sky would rise and fall, also suggesting Leonardo's use of a mirror.

Detail, folio 70v1

Jim Finn from Carolina, US, has struck the ball harder than most over the ball-park fencing with a theory that also focuses on a reversed image of the night sky and once again takes a single page in the manuscript as the starting point for his musings, in this case folio 68v3, the very same that intrigued Professor Newbold. The spiral image presented there approximates to a schema of our own galaxy, the Milky Way, except for one feature – it is facing the wrong way round, as if seen from the outside looking in! This seemingly incredible deduction is explained by Finn's own, highly detailed hypothesis, involving the end of the world and the wisdom of extraterrestrials:

For thirty years I have traced one enigmatic vein of history that is roughly 15,000 years long from start to finish. This vein of history deals with what we today now call 'the end of the world'. I have identified the ancient script that isolates the exact place in the sky from which this destruction event is going to come. That place in the sky points to the center of our Milky Way Galaxy. Our ancient ancestors preserved this information faithfully, generation after generation. Then, one day, 5300 years ago, this information was deliberately taken out of circulation, along with the Goddess Culture that preserved it.

For the last 5300 years, some unknown group that I have come to call the Elders has tried to secretly preserve this end times information, only to ultimately succumb to the religious rhetoric that had replaced it. By the time of Constantine, they had given up and disbanded because they had failed to preserve the truth of their message to humanity. By AD 1000, Western culture was so lost concerning what they now called The Day of the Lord, a single clap of thunder would send people to the ground, trembling in fear, because they believed the time of the END had come. Humanity no longer knew what this 'END' was, nor did they know 'WHO' was coming to save them from it. By the 1500s, two odd things were in progress. UFOs were being painted into the artwork of the times, and a man named Michel de Notredame had accurately put to writing, hidden very well in the 'Preface' to his son Cesar, as well as his Quatrains, the actual history of the 'end of all time'. Question: Who was Nostradamus' 'god that sits nearby'? Nostradamus' reputation has suffered much because of modern tabloid publicity. Nevertheless, the information is there in his work, neatly obscured, but 100 per cent accurate. What other writings/works did Nostradamus have tucked away? Were they claimed by his son Cesar when his father died?

Cesar died in 1631. In 1637 an odd manuscript [VMS] surfaces. Within its pages are drawings. One of these drawings is a depiction of a spiral galaxy. Nostradamus spoke Hebrew. The text is visually obscured Hebrew. The VMS text (like Nostradamus' work) speaks of a 'vast destruction'. The VMS shows that it comes from the center of the galaxy depicted in the drawing. The times are correct. The language is correct. The herbal representations are correct (Nostradamus was an herbalist). The 'naked nymphs' are correct as symbols of life in the 'veins and organs' of the person healed (see the etymology of the Hebrew letter 'H' – the birthing woman/sign of LIFE). The end times information is 100 per cent correct.

Question: Do we dare put two and two together? Is the VMS a work of Michel de Notredame? Total time frame for Michel and Cesar: 1503–1631. Or, is this one of the very OLD books that Nostradamus talks about? Books that he used. Books that he says he burned for fear of discovery. Did he sell one? According to the experts: 'There is no solid evidence to locate the manuscript in any particular region or date.' The plot only seems to thicken during the life, or after the death of either Michel or Cesar de Notredame. It just depends on how one interprets the data.

For so many years the Voynich manuscript has remained silent, like some grand, impenetrable monolith, impervious to all the attentions of the barrage of dedicated and occasionally obsessive inquirers. At the same time, however, like tendrils growing quietly from some creeping ivy, knowledge of the Voynich manuscript has seeped into the wider world outside the realms of cryptology and medieval history. Others have been touched by its mystery, and become inspired, not to attempt yet more explanations or decryptions but rather to use the Voynich manuscript as a starting point for their own creativity.

'The Voynich Cipher Manuscript', for mixed choir and orchestra by Hanspeter Kyburz (Kairos 0012152k) is a piece of music almost as impenetrable as the manuscript itself. Apparently Kyburz, like many another, is obsessed by the Voynich manuscript and elicits from its opacity a wafty, indeterminate tone in which, a reviewer comments, he 'sets rows of numbers deriving from scholarly attempts to crack the code, and poems in a "futuristic-archaistic" "star-language" by Chlebnikov'. Not for him the watery gurgles and pipings of a female choir of sprites. The reviewer continues, 'It is a typically avant-garde collage of choral and instrumental music, at once fascinating for its sheer sound, and inevitably, and no doubt designedly, perplexing.'

Far more intriguing is the mix of fantasy and reality in the literary worlds of H. P. Lovecraft (1890–1937) and Colin Wilson. Lovecraft wrote a number of dark horror stories whilst based in New England, but most famously invented a supposedly arcane opus, *The Necronomicon*, 'written' in the eighth century AD by a mad poet, Abdul Al-Hazred, which served as a basis for a whole genre of tales about an ancient race of malevolent beings, the Great Old Ones. It seems evident that Lovecraft, although not mentioning the Voynich manuscript specifically, must have been aware of it. In the short story 'The Haunter of the Dark', the hero, Robert Blake, makes a surprising discovery whilst exploring a deserted church: 'a small leather-bound record-book filled with entries in some odd cryptographic medium'. Fascinated, he works feverishly to understand it, but 'The cipher he soon saw was no simple one…he would have to draw upon the deepest wells of his strange erudition.' In doing so, tempting providence, however, he calls forth a 'monstrous thing of the night…out of the ultimate black spaces', which finally engulfs him.[1]

Curiously, the fabled *Necronomicon* has become intertwined

with the real manuscript, appearing in two books by Colin Wilson. In *The Return of the Lloigor*, a professor of English, Paul Lang, comes across the volume and discovers that it is written in an Arabic based on Greek and Latin. He realises that it is in fact *The Necronomicon*. The Voynich manuscript reappears yet again as an aid to Wilson's imagination in *The Philosopher's Stone*. Howard Lester and Sir Henry Littleway come under the spell of the Old Ones and try to break out by studying *The Necronomicon*. Reversing the revelation this time, they realise that the manuscript is the key to understanding – but, just as in the Lovecraft story, in the process of decipherment unleash the power of their enemy.

It comes as little surprise to discover that the most famous of all fictional archaeologist adventurers should also have tangled with the Voynich manuscript. In the 1980s, riding the wave of popularity following the trilogy of blockbuster films, a series of spin-off novels appeared recounting the further adventures of Indiana Jones. In one of the novels, *Indiana Jones and the Philosopher's Stone*, the intrepid academic discovers the secret of alchemy within the pages of Voynich's tome. Unfortunately for fans of Dr Jones and the Voynich manuscript, this novel has been out of print for many years.

Throughout the three years spent studying the Voynich manuscript and the subsequent writing of this book, one question has been asked of the authors more frequently than any other: 'What do *you* think it is?' Naturally, our opinions have shifted and changed over this period, one idea holding sway for a number of weeks or months, only to be replaced later by a newly discovered and equally appealing hypothesis. Often such a theory can lure the unwary into areas of research which, however hopeful they appear at first, will suddenly prove fruitless. Researchers can land themselves stranded at the end of an investigative cul-de-sac with no option but to retrace their steps to the recognised path of Voynich thought. Even there, the ground is not always safe. The vast array of ideas and explanations that has been put forward over the years presents any researcher with an intriguing and sometimes overwhelming spectrum of opinion from which to pick and choose; the problem, of course, is how to judge the relative merit of these conflicting theories. Such assessment, though largely governed by rational, intellectual criteria, can also be influenced by the less than scientific concepts of gut feeling and a certain inclination towards the more romantic and dramatic tales that weave in and out of the Voynich story. Inevitably, though, through a combination of all the above elements, a preferred theory eventually presents itself as being either the most likely or most attractive.

Gerry Kennedy

It is now two years since my tryst on the other side of the Atlantic with the Voynich manuscript at Yale – has the love affair prospered? As with all such fleeting encounters, undernourished images of the beloved tend to dim ardour following an initial passion. The black-and-white reproductions offered by the Beinecke Library are rather inadequate to maintain the appeal of a wrinkled and creased skin, beneath which, nevertheless, lies the charm of an ancient but unequivocally feminine presence. A haunting allure continues to linger; the Voynich manuscript is the Mona Lisa of its kind.

Perhaps it is this 'femme fatality' that ensures the overwhelming maleness of its devotees; it cannot merely be the male attraction towards the cold pastimes of problem-solving and code-breaking. For some the desire must lurk to master this wayward damsel; or maybe it is just the thrill of the chase. Possessing neither the cryptographic skills nor the impulse to conquer and pursue, I tend to rely on intuition. The irony, however, of engaging this facility has been to cloud any romantic attachment to the manuscript by declaring it to be false and a sham. I just *feel* the manuscript is a hoax.

During the research for this book, I contacted a number of specialists in many relevant fields but had little response. This may, of course, have been due to other commitments, but the impression gained was that few academics want to give an opinion and risk sticking their necks out. This is something, however, that the Voynicheros, gallantly on their quest to unmask the manuscript, are prepared to do and enjoy. It was in this spirit that the notion of a hoax by Voynich himself was offered in chapter 8.

Tim Mervyn is not alone in advancing the idea that Edward Kelley fabricated the manuscript. Most of the evidence seems based on the fact that Kelley was a rogue and a trickster, who, regardless of skill and opportunity, was motivated by Mammon to concoct the manuscript. Ignoring the general assumption that the Voynich manuscript was created in the mid-fifteenth century, he was, of course, historically close to the date of the Marci letter that appears to provide a vital clue to its existence. On these grounds Wilfrid Voynich is an equal contender for villainy; his jack-the-laddishness is unchallenge-able, and unlike Kelley, we know for sure that the manuscript actually passed through his hands.

There may well be other hoax contenders, but it is significant, I think, that research has not dwelt in the general area of artistic fraud, about which much material is available. Other much wackier avenues have been trodden, but in this case there is a definite disinclination to take any steps – no one really wants the journey to end with a hoax. It seems to me, however, that any artifact that appears to have evident meaning and exhibits a wealth of aspects capable of study, but that has defied all unflagging efforts to interpret, looks suspi-ciously like the product of someone who has manufactured those characteristics quite deliberately.

Should the manuscript eventually turn out to be the work of a fraud, I would like the perpetrator to be Wilfrid Voynich. Apart from my distant kinship to him, I have also grown quite attached to the old devil, certainly more so than my actual blood-relative, Ethel Boole. Unlike her rather cold and intellec-tual ways, Voynich was manifestly a man of passion and action, driven by ideology and *la belle vie*. One can almost forgive his arrogance and dubious dealings in the light of his unabashed acclamation of them. Underworld Pimpernel char-acters always exert a stronger fascination than those possibly far worthier but less flamboyant.

Anecdotes continue to emerge about Voynich. Joan Hinton, his great-niece by marriage, recalls being told that he escaped from Siberian exile, 'though guards had a picture of him but never recognised him'. Did this kind of episode form the spur perhaps for the coat-of-arms that, one presumes, was devised by him and heads his catalogues and letters. It consists of an elaborate crown poised over a possibly ironic drawing of a dog or cat gripping a rat in its mouth. Is this how he saw himself – a would-be aristocrat and man-of-the-world pursued by author-ity and the fear of being caught? Intriguingly the amateurish

Wilfrid Voynich's crest

artwork has an odd style reminiscent of the manuscript. Even visitors to his shop in Piccadilly embarked on a cloak-and-dagger adventure to make their purchases. It consisted of two large rooms and a back room with high bookcases arranged so that customers had to thread themselves in and out, not only giving the illusion of going on an exploration, but providing stopping places where they could discreetly inspect the sprinkling of 'top-shelf' volumes on magic and pornography.

All of this mixed spice does not, of course, add up to a clear indictment of Voynich as hoaxer. We would need to know much more about his movements and contacts between 1896 and 1912. This is unlikely to be forthcoming; passports were not compulsory and his travels would be difficult to reconstruct. There remains, however, a consideration that might modify the picture so far maintained.

A less encompassing version of the theory is tenable. Voynich may, of course, have come across the historically genuine manuscript at Mondragone, but tacked on his home-produced Marci letter of 1665/6, in order to steer the world towards a well-researched trail that would lead to the priceless pen of Roger Bacon. Barlow was horrified at this idea, thinking it, 'more immoral than the manuscript hoax itself'.[2] Yet the Marci letter does raise questions. Why, one might also ask, had this letter to Kircher, if genuine, and later the pivotal basis of all subsequent research, not been bound as a matter of course with the others? Perhaps merely a matter of secretarial convenience; the letter, however, had an air of fraudulence about it, of conveniently and wilfully directing the reader's attention to the star of the show. In other words, we might entertain a partial hoax hypothesis.

Rob Churchill

The various cryptological conjectures and translations of the Voynich manuscript were examined in detail in chapters 4 and 5, and need not be discussed again here in any detail. However, one might judge the likelihood of a correct analysis by examining the cipher-breaking credentials of the person offering it. If one adopts this method, then a lone, calm figure looms head and shoulders above all other Voynich investigators and theorists: William Friedman, whose undoubted genius in exposing the devious art of secret writing makes him most worthy of attention. Not for him the extravagant claims of successful decipherment so often made by far less able researchers; rather the credible and sober judgement that the manuscript probably represents a long-forgotten synthetic language with little chance of being decoded.

Yet while Friedman's hypothesis commands respect because of the lifetime of cryptanalytical expertise he brought to bear on the conundrum, it does little to advance our understanding of the manuscript as a whole. Indeed, the majority of theories that suggest a rational, and therefore identifiable creative input behind the Voynich language seem incapable of providing an encompassing explanation of the bizarre illustrations that also fill the codex. Once again, rational speculation and logical investigation wrestle with intuition and a certain gut feeling. For example, it has been pointed out by a number of commentators that the entropy, the variations in character or word order, of Voynichese is too low to be a European language, but does correlate to the entropy found in Polynesian tongues. An interesting fact no doubt, but common sense surely dictates that the manuscript cannot be the product of islanders in the South Pacific.

Furthermore, two of the pre-eminent modern Voynich researchers, Gabriel Landini and René Zandbergen, have carried out a number of statistical analyses of the manuscript, including one developed in the 1940s by the Harvard linguist George Zipf, and which still bears his name. By determining the frequency with which different letters appear in a sample text, and plotting their occurrence on a graph, Zipf demonstrated the basic relationships between letters, words and even patterns of speech that underpin most languages. The application of 'Zipf's Law' allows one to identify coherent patterns of writing or speech (which produce a gradient of –1 on the graph), from meaningless or random strings of characters. The test, when applied to the Voynich manuscript, produced the appropriate gradient to suggest an underlying linguistic structure. This is all well and good when such evidence is considered with a cool and scientific detachment, but just take a look at a sample of the Voynichese language and such certainties begin to slip away. We may rationally appreciate that Voynichese exhibits a statistical linguistic foundation, but, with its strings of repeated words unlike anything one recognises in a normal language, it just does not *look* right.

Such a desire to find structure and logic behind the Voynich script is eminently understandable. Almost everyone who has seen the manuscript, either with their own eyes or in photographs, has an instantaneous thrill as the thought occurs to them: 'Perhaps I shall spot something that all the others have overlooked.' We all want there to be a hidden meaning in the Voynich manuscript because we would all love to be the first to find it. Yet because of the failure of cryptanalysis to produce a decipherment that has met with universal approbation, and because the illustrations still lack a unified understanding, one begins to wonder if an intelligible plain text ever existed at all. All of which suggests to me two other options for investigation: the Voynich manuscript as deliberate hoax or forgery, or the Voynich manuscript as a product of mental illness or delusion.

The idea of a hoax or deliberate forgery for money is very alluring, and goes a long way to explaining the impenetrable script and extraordinary drawings. Of the two versions of this theory, a late-medieval or Renaissance hoax versus a modern forgery, the early version seems to me the more probable. It does, however, seem that the creator of the manuscript is just as likely to be a long-forgotten or anonymous author rather than any of the more glamorous and famous historical names with which it has been connected. Much has been made over the years of the possible links between the manuscript and Roger Bacon, John Dee and Edward Kelley, yet it seems to me that rather too much emphasis has been placed on these tenuous leads and the scant evidence produced to support them. We must not forget that the suggestion of Bacon's involvement comes from one mention in the Marcus Marci letter, and even then it is only based on the testimony of 'Dr Raphael'. There is no mention whatsoever in the Marci letter of Dee or Kelley, their involvement first being suggested by Voynich to provide a convenient and somewhat glamorous bridge between seventeenth-century Bohemia and medieval England. Many complex and convoluted theories have been woven around these romantic assumptions, without, perhaps, enough consideration being given to the likelihood of them being true. Yet again, an example of the heart ruling the head in the world of the Voynich manuscript?

A modern forgery is another possibility, with Wilfrid Voynich standing out as the most probable culprit. Yet for all his mysterious and secretive early life, not to mention his somewhat dubious morals, there seems to to be one rather compelling argument *against* Wilfrid's authorship. Throughout his period of ownership, Voynich believed that Roger Bacon was the creator of his strange manuscript, and he spent considerable time and effort in his attempts to establish this as fact. Yet as we have seen in chapter 2, the Voynich manuscript bears little physical resemblance or thematic similarity to any other work in the Bacon canon. Surely if Voynich were to have attempted such an audacious hoax, from which he undoubtedly expected great financial reward, he would have at least produced a document that looked a little more like the known works of the English friar, or seeded the manuscript with a few obvious 'clues' which would guide an investigator towards Bacon. As it is, no concrete link between the manuscript and Roger Bacon has ever been established, which suggests either an under-researched and slipshod attempt at forgery by Voynich, or perhaps no forgery at all.

But let us not, however, exonerate Voynich too quickly. Supposing the manuscript were genuine, there are still a number of mysterious circumstances surrounding its acquisition. Firstly there is Voynich's refusal to divulge the exact location of the 'castle in Southern Europe' in which he discovered the manuscript, with the Villa Mondragone only being identified upon the death of his wife Ethel in the 1960s. Then there is the absence of a label identifying a likely previous owner of the Voynich manuscript. Of the thirty other volumes Voynich *is* known to have purchased from the Villa Mondragone, almost all had a note attached to the cover acknowledging Petrus Beckx as their former owner. During political upheavals in Rome in the 1870s, Beckx, then the General Secretary of the Jesuits, transferred his library to the Villa Mondragone. Is there any possible reason why Wilfrid Voynich might have removed a label which provided a clear indication of his manuscript's provenance?

Finally, there is a strange footnote in the story of the Voynich manuscript that has never been adequately explained. H.P. Kraus, the New York book dealer who was to be the last private owner of the manuscript before it was donated to Yale University, recounts in his autobiography a trip to Rome in 1963, and a visit to the Vatican Library. There he met Monsignor Jose Ruysschaert, who had prepared a list of the books acquired by the Library from the Collegio Romano in 1912. Kraus recounts the following:

> I knew that he had published the catalogue of the Mondragone Library and I hoped to get information about the Cipher manuscript. To my great surprise he thought that the manuscript was still in the library.
>
> I asked him: 'Can you show it to me?'
>
> 'Yes,' he replied, and headed for the stacks. Soon he returned without it. I had to tell him that I owned the codex, and how it came to me.[3]

How, then, can we interpret Ruysschaert's extraordinary confusion? There appears at first to be no explanation other than a simple mistake in a catalogue, but when one takes into account the other anomalies described above, might one detect the less than innocent hand of Wilfrid Voynich at work?

Let us not forget the wily methods Voynich regularly employed in order to obtain rare books, especially the story related by Giuseppe Orioli when Wilfrid convinced a Father Superior to hand over his monastery's entire collection of valuable manuscripts in return for 'a cartload of modern trash'. If forging a manuscript might have been beyond Voynich's abilities, procuring one via dishonest means clearly was not.

If we look again at the three seemingly disconnected facts above, perhaps another scenario suggests itself. Imagine Voynich sifting through the chests of dusty old books at the Villa Mondragone sometime in early 1912. Suddenly he chances upon a bizarre volume, like no other he has seen before, accompanying which is a tantalising letter which seems to indicate that it might be a lost work by Roger Bacon. Such a book, if genuine, would be worth a fortune on the open market; a fact that would not have escaped the ever cash-strapped Voynich. And now he puts his crafty mind to work. He must procure this astonishing artifact without alerting the current owners to its potential worth, thereby sending their asking price sky high, or perhaps even preventing the sale altogether. So, he spirits it away without the Jesuits of Mondragone ever knowing.

Of course, Voynich must erase any evidence that could link his 'ugly duckling' with its true owners. The label of Petrus Beckx is removed from the book, and the exact location of his discovery never divulged. The remainder of the Mondragone collection, meanwhile, returns to Rome and the Vatican Library, where the librarian, unaware that the cipher manuscript has been secretly purloined, includes it in the catalogue of 1937. It is only in the early 1960s, at the request of Kraus, that Monsignor Ruysschaert physically goes in search of the manuscript, only to discover it is no longer in the Vatican Library, and has not been for over fifty years.

A fanciful theory spun out of a few scant and unrelated facts? Or another twist in the tale of the Voynich manuscript? Either way, it brings us no closer to understanding who might have created the Voynich manuscript, or why. Any theory must convincingly explain the strange nymphs and the mind-boggling 'rosettes'. Although the individual illustrations within the botanical and astrological sections are unquestion-ably fantastical, they do not seem as completely unworldly as the gynaecological plumbing, naked ladies and swirling man-dalas, which seem to offer no sensible foundations on which to build a credible theory.

We are left, through a process of elimination, in the hands of the visionary, the mad and the hallucinatory, and it is to this conclusion that I am intuitively drawn. In the opening chapter of this book the authors suggested that 'The overriding sense is that the creator of the manuscript had a purpose *other* than to create something of "beauty", and was driven rather by a desire to convey meaning.' Might it just be that this 'meaning' is beyond our comprehension because the mind that created the Voynich manuscript was irrational or insane? There is little or no hard evidence for this assumption, except the fact that hallucinosis of one form or another seems to provide a possible interpretation for the more baffling elements of the book. The Voynich rosettes, just like the 'Outsider Art' hypothesis, have never been fully investigated or explored. Perhaps it is within these strange offshoots from the main body of Voynich research that the long-sought-after understanding and explanation lies?

How can the many years of research into the Voynich manuscript, and the bewildering array of hypotheses relating to its meaning and origin, be summed up? Just as with the manuscript itself, there can be no single, all-encompassing conclusion. In fact, the multiplicity of theories, such as exists even today among the current Voynich internet circle, is one of the unique and joyous aspects of the manuscript. The many and varied interpretations of the codex, none of which appears to provide a totally satisfying explanation, continue to provoke intellectual debate rather than scholarly consensus. This is hardly surprising when one remembers that even individual pages are open to wildly differing explanations. How can one hope to assess which of the competing readings is likely to be closest to the truth?

The conflicting opinions of the many Voynich scholars arise not just because of the strange and inexplicable nature of the manuscript itself, but also due to the diverse and conflicting personalities who have applied their particular intellectual skills to the conundrum. In Hamlet's instructions to the Players, Shakespeare provided us with the defining purpose of their art, namely: 'to hold as t'were a mirror up to nature'. The 'art' of the Voynich manuscript is to hold a mirror up to each and every investigator, in which he or she often sees, instead of the truth underpinning the manuscript, a reflection of their own preconceptions and beliefs. And herein lurks the danger for all Voynich researchers, because the manuscript is not some pristine looking glass, rather a distorting mirror from a fairground house of fun, throwing back a twisted and almost unrecognisable image. It is an alchemical mirror, in which the object viewed is transmuted into something rich and strange.

For so many who have studied the Voynich manuscript, and

believed their researches to have uncovered its dark secrets, they have in fact seen only a misshapen reflection of their own hopes and desires. The most obvious example is poor Professor Newbold. Perhaps driven by the need to prove his academic worth, he saw the manuscript as an opportunity to attain the long-hoped-for intellectual recognition. The more he peered through the lenses of his microscope, the more certain his beliefs became. But his hopes, just like the imaginary short-hand letters he perceived, were phantoms conjured up by his own excitement and ambition. The Voynich manuscript, meanwhile, gave up none of its secrets.

The list, of course, goes on. What of James Martin Feely, the Rochester lawyer whose hubris led to the publication of his findings at his own expense, and an inevitable critical mauling? He too was surely driven by ambition rather than any great gift for cryptology, and his decipherment was only made possible by the strangely flexible nature of Voynichese. This might also explain the curious silence of Athanasius Kircher. When faced with the inscrutability of this strange gift of a manuscript from Marcus Marci, did he perhaps perceive his own cryptological shortcomings and the weakness of his hieroglyphic transcriptions? Could he have realised that his own reputation was built upon guesswork rather than ability, and that this odd manuscript was more likely to bring intellectual ruin than provide the pinnacle of a scholarly career?

Possibly the best analogy can be drawn with a famous paradox from quantum physics, known today as 'Schrödinger's cat'. Erwin Schrödinger devised his well-known 'thought experiment' in an attempt to disprove the kind of extraordinary and seemingly illogical conclusions that were being reached by other scientists in the field of quantum theory. He was bothered, as incidentally was Albert Einstein, by the way quantum theory suggested the importance of *probabilities* rather than absolutes, and particularly by the influence of external observation on the actions of the quantum world. In the hypothetical experiment devised by Schrödinger, a cat would be placed in a box alongside a phial of poison gas. As well as the unfortunate feline and the deadly phial, the box would also contain a lump of radioactive material and a detection device such as a Geiger counter linked to the poison container. The experiment is so designed that there is a fifty-fifty chance of the lump of material emitting a radioactive particle, which would be detected by the Geiger counter, in turn triggering the release of the poison gas, thus killing the cat. The box is sealed, and at that point there is an equal probability that a particle has or has not been released through radioactive decay, and therefore a fifty-fifty probability that the phial of poison gas is either intact or broken, and that the cat is dead or alive. The only way to ascertain which of these two possibilities has occurred is to open the box and observe the outcome of the experiment. However, the situation is not so straightforward as it may at first seem, as science writer John Gribbin explains:

> But now we encounter the strangeness of the quantum world. According to the theory, *neither* of the two possibilities open to the radioactive material, and therefore to the cat, has any reality unless it is observed. The atomic decay has neither happened nor not happened, the cat has neither been killed nor not killed, until we look inside the box to see what has happened. Theorists who accept the pure version of quantum mechanics say that the cat exists in some indeterminate state, neither dead nor alive, until an observer looks into the box to see how things are getting on. Nothing is real unless it is observed.[4]

Such an 'indeterminate state' is precisely the situation in which we find the Voynich manuscript. In its current resting place at the Beinecke Library, the manuscript exists in a conceptual limbo not dissimilar to the state of non-being experienced by Schrödinger's cat. With its true meaning still unknown, and with its seemingly unique ability to provide corroborating evidence for almost all of the various hypotheses that have ever been suggested, at a fundamental level the Voynich manuscript fits all the theories that have ever been put forward about it, and at the same time, none of them. At this moment the manuscript could be considered simultaneously to be the work of Bacon, Dee, Kelley, Voynich or any number of other, long-forgotten authors, because, following the quantum logic of Schrödinger's experiment, we have no way of 'opening the box' to determine which of these possibilities represents the truth.

For the observer in Schrödinger's experiment, the action of peering inside the box to check on the wellbeing or otherwise of the cat immediately resolves the 'neither-alive-nor-dead' paradox; but with the Voynich manuscript, things are not so clear-cut. We cannot simply accept a particular theory at face value, thereby instantly eliminating the myriad competing and complementary hypotheses, because there must first be a clear set of criteria by which to judge the veracity of an explanation. Many researchers over the years have believed in all good faith that they have discovered either a decipherment of the Voynichese language or the real meaning of the strange illustrations. Many more such theories will inevitably be presented in years to come by scholars equally convinced of the correctness of their methodology and conclusions. One step towards a better understanding of the manuscript might be the granting of permission by Yale University to allow radio-carbon dating of the vellum or chemical analysis of the pigments. But until such time as these tests are carried out, thereby prising open the lid of Schrödinger's box, the Voynich manuscript remains at once both a forgery *and* genuine, the product of genius *and* delusion, priceless *and* worthless.

There is perhaps a final thought one should bear in mind when considering the manuscript. For almost all who have tackled the subject, there is an overwhelming desire to be the first to break the code of the Voynichese language and to understand the meaning of the tantalising illustrations. This has inevitably led to a somewhat reductionist approach, in which the manuscript is broken down to its various constituent parts and sections in an attempt to solve the mystery. In doing so, we forget the beauty of the manuscript in its totality. Like schoolboys who pull apart their toys to understand how they work, only to discover later that they are unable to piece them back together, we are in danger of pulling apart the Voynich manuscript and seeing it only as a combination of unconnected and discrete parts lacking a larger, meaningful whole. Surely a holistic approach will produce the all-encompassing explanation the codex so richly deserves. Or perhaps we should step back a moment, and ignore the incessant din of academic debate that continues to roar around the manuscript. Maybe, just for a short while, we should pause and appreciate the Voynich manuscript for what it truly is: a beautiful object, an enigmatic, alluring and enduring mystery that is, in the final reckoning, perhaps better left unsolved?

✦ NOTES ✦

INTRODUCTION
1. D'Imperio, Mary, *The Voynich Manuscript: an Elegant Enigma*, p.11.

CHAPTER 1
1. Sowerby, E.M., *Rare Books and Rare People*.
2. ibid, p.9.
3. ibid, p.11.
4. Kraus, H.P., *A Rare Book Saga: the Autobiography of H.P. Kraus*, p.219.
5. Sowerby, p.33.
6. 'A Preliminary Sketch of the History of the Roger Bacon Cipher', Wilfrid Voynich. *Transactions of the College of Physicians of Philadelphia*, 3rd series, vol. 43 (1921), p.415.
7. Newbold, William Romaine, 'The Voynich Roger Bacon Manuscript'. *Transactions of the College of Physicians of Philadelphia*, 3rd series, vol. 43 (1921), p.461.
8. Carter, A.H. (1946), as quoted by Mary D'Imperio, *The Voynich Manuscript: an Elegant Enigma*, p.12.
9. D'Imperio, p.23.
10. Kahn, David, *The Codebreakers*, p.864.
11. D'Imperio, p.23.
12. Sowerby, p.13.

CHAPTER 2
1. Bridges, J.H., *The Life and Work of Roger Bacon*, p.28.
2. Bacon, Roger, Opus Majus. R. Belle Burk (Kissinger, 1998).
3. Clegg, Brian, *The First Scientist: a Life of Roger Bacon*.
4. ibid, p.135.
5. ibid, p.133.
6. ibid, p.133.
7. Newbold, William Romaine, 'The Voynich Roger Bacon Manuscript'.
8. Kent, R.G., from Foreword to Newbold, William Romaine, *The Cipher of Roger Bacon*, p.xiii.
9. Newbold, *The Cipher of Roger Bacon*, p. 73.
10. ibid, p.74.

11. D'Imperio, Mary, *The Voynich Manuscript: an Elegant Enigma*, p.60.
12. Newbold, *The Cipher of Roger Bacon*, p.108.
13. ibid, p.xxiii.
14. ibid, p.xix.
15. ibid, p.xvii.
16. *Harper's Magazine*, 143 (1921), pp.186–97.
17. Manly, J.M., *Speculum* (1931).
18. Kahn, David, *The Codebreakers*, p.868.
19. *Speculum*, p.350
20. Kahn, p.869.
21. Singh, Simon, *The Codebook*, p.7.
22. *Speculum*, p.353.
23. ibid, p.354.
24. ibid, p.355.
25. ibid, p.355.
26. Newbold, 'The Voynich Roger Bacon Manuscript', p.465.
27. *Speculum*.
28. Newbold, 'The Voynich Roger Bacon Manuscript', p.465.
29. ibid, p.465.
30. *Speculum*, p.355.

CHAPTER 3
1. Voynich, Wilfrid, 'A Preliminary Sketch of the History of the Roger Bacon Cipher Manuscript'. Transactions of the College of Physicians of Philadelphia, 3rd series, vol. 43 (1921), p.424.
2. Wormald, Francis, and Wright, C.E., eds., *The English Library Before 1700: Studies in History*, p.152.
3. Woolley, Benjamin, *The Queen's Conjuror: the Life and Magic of John Dee*, p.23.
4. ibid, p.51.
5. Suster, G., *John Dee: Essential Readings*, p.100.
6. Clulee, N., *John Dee's Natural Philosophy: Between Science and Religion*, p.30.
7. Suster, p.30.
8. Deacon, R., *John Dee*, p.120.
9. Casaubon, M., *A True and Faithful Relation...* (London, Askin, 1974).
10. Evans, R.J.W., *Rudolf and His World*, p.7.
11. Clulee, p.226.
12. Evans, p.224.
13. Clulee, p.252.
14. Fenton, E., ed., *The Diaries of John Dee*, p.186.
15. ibid, p.188.
16. Evans, p.225.
17. Woolley, p.281.
18. Harkness, Deborah, *John Dee's Conversation with Angels*, R.J. Roberts and A.G. Watson, John Dee's Library Catalogue.

20. ibid, p.24.
21. Bodleian Library, Oxford Ashmole Collection, f19v and 847 passim, p.54.
22. Roberts and Watson, p.54.
23. Woolley, p.263.
24. ibid, p.267.
25. Evans, p.182.
26. ibid, p.239.
27. Voynich, 'A Preliminary Sketch...', p.430.
28. Brumbaugh, R.S., *The World's Most Mysterious Manuscript*, p.136.
29. Voynich, 'A Preliminary Sketch...', p.417.
30. Godwin, Jocelyn, *Athanasius Kircher*, p.5.
31. Pope, M., *The Story of Decipherment*, p.30.
32. ibid, p.22.
33. As quoted from Pope.

CHAPTER 4
1. Brumbaugh, R.S., *The World's Most Mysterious Manuscript*, p.115.
2. ibid, p.31.
3. Singh, Simon, *The Code Book*, p.29.
4. Kahn, David, *The Codebreakers*, p.870.
5. Feely, J.M., *Roger Bacon's Cypher: the Right Key Found*, p.9.
6. Reeds, Jim, 'William F. Friedman's Transcription of the Voynich Manuscript', p.7.
7. Feely, pp.15–17.
8. Kahn, p.870.
9. McKaig, as quoted by Mary D'Imperio, *The Voynich Manuscript: an Elegant Enigma*, p.36.
10. Brumbaugh, *The World's Most Mysterious Manuscript*, p.91.
11. D'Imperio, p.36.

CHAPTER 5
1. Kahn, David, *The Codebreakers*, p.374.
2. ibid, p.376.
3. ibid, p.22.
4. Reeds, Jim, 'William F. Friedman's Transcription of the Voynich Manuscript', p.5.
5. Reproduced from Brumbaugh, R.S., *The World's Most Mysterious Manuscript*, pp.102–3.
6. Kahn, p.391.
7. Clark, R.W., *The Man Who Broke the Purple*, p.168.
8. D'Imperio, Mary, *The Voynich Manuscript: an Elegant Enigma*, p.37.
9. Brumbaugh, p.119.
10. ibid, p.120.
11. ibid, p.127.

12. ibid, p.131.
13. Levitov, L., *The Solution of the Voynich Manuscript*, p.21.
14. ibid, p.12.
15. ibid, p.22.
16. ibid, p.15.
17. ibid, p.67.
18. D'Imperio, p.45.
19. Kahn, p.759.

CHAPTER 6
1. Rawcliffe, Carole, *Medicine in Later Medieval England*, p.3.
2. Blunt, W., and Raphael, S., *The Illustrated Herbal*.
3. Collins, M., *Medieval Herbals*.
4. *The Voynich Mystery*, BBC/Mentorn Films, 9 December 2002.
5. D'Imperio, Mary, *The Voynich Manuscript: an Elegant Enigma*, p.61.
6. Riddle, John M., *Contraception and Abortion from the Ancient World to the Renaissance*.
7. Riddle, John M., *Eve's Herbs: a History of Contraception and Abortion in the West*.
8. Culpeper, Nicholas, *Culpeper's Complete Herbal and English Physician*.
9. Kauffmann, C.M., *The Baths of Pozzuoli*.
10. Caviness, Madeline H., *Visualising Women in the Middle Ages*, p.99.
11. D'Imperio, p.170.

CHAPTER 7
1. Rhodes, Colin, *Outsider Art: Spontaneous Alternatives*, pp. 7–8.
2. Cardinal, Roger, *Outsider Art*, p.17.
3. Rhodes, p.61.
4. as quoted, Rhodes, p.62.
5. ibid, p.61.
6. ibid, p.108.
7. ibid, p.151.
8. Sacks, Oliver, *Migraine: Understanding a Common Disorder*, p.53.
9. D'Imperio, Mary, *The Voynich Manuscript: an Elegant Enigma*, p.70.
10. Beer, Frances, *Women and Mystical Experiences in the Middle Ages*, p.16.
11. Flanagan, Sabina, *Hildegard of Bingen*.
12. Beer, p.15.
13. Flanagan, p.193.
14. ibid, p.189.
15. Sacks, *Migraine…*, p.275.
16. Beer, p.16.
17. Flanagan, pp.204–5.
18. Hildegard of Bingen, as quoted by Sacks, Oliver, *The Man Who Mistook his Wife for a Hat*.

19. Flanagan, pp.202–4.
20. Sacks, Oliver, *The Man Who Mistook His Wife...*, pp.161–2.
21. D'Imperio, p.21.
22. Sacks, *Migraine...*, pp.273–4.
23. ibid, p.276.
24. ibid, p.279.
25. Sacks, *The Man Who Mistook His Wife...*, p.129.
26. D'Imperio, p.70.
27. Baker, Robert, *Hidden Memories*, p.115.
28. Christie-Murray, David, *Voices from the Gods*, p.83.
29. ibid, p.84.
30. Baker, p.115.

CHAPTER 8
1. Barlow, Michael, 'The Voynich Manuscript – by Voynich?' *Cryptologia*, vol. 10, no. 4 (October 1986).
2. D'Imperio, Mary, *The Voynich Manuscript: an Elegant Enigma*, p.6.
3. *The Voynich Mystery*, BBC/Mentorn Films (9 December 2002).
4. D'Imperio, p.5.
5. Worrall, Simon, *The Poet and the Murderer* (Fourth Estate, 2002).
6. D'Imperio, p.38.
7. Barlow, p.216.
8. Sensese, Donald, *Sergei Stepniak-Kravchinskii: the London Years* (Oriental Research Partners, Newtonville, Mass., 1987).
9. Cook, Andrew, *On His Majesty's Secret Service: Sidney Reilly, Codename ST1*.
10. Lockhart, Bruce, *Ace of Spies* (London: Quartet, 1992).
11. Cook, p.34.
12. Taratuta, E., *Ethel Lilian Voynich – The Fate of a Writer and the Fate of a Book*, (Moscow, 1964: unpublished translation by M. Kravchenko).
13. Orioli, Giuseppe, *Adventures of a Bookseller* (privately printed, London, 1937).
14. ibid, p.95.
15. ibid, p.94.
16. ibid, p.93.
17. Sowerby, E.M., *Rare Books and Rare People*, p.16.

CHAPTER 9
1. Lovecraft, H.P., *The Haunter of the Dark* (London: Voyager, 2000), p.293.
2. Barlow, Michael, 'The Voynich Manuscript – by Voynich?' *Cryptologia*, vol. 10, no. 4, p.215 (October 1986).
3. Kraus, H.P., *A Rare Book Saga: the Autobiography of H.P. Kraus*, p.222.
4. Gribbin, John, *In Search of Schrödinger's Cat*, p.2.

✦ SELECT BIBLIOGRAPHY ✦

Books

Anderson, F.J., *An Illustrated History of Herbals* (Columbia, 1977).

Baker, Robert A., *Hidden Memories: Voices and Visions from Within* (Buffalo, NY: Prometheus Books, 1992).

Beer, Frances, *Women and Mystical Experience in the Middle Ages* (Rochester, NY: Boydell Press, 1992).

Blunt, Wilfrid, and Raphael, Sandra, *The Illustrated Herbal* (London: Thames and Hudson, 1979).

Bridges, John Henry, *The Life and Work of Roger Bacon* (London: Williams and Norgate, 1914).

Brumbaugh, Robert S., *The World's Most Mysterious Manuscript: The Voynich 'Roger Bacon' Cipher Manuscript* (Carbondale: Southern Illinois University Press, 1978; London: Weidenfeld and Nicholson, 1977).

Bryer, Robin, *The History of Hair* (Philip Wilson, 2003).

Cardinal, Roger, *Outsider Art* (London: Studio Vista).

Caviness, Madeline H., 'Hildegard as Designer of the Illustrations to her Work', from Hildegard of Bingen, *The Context of Her Thought and Art*, eds. Charles Burnett and Peter Dronke (Warburg Institute, 1998).

Caviness, Madeline H., *Visualising Women in the Middle Ages* (University of Pennsylvania, 2001).

Christie-Murray, David, *Voices from the Gods: Speaking with Tongues* (London: Routledge and Kegan, 1978).

Clark, Ronald W., *The Man Who Broke the Purple: the Life of the World's Greatest Cryptologist, Colonel William F. Friedman* (London: Weidenfeld and Nicolson, 1977).

Clegg, Brian, *The First Scientist: a Life of Roger Bacon* (London: Constable, 2003).

Clulee, Nicholas H., *John Dee's Natural Philosophy: Between Science and Religion* (Routledge, Kegan and Paul, 1988).

Collins, Minta, *Medieval Herbals* (London: British Library, 2000).

Cook, Andrew, *On His Majesty's Secret Service: Sidney Reilly, Codename ST1* (Tempus Books, 2002).

Deacon, Richard, *John Dee, Scientist, Geographer and Secret Agent to Elizabeth I* (London: Frederick Muller, 1968).

Di Rola Klossowski, Stanislav, *Alchemy (Art and Imagination)* (London: Thames and Hudson, 1973).

D'Imperio, Mary E., *The Voynich Manuscript: An Elegant Enigma* (Laguna Hills, California: Aegean Park Press, 1978).

Drey, Rudolf, *Apothecary Jars* (London: Faber, 1978).

Easton, Stewart C., *Roger Bacon and His Search for a Universal Science* (Oxford: Blackwell, 1952).

Evans, Robert J.W., *Rudolf and His World* (Oxford: Clarendon, 1984).

Feely, James Martin, *Roger Bacon's Cypher: the Right Key Found* (Rochester, 1943).

Fenton, Edward, ed., *The Diaries of John Dee* (Charlbury: Day Books, 1998).

Flanagan, Sabina, *Hildegard of Bingen, 1098–1179: a Visionary Life* (London: Routledge, 1989).

French, Peter, *The World of an Elizabethan Magus* (London: Routledge, Kegan and Paul, 1972).

Gascoigne, Bamber, *A Brief History of Christianity* (London: Robinson, revised edition, 2003).

Godwin, Jocelyn, *Athanasius Kircher: a Renaissance Man and the Quest for Lost Knowledge* (London: Thames and Hudson, 1979).

Greene, Brian, *The Elegant Universe* (London: Vintage, 1999).

Gribbin, John, *In Search of Schrödinger's Cat: Quantum Physics and Reality* (London: Black Swan, 1984).

Griffenhagen, George, and Bogard, Mary, *The History of Drug Containers and Their Labels* (Madison: American Institute of the History of Pharmacy, 1999).

Harkness, Deborah, *John Dee's Conversations with Angels* (Cambridge University Press, 1999).

Kahn, David, *The Codebreakers* (New York: Macmillan, 1967).

Kauffmann, C.M., *The Baths of Pozzuoli* (Oxford: Bruno and Cassirer, 1959).

Kraus, H.P., *A Rare Book Saga: the Autobiography of H.P. Kraus* (New York: Putnam, 1978).

Levitov, Leo, *The Solution to the Voynich Manuscript: a Liturgical Manual for the Endura Rite of the Cathari Heresy, the Cult of Isis* (Laguna Hills, California: Aegean Park Press, 1987).

Lupton, Deborah, *Medicine as Culture, Illness, Disease and the Body in Western Societies* (London: Sage, 1994).

Maddocks, Fiona, *Hildegard of Bingen: the Woman of her Age* (London: Headline, 2001).

Morin, France, *Heavenly Visions: Shaker Gift Drawings and Songs* (New York: Drawing Centre, 2001).

Newbold, William Romaine, *The Cipher of Roger Bacon*, ed., with foreword and notes, Roland Grubb Kent (Philadelphia: University of Pennsylvania, 1928).

Norris, Herbert, *Medieval Costume and Fashion* (Dover, 1999).

Norwich, John Julius, *Byzantium: the Apogee* (London: Viking, 1991).

O'Shea, Stephen, *The Perfect Heresy: the Life and Death of the Cathars* (London: Profile Books, 2001).

Page, Sophie, *Astrology in Medieval Society* (London: British Library, 2002).

Pratt, Fletcher, *Secret and Urgent* (New York: Bobbs Merrill, 1939).

Pope, Maurice, *The Story of Decipherment* (London: Thames and Hudson, 1975).

Poundstone, William, *Labyrinths of Reason* (New York: Doubleday, 1988).

Rawcliffe, Carole, *Medicine and Society in Later Medieval England* (Stroud: Sutton, 1995).

Regrove, H. Stanley, *Roger Bacon: the Father of Experimental Science and Medieval Occultism* (London: William Rider, 1920).

Rhodes, Colin, *Outsider Art: Spontaneous Alternatives* (London: Thames and Hudson, 2000).

Riddle, John M., *Contraception and Abortion from the Ancient World to the Renaissance* (Harvard University Press, 1992).

Riddle, John M., *Eve's Herbs: a History of Contraception and Abortion in the West* (Harvard University Press, 1997).

Roberts, R.J., and Watson, A.G., *John Dee's Library Catalogue* (London Bibliographical Society, 1999).

Sacks, Oliver, *The Man Who Mistook His Wife for a Hat* (London: Picador, 1985).

Sacks, Oliver, *Migraine: Understanding a Common Disorder* (London: Picador, 1993).

Suster, Gerald, *John Dee: Essential Readings* (Crucible, 1986).

Singh, Simon, *The Code Book* (London: Fourth Estate, 1999).

Sowerby, E.M., *Rare Books and Rare People* (Williamsburg: Constable, 1967).

Watson, Gilbert, *Theriac and Mithridatium: a Study in Therapeutics* (London: Wellcome Historical Medical Library, 1966).

Westacott, E., *Roger Bacon, His Life and Legend* (London: Rockliff, 1953).

Whitfield, Peter, *Astrology: a History* (London: British Library, 2001).

Woolley, Benjamin, *The Queen's Conjuror: the Life and Magic of John Dee* (London: Flamingo, 2000).

Yates, Frances, *The Rosicrucian Enlightenment* (St Albans: Paladin, 1975).

Articles and Papers

Barlow, Michael, 'The Voynich Manuscript – by Voynich?', *Cryptologia* (vol. 10, no. 4, October 1986).

Guy, Jacques B.M., 'On Levitov's Decipherment of the Voynich Manuscript' (9 December 1991).

Nadis, Steve, 'Look Who's Talking', *New Scientist* (vol. 179, issue 2403, 12 July 2003).

Newbold, William Romaine, 'The Cipher of Roger Bacon', *Proceedings of the College of Physicians and Surgeons of Philadelphia* (Philadelphia, 1921, pp.431–74).

Reeds, Jim, 'William F. Friedman's Transcription of the Voynich Manuscript', *Cryptologia* (vol. 19, 1995, pp.1–25).

Stallings, Dennis J., 'Catharism, Levitov, and the Voynich Manuscript'.

Voynich, Wilfrid Michael, 'A Preliminary Sketch of the History of the Roger Bacon Cipher Manuscript', *Proceedings of the College of Physicians and Surgeons of Philadelphia* (Philadelphia, 1921, pp.415–30).

Zandonella, Catherine, 'Book of Riddles', *New Scientist* (vol. 172, issue 2317, 17 November 2001).

Internet Sites

www.geocities.com/voynichms/
A comprehensive and invaluable website for any would-be Voynich researcher (containing both a 'long' and 'short' tour of Voynich history and ideas). Created and run by René Zandbergen.

www.voynich.no-ip.com
Takeshi Takahashi has assembled a very useful selection of Voynich folios. The folio numbering throughout this book has been taken from this site.

✦ INDEX ✦

mental illness/insanity, 190–2, 254–5
Mercator, Gerard, 54
Merovingians, 141
Mervyn, Tim, 216–20, 247
Mezentsev, General, 6
microscope, 27, 37, 38, 50
Middle High German, 242
migraines/migrainous hallucinations,
    196–202
Milan, 129
Milky Way, 243
Mirbel, Alexis, 206, 207
Missowsky, Dr Raphael (referred to as
    'Dr Raphael'), 18, 69–70, 73, 252
mnemonic key, 93–4, 99
monad, 55, 55
Mondragone see Villa Mondragone
monoalphabetic substitution ciphers,
    86, 88–91, 96, 143–4, 146
Montsegur, 135, 141
Mormon Church, 212–13
Morris, William, 7
Mortlake, 52, 56, 63, 68
Moscow University, 5
Mother Ann (Ann Lee), 187, 188
Mother Ann's Work, 188, 205
Mülle, Catherine Elise see Smith,
    Hélène
multialphabetic/polyalphabetic
    substitution ciphers, 94–108,
    147–8
Murifri, 60
Museo Kircheriano, 71, 80
mystical/visionary experience, 193–7,
    198–200, 201, 254

Nalvage, 60
National Museum of Pakistan, 213
National Security Agency, 120
Necronomicon, The, 245–6
New England, 186, 213, 245
New Testament, 204
New York, 16, 151, 187, 221, 233, 234
    State, 212, 232
New York Guarantee Trust, 233
Newbold, William Romaine, 17, 27–50,
    69, 81, 82, 87, 109, 114, 120, 124,
    128, 148, 174, 175, 176, 180, 202,
    214, 226, 232, 233, 234, 243, 256
Newton, Isaac, 74–5
Nicetas, 135
Nill, Anne, 233, 234
Noah, 77, 78
Northumberland, John Dudley, Duke
    of, 20, 53, 140, 224
Nostradamus, 244
Notarikon, 31
Notredame, Cesar, 244

Notredame, Michel de (Nostradamus),
    244
nudes/nymphs, 10–11, 12, 37, 132,
    168–9, 172, 174, 177, 179
nudity, attitudes to, 170–2
nulls, 93, 147
'numerological box cipher', 129–30,
    133, 213, 215–16
nymphs see nudes/nymphs

Okhrana (Russian Secret Police), 223
Old Order Amish (Anabaptist
    Mennonites), 187
Old Testament, 30, 77, 204
Omort, H., 17
O'Neill, Dr Hugh, 116, 117, 157
Oriental Cycle of séances, 206, 207
Orioli, Giuseppe, 224, 225, 253
O'Shea, Stephen, 141
Osiris, 79
Outsider Art, 189–93, 255
Oxford, 21, 26
    University, 21

Paderborn, 74
Paderewski, Ignace, 221
Pakistan, 213
    National Museum of, 213
Paracelsus, 162
Paris, 8, 16, 20, 21, 23
    Bishop of, 20
    University of, 20
Parkin, Stephen, 224
Pasammetichus, Pharaoh, 79
Paul, St, 204
Paulicians, 135
Pennsylvania, University of, 28, 35
Pentateuch, 30
Pentecost, Day of, 204, 205
Pentecostals, 205
Perfect, 136, 138, 140, 141
Persian astronomers, 48, 49
Peter of Castelnau, 134, 136
Peter of Eboli: Balneis Puteolanis, 170,
    171
Peter of Maricourt, 21–2
Petersen, Father Theodore C., 116, 123
pharmaceutical jars (apothecary jars),
    11, 166–8, 168
Philological Quarterly, 123, 126
Piccadilly, London, 8
Pisces, 177, 179
plants and herbs, 10, 11–12, 116, 117,
    132, 151, 152–3, 154–66, 173–4,
    180, 193
Plato, 53
Platts, Matthew, 239–40
'Pleiades' folio, 181, 181, 182